Growing Up *in*
MINNESOTA

Ten Writers Remember Their Childhoods

Ten writers tell what it meant to them to grow
up in Minnesota. Their reminiscences range
from northern Minnesota to north Minneapolis, from the snug comfort of a Victorian
home to the struggles of a poor black family.

All say something not only about a particular
time and place but also about the experience
of growing up.

Harrison Salisbury
Meridel Le Sueur
Robert Bly
Gerald Vizenor
Toyse Kyle
Keith Gunderson
Shirley Schoonover
Edna and Howard Hong
Mary Hong Loe

When you mention Minnesota, most Americans would probably respond: cold, snow, Indians, north woods. They picture a state peopled almost entirely by blond, lumbering Swedes....What jumps from the pages of *Growing Up in Minnesota* is that the state defies the old stereotypes. It has immense diversity.

Steve Berg
Minneapolis Tribune

An excellent book about "growing up in Minnesota."

Frederick Manfred
Moons and Lion Tailes:
A Midwestern Journal of
Poetry and Comment

Intense, sharply etched, and extremely varied reports of life in the Gopher State....Because of their honesty, these essays are absorbing and affirmative commentaries on the history and culture of Minnesota.

Kirk Jeffrey
Indiana Magazine of History

What each of the ten accounts of the Minnesota childhoods in this collection have in common is the effect of place, for better or worse, on the child who grew up in that place....These are simple, clear stories, clearly and simply told, which is the book's best asset.

Andrew Allegretti
North Dakota History

Growing Up in Minnesota is the kind of charmingly truthful book that can be read and reread with enjoyment for years to come.

Robert L. Girouard
The Free Press, Mankato

A marvelous collection of memories and ideas.

Barbara Flanagan
Minneapolis Star

In case you think that this book would have no appeal outside
the state of Minnesota, you are wrong. The joys and sorrows of
growing up are universal....Rich, poor, white, black, Indian,
city, country, all of these backgrounds are here. Every reader
will have a favorite, but all of these memoirs are worth reading.

Kliatt Paperback Book Guide

You are attentive to anything that might have shaped a Minnesota writer from the mix and tangle of racial and ethnic and
religious roots, the rural and urban backgrounds, and their
modes of expression. A growing sense of place surrounds
you....You follow the course pain or joy takes throughout each
childhood until it leads unmistakably into your own.

Chet Corey
Great River Review

Growing Up in Minnesota...opens the variety of life that is Minnesota. Too often in small town America one begins to view his
own life style as the norm, and this myth is pleasantly destroyed.

Ed Shannon
Montevideo American News

As I write this, the temperature has dipped below zero and the
enforced solitude of another Minnesota winter is beginning.
Perhaps that accounts for the feeling I am left with—this would
be an excellent book to curl up with by the fire.

Susan Gyneth Grieger
The Minnesota Daily

Growing Up *in*
MINNESOTA

Ten Writers Remember Their Childhoods

Chester G. Anderson, Editor

University of Minnesota Press
Minneapolis
London

Cover montage and design: Patricia M. Boman

Photographs used in the montage are courtesy of the Minnesota Historical Society. *Foreground*: Looking northwest
along Washington Avenue past railroad yards, Milwaukee
Depot, ca. 1920. Photographed by C. P. Gibson.
Background: Farm scene, possibly Swift County, ca. 1948.

Library of Congress Catalog Card Number 75-40546

ISBN 0-8166-0921-7

Eighth printing, 1994

Contents

Growing Up in Minnesota:
Ten Writers Remember Their Childhoods

Introduction: From Tepee to Ax and Stump

by Chester G. Anderson

The Great Seal of Minnesota, dating from 1849 when the state was still a territory, tells its story succinctly. In the left foreground a farmer plows up the prairie. Near him in the right foreground stands the stump of a tree with an ax embedded in it and a rifle, with a powder horn slung from the barrel, leaning against it. In the background St. Anthony Falls (named by Father Hennepin in 1680) awaits the arrival of the millers, and beyond the falls the forests are as yet untouched by the stroke of the lumbermen. In the middle distance a warrior on horseback, lance in hand, rides away toward the setting sun.

Women are represented on the seal only by their absence. Maybe they are at home cooking dinner for warrior and worker, filling the pipe of peace, helping the children grow up. Or did the earliest political fathers dimly descry mother and family in that poor stump, the plowed virgin soil, the river ready for harnessing, the forests awaiting the saw, the lay of the land, as some evidence suggests? One draft version of the seal, for instance, showed a tribal family with a lodge and another showed a cabin and a haystack. The last letter that we have on the subject of the drafts was from Alexander Ramsey, the territorial governor, to Henry H. Sibley, the congressional delegate, on December 28, 1849. In it Ramsey argued for the inclusion of a tepee in the design:

Upon a more careful examination of the designs & mottoes for our seal, I come to these conclusions viz: that in the drawing by Capt. Abert Civilization in the number & prominence of the objects predominates too much over the Indian state which at least for the present is our more distinctive characteristic. In Capt. Eastmans design the equilibrium is better preserved; his is also more bold grand & striking—if you think it better to adopt Aberts design would it not be well to take out some of the improvement ideas say the stump & axe and in some appropriate part locate a "teepee" this would make the Indian life in the seal more striking & attractive.*

But "Civilization" won: no location could be found for the tepee (the woman, the family), and the rifle and the powder horn were added to the "improvement ideas" of the ax and the stump.

The Latin motto on the seal seems meant to assure us that, European civilization having arrived in the Mississippi Valley, everything is going to be all right. Yet the motto contains two errors. The founding fathers intended to say "I wish to see what is beyond" (*quo ultra volo videre*) and instead they said "I wish to see what is above" or "what rises from below" (*quo sursum volo videre*). Well, almost. The engraver or someone else made a mistake and *volo* came out *velo*, which is gibberish. Was this double slip freudful, suggesting conflicting intentions? Guilty uneasiness about what culture does to nature? To try to answer such questions would be, no doubt, to pursue truth too far into its thicket.

But what has it been like to grow up in a state so represented by its earliest political fathers? The contributors to *Growing Up in Minnesota*, to whom I will introduce you in a moment, give us their own heartfelt answers to this question.

If rifle, ax, plow, and other machines of civilization have proved less benign than Governor Ramsey's category of "improvement ideas" suggests, Minnesota remains, nevertheless, a comely place, its nature less blasted than nature elsewhere. It is very easy to love. Although one is rarely astounded by single natural wonders, the

---

*William Watts Folwell, *A History of Minnesota*, vol. I (Minnesota Historical Society, 1921), pp. 460-461.

plethora of comfortable loveliness is impressive. Here and there, as on the shores and islands of Lake Superior, it can be pretty exciting. The most spectacular views along Lake Superior, however, are on the North Shore, in Canada.

Northwest and southwest of Lake Superior there are some three million acres of lakes and forests of spruce and jack pine and hardwoods, with an occasional tamarack swamp. Among the over fifteen thousand lakes in Minnesota that cover more than ten acres of land, a few lakes in the north — Mille Lacs, Leech Lake, Lake Winnibigoshish, Red Lake, Rainy Lake, and Lake of the Woods — are fifteen, twenty, or even thirty miles across. And they are relatively unspoiled, in spite of motorboats, snowmobiles, and seaplanes. I could say beautiful beyond belief. Surely it would be niggling to hanker here for mountains, to grouse about an absence of ocean. Minnesota is comely.

In the southern and western parts of the state there is agriculture, the rich, abundant land flat or gently rolling as one goes toward the Fergus Falls neighborhood painted by Charles Beck or the Waterville area shown us years ago in the watercolors of Adolf Dehn. And of course there are the railroads and the villages and cities that grew up alongside them, with elevators rising from below to beyond and railway stations — those buildings that Sinclair Lewis called derisively the final aspiration of architecture — many now abandoned. And the highways, the highways, the highways we are on.

Few locations in Minnesota are more than a few miles from a lake, a creek, or a part of one of the three great river systems flowing contrary to one another toward far-off seas. The Mississippi River rises near Lake Itasca — one can jump across its clear waters there — and heads toward the Gulf of Mexico. The Red River of the North, which forms part of the western boundary of Minnesota, flows into Canada's Lake Winnipeg, thence to Hudson Bay. And the St. Louis River, with the others in its system, flows into Lake Superior and ultimately the Atlantic. There are so many lakes that ninety-nine are called Long Lake, ninety-one Mud Lake, seventy-six Rice Lake, forty-three Bass Lake, and so on.

Even within Minneapolis there are twenty-one fine lakes, and some twenty-five miles of the twenty-five thousand miles of rivers in the state have been measured within the city. The Mississippi drops fifty feet at St. Anthony Falls, and Minnehaha Creek cascades fifty-four feet within the city — a fall that inspired Longfellow to write about it. The Minnesota River, flat and murky and tending to overflow its banks each spring, gave its name to the state. Nobody knows exactly what the name means, and opinions range from "sky-blue water" to "milky water," as suggested by an old tribal woman (now long dead) who may not have known the word "mucky."

Not quite sublime, the scenery of the state has its own middle-of-the-road beauty. Even the wildlife of the state fits the image of moderation. If we look hard enough in northern Minnesota, of course, we can see moose, timber wolves, and eagles, although we are more likely to find them stuffed in the IGA store or the local saloon. But there are no giraffes or yaks or armadillos or kiwis here. It is the relatively ordinary critters that are plentiful: deer, bears, skunks, raccoons, beavers, muskrats, foxes, and wildfowl. Pheasants and ducks are common even within cities, with geese, herons, and owls nearby. And we are surrounded by fish. For the loon, the state bird, we must visit a country lake. It's worth the trip, especially for kids, to hear the loony laughter. First the loon laughs. A kid will laugh back, naturally, and the loon will reply, joining in an endless exchange of echoing fun. Minnesota is a good place in which to grow up.

The earlier generations of Minnesotans who found the middling nature of the state to their liking — tribal peoples in ancient times, more recent settlers from Europe and elsewhere, and blacks whose ancestors were brought to America by force — busily added to it their own temperate cultures. And we who continue to shape the middle-of-the-road image of Minnesota also like it that way. More or less.

That Minnesota is a good place in which to grow up is the consensus of those who have written accounts of their growth for this book. Before I introduce them to you, however, I would like to say a few words about the sense of place, as I understand it, and about the assumptions on which this book is based.

Love for the natal place is not new. Since human beings first began to assert themselves as individual identities — to say "I am" — they have done so in relation to their parents and their place of birth. Homer is said to have been a blind man and a wanderer on the earth. However that may be, his great character Odysseus clearly proclaims his identity in relation to his parents and his place of birth. Far from home and fearing the foreign, cannibalistic Cyclops, he says that his name is "Nobody" or "Noman" — a pun (*"Outis"*) on his name. But when he has burned out the wicked giant's eye, he cries his selfhood from the ship as he and his men escape amid the hail of boulders hurled by the Cyclops: "It is I, Odysseus, son of Laertes, from Ithaca!"

The love Americans feel for their birthplace, however, involves relatively little local patriotism. An American is born, let us say, in Schenectady and grows up there. One day the boss says, "We're going to have to transfer you to the home office in Tulsa, but it will be a step up the ladder." Why not? Who cares whether we live in Pittsburgh or Los Angeles? The ground of concrete and black-top provides sparse root-room for our rubber wheels. The metal, glass, and cement heaps of our skylines support only the vaguest of infantile dreams, which are easily transferable from one city to another.

The transferability of our weak affection for place is also evident in small-town America. The writings of Willa Cather, Sinclair Lewis, Zona Gale, Sherwood Anderson, and others confirm our suspicion that life along Main Street is much the same from Gopher Prairie, Minnesota, to Winesburg, Ohio. Emptiness is emptiness. The way to solve the problem of being born in a small town is to leave it for the city — Minneapolis, Pittsburgh, Buffalo — what's the difference? Even childhood on an American farm does not necessarily instill the attachment to place that Odysseus feels for Ithaca, much less what Aleksis Kivi feels for Karelia, Charles Péguy for the Lorraine, or Nikos Kazantzakis for Crete. Hamlin Garland's *Main-Travelled Roads* could run anywhere through the grubby Middle Border, and his characters — whom William Dean Howells referred to as "those gaunt, grim, sordid, pathetic, ferocious figures . . . so easy to caricature as Hayseeds" — could fit into the nineteenth-century American landscape anywhere from Ohio to the Dakotas, from West Virginia to Nebraska. In fact, they were likely to be on the move, like their urban or small-town counterparts, from one place to another. I heard somewhere that nowadays Americans move, on the average, once every five years.

Our patriotism is less for *patria* (or *matria*, as Plato was surprised to learn that the Cretans termed it) than for symbols and ideals — the flag, the Declaration of Independence, the Constitution, liberty, justice, equality, bravery. While the Norwegian sings "Ja, vi elsker dette landet . . ." ("Yes, we love this land . . .") or the Finn sings "Oi maame, suomi, synnyinmaa . . ." ("O land, Finland, native land . . ."), we proudly hail a star-spangled banner illuminated by the red glare of war. And our war songs describe even more precisely the kinetic rolling of our patriotism "from the halls of Montezuma to the shores of Tripoli" as "those caissons go rolling along." Movement is our thing, the world our oyster — westward to the Pacific, to Hawaii and the Philippines, to Vietnam, to the moon and beyond.

We could not understand, therefore, during the last century or so, why the tribal peoples did not want to be moved to just any old set of acres "reserved" for them, why they insisted, ineffectually, that they must keep the burial grounds. Chief Shakopee, during the great and despicable theft of treaty lands in Minnesota by politicians and traders in 1851, spoke up with a small voice in an attempt to retain Wayzata for his people. The name that the rich exurb of Minneapolis still bears means "the beautiful aspect of the Spirit." But of course Shakopee and his people lost that, too, through the action of the legislatures and the Great White Fathers.

In 1966 Bob Dylan, who grew up in Minnesota, described his feelings about his home state in an interview published in *Playboy*: "I didn't run away from it; I just turned my back on it. It couldn't give me anything. . . . So leaving wasn't hard at all; it would have been much harder to stay. I didn't want to die there." Yet even as he decried, like Carol Kennicott in *Main Street*, the voidlike aspect of Minnesota, he knew that his own sense of being-in-the-world was fashioned here: "As I think about it now, though, it wouldn't be such a bad place to go back to and die in. There's no place I feel closer to now, or get the feeling that I'm part of, except maybe New York; but I'm not a New Yorker. I'm North Dakota-Minnesota-Midwestern. I'm that color. I speak that way. I'm from someplace called the Iron Range. My brains and feelings have come from there. I wouldn't amputate on a drowning man; *nobody* from out there would."

It seems less a question of literary influence than of shared experience that Bob Dylan's comments about his Midwestern roots call to mind not only the sentiments of Carol Kennicott but also those of Nick Carraway at the end of *The Great Gatsby* (Charles Scribner's Sons, 1925). Carraway has just finished telling the story of Gatsby and the others against the backdrop of Long Island and Manhattan. He recalls earlier days when he had returned to Minnesota from prep school or college. In his recollection he is leaving the train depot in Chicago:

> When we pulled out into the winter night and the real snow, our snow, began to stretch out beside us and twinkle against the windows, and the dim lights of small Wisconsin stations moved by, a sharp wild brace came suddenly into the air. We drew in deep breaths of it as we walked back from dinner through the cold vestibules, unutterably aware of our identity with this country for one strange hour, before we melted indistinguishably into it again.
>
> That's my Middle West — not the wheat or the prairies or the lost Swede towns, but the thrilling returning trains of my youth, and the shadows of holly wreaths thrown by lighted windows on the snow. I am a part of that, a little solemn with the feel of those long winters, a little complacent from growing up in the Carraway house in a city where dwellings are still called through decades by a family name. I see that this has been a story of the West, after all — Tom and Gatsby, Daisy and Jordan and I, were all Westerners, and perhaps we possessed some deficiency in common which made us subtly unadaptable to Eastern life.

It may be a place to be from, but it is impossible to leave behind.

Based on every instant of that childhood we never entirely relinquish, our lives are never entirely free of its forms. The eight accounts of childhood and early youth in this book reveal a wide variety of these shapes — the cosmic lyricism and rounded portraiture of Meridel Le Sueur, the subtle journalistic rhythms of Harrison Salisbury, the incisive vignettes and fantasies of Gerald Vizenor, the confined hallscapes and tentative outrides of Keith Gunderson's prose (complemented by the liberating play of his prose poems), the sensuous exuberance of Shirley Schoonover, the ironic gaiety laid over the agony of Toyse Kyle, the memorable images of Robert Bly, and the family chorus of the Hongs — Edna, Howard, and Mary Hong Loe. The accounts are arranged in the order that I have just described, proceeding generally from age to youth with a few exceptions to provide an alternation between country life and city life and to save the family tandem for the end.

There is not a crybaby in the bunch. And it is not because there are not plenty of losses — abandonments, desertions, a murdered father, a suicidal mother, the guilt of the newly come, the destruction of the environment, declining fortunes, difficulties at role-playing. But the losses are socialized. Griefs become grievances. The creative self "comes through" to wisdom, care, and love, those ripe strengths so hard to attain.

Meridel Le Sueur talks about the communication she felt in her childhood with the curved unconscious — the realm of the ancient mother, the time, as she calls it, of wood before metal. With the help of Zona (the Indian woman) and her ancestral wisdom, and with the mothering prairie in her bones and flesh, she felt intuitively as a child that the world was a maternal round, that the patriarchal forgery of history (the birth of Eve from Adam's rib and of Athena from the head of Zeus) was a lie. (There is no such derivative genesis for women in the stories of the American tribal peoples.) She was present at the end of the last great conflict between the new culture of the West and the old culture of Asia — the imposition by force of the Greek-Christian-puritanical-patriarchal rectangular house on the Asian-Indian-pagan-matriarchal curve of the plains. The patriarchy won again, as everyone knows, just as it had in ancient Israel and Greece, bringing law and order, property and marriage, technological dominance over nature. Bringing, too, airplanes, bombs, snowmobiles, pollution, and the knowledge of death; skyscrapers, freeways, parking lots. The enormous erection of the IDS Tower in Minneapolis stands as our *lingam* to the local victory.

If Meridel Le Sueur is our Sappho and Teiresias, Harrison Salisbury is, I think, our Thucydides and Sophocles. He recreates for us a Victorian family in a Victorian house in the Victorian city of Minneapolis, early in the present century. Lamenting losses to the great god Progress, he bravely declines to deny his own childhood assent to the theology of the Victorian era and instead shows us himself and his society inside the myth.

Salisbury's childhood vision of Minneapolis included its essence. It remains an imperial city, long after the decline of the European empires, although to my eye now it seems less like London than like Lübeck or Munich: rich, energetic, well arranged, clean, comfortable, set amid and upon its considerable natural comeliness. It breathes Thomas Mann more than Dickens. A touch of *A Christmas Story* remains, as Salisbury suggests it did in his childhood, but the prevailing image nowadays recalls the dull complacency of *Buddenbrooks* more than the exciting variety of *David Copperfield*. The empire is not run by emperor or empress, however, but by mercantile, financial, and industrial giants — in food manufacture, abrasives, electronics, and diversified services.

It is against such giants and their smaller imitators that Gerald Vizenor sets his childhood fantasies of the "little people from the woodland of love." The giants need not be those entrepreneurs who took the land, the furs, the woods, and the metals, nor those who continue such work in our time. They need not even be the unknown murderers of the young father or the bureaucrat who twenty-five years later dismissed Vizenor's question about his father's death with, "We never spent much time on winos and derelicts in those days . . . one Indian vagrant kills another." They include Mean Nettles, the young bully, as well as the flatulent stepfather — all "terminal believers" who have but one vision of the world. The terminal believers and giants cannot have the more ancient and valuable roles of trickster, of mocker, of self-ironist. They can see neither the little people from the woodland of love nor the blackhead in the lover's ear.

Keith Gunderson, too, is concerned, but more literally, with "little people" — that is, with himself as a young child growing up in a small Minneapolis apartment — and with the toys and books that helped him to grow. In spite of the prairies to the south and west, the coulee country to the east, and the great woodlands up north, his early experience of the world was set against the hall-scape of 3142 Lyndale Avenue South, named by its builder, with superlative Midwestern turgidity, the Upland Apartments.

Inside the apartment his space was even smaller — the bedroom which he shared for fourteen years with his younger sisters. There his own territory shrank to his bed, the gap between the bed and the wall, two closet shelves, and a cardboard box. Naturally enough, he "developed survival tactics best suited for close-quarter confrontations." In his outdoor travels on his marvelous broomstick horse Neigh-Neigh he never ventured beyond a three-block radius. But on one of his two closet shelves he kept his collection of issues of the *National Geographic*, and he learned at an early age to range widely in thought and imagination, such interior journeys apparently led by the muses of philosophy and poetry.

Shirley Schoonover did not have a broomstick horse — she had a real one named Valko, along with a goose named Petrice and assorted cats, dogs, cows, and scary owls. And her personal world in northern Minnesota was, almost from its beginning, at least as big as a farm. Movement was her way of life — walking, running, climbing, skiing, skating, sliding, swimming, riding. As a youngster she was a tomboy and a daredevil who flirted with Kalma, the god of death, by swimming the Finnish initiation rite underwater between two holes in the ice, diving in from the boiling heat of the sauna. Perhaps it is this restless self, developed in childhood, that has taken her out of Minnesota to live in Nebraska and New York and (now) Missouri. Or maybe she is still moved by her passion for new sensations — the smells and tastes and sounds and sights and tactile delights that she so relished in her childhood and that she here remembers for us in a rush of kinetic prose.

Toyse Kyle's early memories are of a more austere sort, recalling deprivation and malnutrition in a world that was something like hell. Good food came as a result of theft, or as guilty reparation from community institutions, or as a bribe from the church. Her brush with death was not part of a ritual or a game but instead was a terribly real adventure, when her mother, temporarily maddened by her own burdens, tried to pull her off a Minneapolis bridge into the Mississippi River.

Both before and after this night of terror, Kyle's unattainable goal as a child was "to please Mama," and the powerful character of her mother dominates her story of survival and endurance. Her account of what it was like to grow up black in Minnesota is the best I have read, and I should think that her mother (now dead) would indeed be pleased at last.

If Toyse Kyle's story is essentially of the mother, Robert Bly's is all of the father. This emphasis will surprise readers of some of his recent books and essays (such as *Sleepers Joining Hands* and *Leaping Poetry*), with their stress on the Great Mother. For here she fades, in both her bountiful and destroying aspects, into background images of snow and smokehouse, haymow and harvest, waitress and threshing machine. In his new view of past and present Bly sees a child held up by the father over the snow. He sees the Good Father actually going to the judge himself, in defiance of the sheriff-devil and his wicked *fait accompli*, to rescue the Bad Father who has physically attacked the Bad Mother in a reenactment of the primal scene. This is not, I think, the childish dream of rescuing the Good Mother. Rather, it is at once the mature recognition and renunciation of that oedipal wish in the affirmation of choice: "One moral act will last a lifetime" for the son of the father who does it.

One of the most absorbing parts of Bly's account of his childhood is the group of unedited entries from the diary that he kept when he was in the sixth grade. In the entries and between the lines we can read that the wisdom and harmony mentioned above were not easily won.

The Hongs – Edna, Howard, and Mary – write as a family and try to "remember forward." This collaboration is as it should be, because the Hongs in life typify all that is closest to the family ideal. Howard and Edna built their beautiful and locally famous stone house with their own hands thirty-five years ago on Pop Hill in Northfield, and when the college took the hill, they moved the house westward to Heath Creek. The house was a nest from the beginning, for their own children and their adopted offspring as well as for neighborhood children and students. Their whole life has been a collaboration of which their co-authored and co-translated books are but the most public sign. Yet few families give the lie so directly to possessiveness and "togetherness" in their stress on space, on solitude, and on faith in God.

When strangers come to Minnesota to try to form an image of the state to present to the readers of *Time* (the cover article to which Toyse Kyle refers) or the *Christian Science Monitor*, they see the natural beauty of the state and the essentially urban cultural elements such as the theaters and art museums, the university, the professional sports teams, and so on. Most of all they see a state where agriculture is rich, where industry is booming, where politicians are honest, where the business community and the people themselves have a social conscience. They see the good life and the essential spirit, as the writer in *Time* put it, of "courtesy and fairness, honesty, a special capacity for innovation, hard work, intellectual adventure and responsibility." They observe that Minnesota has less of drugs, crime in the streets, pollution, and traffic jams than many cities have. There is a good ethnic mix and a balanced economy. They say that although blacks and tribal peoples may not share fully in the good life these minorities make up only two percent of the population and their lot is looking up. If anything works against this image, according to the writers in the periodicals, it is the hard winters and the mosquitoes, from the side of nature, and the old threat, from the side of culture, that the contentment of the good life will dwindle to complacency and blandness.

This public image — proudly as it may have been hailed on the day the magazine or the newspaper appeared — is rarely part of the private childhoods described in the accounts that follow. The mirror that reflected the modern image seems to have been as much askew as the one that recorded the image used in the design of the Great Seal 127 years ago. The tension that informs the narratives in this book comes from the disparity between the journalistic image and the reality. Minnesota may be Eden with hard winters and mosquitoes, but it is Eden, as a wag said, the day after the fall.

MERIDEL LE SUEUR

The Ancient People and the Newly Come

by Meridel Le Sueur

Born out of the caul of winter in the north, in the swing and circle of the horizon, I am rocked in the ancient land. As a child I first read the scriptures written on the scroll of frozen moisture by wolf and rabbit, by the ancient people and the newly come. In the beginning of the century the Indian smoke still mingled with ours. The frontier of the whites was violent, already injured by vast seizures and massacres. The winter nightmares of fear poisoned the plains nights with psychic airs of theft and utopia. The stolen wheat in the cathedrallike granaries cried out for vengeance.

Most of all one was born into space, into the great resonance of space, a magnetic midwestern valley through which the winds clashed in lassoes of thunder and lightning at the apex of the sky, the very wrath of God.

The body repeats the landscape. They are the source of each other and create each other. We were marked by the seasonal body of earth, by the terrible migrations of people, by the swift turn of a century, verging on change never before experienced on this greening planet. I sensed the mound and swell above the mother breast, and from embryonic eye took sustenance and benediction, and went from mother enclosure to prairie spheres curving into each other.

I was born in winter, the village snow darkened toward mid-

17

night, footsteps on boardwalks, the sound of horses pulling sleighs, and the ring of bells. The square wooden saltbox house held the tall shadows, thrown from kerosene lamps, of my grandmother and my aunt and uncle (missionaries home from India) inquiring at the door.

It was in the old old night of the North Country. The time of wood before metal. Contracted in cold, I lay in the prairie curves of my mother, in the planetary belly, and outside the vast horizon of the plains, swinging dark and thicketed, circle within circle. The round moon sinister reversed upside down in the sign of Neptune, and the twin fishes of Pisces swimming toward Aquarius in the dark.

But the house was New England square, four rooms upstairs and four rooms downstairs, exactly set upon a firm puritan foundation, surveyed on a level, set angles of the old geometry, and thrust up on the plains like an insult, a declamation of the conqueror, a fortress of our God, a shield against excess and sin.

I had been conceived in the riotous summer and fattened on light and stars that fell on my underground roots, and every herb, corn plant, cricket, beaver, red fox leaped in me in the old Indian dark. I saw everything was moving and entering. The rocking of mother and prairie breast curved around me within the square. The field crows flew in my flesh and cawed in my dream.

Crouching together on Indian land in the long winters, we grew in sight and understanding, heard the rumbling of glacial moraines, clung to the edge of holocaust forest fires, below-zero weather, grasshopper plagues, sin, wars, crop failures, drouth, and the mortgage. The severity of the seasons and the strangeness of a new land, with those whose land had been seized looking in our windows, created a tension of guilt and a tightening of sin. We were often snowed in, the villages invisible and inaccessible in cliffs of snow. People froze following the rope to their barns to feed the cattle. But the cyclic renewal and strength of the old prairie earth, held sacred by thousands of years of Indian ritual, the guerrilla soil of the Americas, taught and nourished us.

We flowed through and into the land, often evicted, drouthed out, pushed west. Some were beckoned to regions of gold, space like a mirage throwing up pictures of utopias, wealth, and villages

of brotherhood. Thousands passed through the villages, leaving
their dead, deposits of sorrow and calcium, leaching the soil, creat-
ing and marking with their faces new wheat and corn, producing
idiots, mystics, prophets, and inventors. Or, as an old farmer said,
we couldn't move; nailed to the barn door by the wind, we have to
make a windmill, figure out how to plow without a horse, and in-
vent barbed wire. A Dakota priest said to me, "It will be from here
that the prophets come."

Nowhere in the world can spring burst out of the iron bough as
in the Northwest. When the plains, rising to the Rockies, swell
with heat, and the delicate glow and silence of the melting moisture fills the pure space with delicate winds and the promise of
flowers. We all came, like the crocus, out of the winter dark, out
of the captive village where along the river one winter the whole
population of children died of diphtheria. In the new sun we
counted the dead, and at the spring dance the living danced up a
storm and drank and ate heartily for the pain of it. They danced
their alien feet into the American earth and rolled in the haymow
to beget against the wilderness new pioneers.

All opened in the spring. The prairies, like a great fan, opened.
The people warmed, came together in quilting bees, Ladies' Aid
meetings, house raisings. The plowing and the planting began as
soon as the thaw let the farmers into the fields. Neighbors helped
each other. As soon as the seed was in, the churches had picnics
and baptizings. The ladies donned their calico dresses and spread a
great board of food, while the children ran potato races and one-
legged races and the men played horseshoes and baseball. Children
were born at home with the neighbor woman. Sometimes the doctor got there. When I was twelve, I helped the midwife deliver a
baby. I held onto the screaming mother, her lips bitten nearly off,
while she delivered in pieces a dead, strangled corpse. Some people
who made it through the winter died in the spring, and we all
gathered as survivors to sing "The Old Rugged Cross," "Shall We
Gather at the River?" and "God Be with You Till We Meet Again."

The Poles and the Irish had the best parties, lasting for two or three days sometimes. But even the Baptist revival meetings were full of singing (dancing prohibited), and hundreds were forgiven, talking in tongues. Once I saw them break the ice to baptize a screaming woman into the water of life for her salvation.

On Saturday nights everybody would shoot the works, except the prohibitionists and the "good" people, mostly Protestant tee-totalers who would appear at church on Sunday morning. The frontier gamblers, rascals, and speculators filled the taverns — drink, women, and gambling consuming the wealth of the people and the land. There were gaming palaces for the rich, even horse racing in Stillwater. In St. Paul Nina Clifford, a powerful figure, had two whorehouses, one for gentlemen from "the Hill" and the other for lumberjacks coming in from the woods to spend their hard-earned bucks. It was said that three powers had divided St. Paul among them — Bishop Ireland took "the Hill," Jim Hill took the city for his trains, and Nina Clifford took all that was below "the Hill."

When the corn was "knee-high by the Fourth of July," and the rainfall was good and the sun just right, there was rejoicing in the great Fourth of July picnics that specialized in oratory. Without loudspeakers there were speeches that could be heard the length of the grove, delivered by orators who practiced their wind. When farm prices fell because of the speculation of the Grain Exchange in Minneapolis, the threatened farmers met on the prairie and in the park, the town plaza, and the courthouse to speak out against the power of monopoly. They came for miles, before and after the harvest, in farm wagons with the whole family. They passed out manifestos and spoke of organizing the people to protect them-selves from the predators.

There is no place in the world with summer's end, fall harvest, and Indian summer as in Minnesota. They used to have husking bees. The wagons went down the corn rows, and the men with metal knives on their fingers cut the ears off the stalks and tossed them into the wagons. Then they husked the ears, dancing after-ward, and if a man got a red ear he could kiss his girl. In August there were great fairs, and the farmers came in to show their crops and beasts, and the workers showed their new reapers and mowers.

There was the excitement of the fall, the terror of the winter coming on. In the winter we didn't have what we did not can, preserve, ferment, or bury in sand. We had to hurry to cut the wood and to get the tomatoes, beans, and piccalilli canned before frost in the garden. It was like preparing for a battle. My grandmother wrapped the apples in newspaper and put them cheek by jowl in the barrels. Cabbage was shredded and barreled for sauerkraut. Even the old hens were killed. I was always surprised to see my gentle grandmother put her foot on the neck of her favorite hen and behead her with a single stroke of a long-handled ax.

The days slowly getting shorter, the herbs hung drying as the woods turned golden. Everything changes on the prairies at the end of summer, all coming to ripeness, and the thunderheads charging in the magnetic moisture of the vast skies. The autumnal dances are the best medicine against the threat of winter, isolation again, dangers. The barns were turned into dance halls before the winter hay was cut. The women raised their long skirts and danced toward hell in schottisches, round dances, and square dances. The rafters rang with the music of the old fiddlers and the harmonica players.

When the golden leaves stacked Persian carpets on the ground and the cornfields were bare, we saw again the great hunched land naked, sometimes fall plowed or planted in winter wheat. Slowly the curve seemed to rise out of the glut of summer, and the earth document was visible script, readable in the human tenderness of risk and ruin.

The owl rides the meadow at his hunting hour. The fox clears out the pheasants and the partridges in the cornfield. Jupiter rests above Antares, and the fall moon hooks itself into the prairie sod. A dark wind flows down from Mandan as the Indians slowly move out of the summer campground to go back to the reservation. Aries, buck of the sky, leaps to the outer rim and mates with earth. Root and seed turn into flesh. We turn back to each other in the dark together, in the short days, in the dangerous cold, on the rim of a perpetual wilderness.

It is hard to believe that when I was twelve it was that many years into the century, fourteen years from the Spanish-American

War, twenty-two years from the Ghost Dance and the Battle of Wounded Knee, and four years until World War I would change the agrarian world.

I hung, green girl in the prairie light, in the weathers of three fertile and giant prairie women who strode across my horizon in fierce attitudes of planting, reaping, childbearing, and tender care of the seed. As a pear ripens in the chemical presence of other pears, I throve on their just and benevolent love, which assured a multiplication of flesh out of time's decay. I knew the first eden light among their flowers and prairie breasts, buttocks, and meadows, in their magnetic warmth and praise.

One was my grandmother from Illinois, whose mother was a full-blooded Iroquois who had married her teacher, an abolitionist preacher. She had come with him to the West and vowed she would die on the day of his death. She did. My grandmother herself was a puritan, fortressed within her long skirts and bathing under a shift. She divorced her husband, an unusual act in her society. He was drinking up the farms her father left her. Afterward she rode over the Midwest in a horse-drawn buggy, a shotgun beside her, for the Woman's Christian Temperance Union, crying in the wilderness for sobriety. We rode in hayracks in temperance parades, dressed in white and shouting slogans — "Tremble, King Alcohol: We shall grow up, and lips that touch liquor shall never touch mine!"

Her daughter, my mother, went to college, with my grandmother cooking for fraternities to earn the money to send her through, and married a Lothario preacher at nineteen. She had four children; one died very young. She had read the works of Ellen Key and had heard Emma Goldman, and by the time her last child was born, she believed that a woman had the right of her own life and body. She took a course in comparative religion and broke away from the Christian church. Because the laws of Texas made women and children chattels with no property or civil rights, my mother kidnapped us in the night and fled north like a black slave woman, hoping to get over the border into the new state of Oklahoma, where the laws were more liberal. My father tried to extradite us as criminals or property but failed.

The third woman was a Mandan Indian we called Zona. She

lived in the grove with the Indians who came in the summer to work in the fields, and she helped us out at canning time. Her husband had died of grief because the buffalo did not come back in the Ghost Dance and because, after the massacre at Wounded Knee, the government had prohibited her people from dancing and smoking the sacred pipe and had suppressed the shield societies. After that, she said, even the blueberries disappeared.

I grew in the midst of this maternal forest, a green sapling, in bad years putting my roots deep down for sustenance and survival. It was strange and wonderful what these women had in common. They knew the swift linear movement of a changing society that was hard on women. They had suffered from men, from an abrasive society, from the wandering and disappearance of the family. They lived a subjective and parallel life, in long loneliness of the children, in a manless night among enemies.

They were not waiting for land to open up, for gold mines to be discovered, or for railroads to span the north. They were not waiting for any kind of progress or conquest. They were waiting for the Apocalypse, for the coming of some messiah, or, like my grandmother, to join their people in heaven after a frugal and pure life. Their experience of this world centered around the male as beast, his drunkenness and chicanery, his oppressive violence.

They carried in them the faces of old seeds, ghosts of immigrants over land bridges, old prayers in prairie ash, nourishing rain, prophecies of embryos and corpses, distance opening to show the burning green madonnas in the cob, doomed radiance of skeletons, concentrated calcium, delayed cries at night, feeding pollen and fire. They carried herbs and seeds in sunbonnets, bags of meal, and lilac pouches.

We sat together after harvest, canning, milking and during cyclones in the cellar, and they seemed like continents, full of appearing children and dying heroines. The three of them had much to do with the primal events of the countryside — death, birth, illness, betterment of roads and schools.

I sneaked out with Zona often, crawling out the window over the summer kitchen and shinnying down the apple tree to go through the pale spring night to the Indian fires, where the Indian workers drummed until the village seemed to sink away and some-

thing fierce was thrust up on the old land. The earth became a circle around the central fire, and the skin stretched over the quiet
and hollow skulls of the old and sacred traditional people of the
Mandans. The horizon grew larger, the sling of the night stars
moved above, and the horizon dilated in the repeating circle of the
dancers.

I sat hidden in the meadow with Zona. She was tall and strong,
like many of the Plains Indians. The structure of her face was Ori-
ental, her woman's cheeks round as fruits, encased nutlike by her
long black hair. She told me of how the grass once moved in the
wind, winey in color — the ancient flesh of the mother before the
terrible steel plow put its ravenous teeth in her. How antelope,
deer, elk, and wild fowl lived richly upon the plains, and how in
spring the plains seethed with the roaring of mating buffalo. How
you could hear the clicking of their horns and the drumbeat of
their feet in the fury of rut. How the warriors went out to slay the
meat for the winter. And the summers of the wild berries and the
plums and the making of pemmican, the jollity and wooing, the
buffalo going south to the salt licks and the Mandans to their great
mounded grass cathedrals where they spent the winter in telling
stories and legends of the mountains and the shining sea to the
west. She said they were the first people in the world. They had
lived inside the mother earth and had come up on huge vines into
the light. The vine had broken and there were some of her people
still under the earth. And she told how the traders threw smallpox-
infected clothing into the Mandan village. Most of them died that
winter. The whole northern plains stank with the unburied dead.

She showed me that the earth was truly round, sacred, she said,
so that no one could own it. The land is not for taking, she said,
and I am not for taking. You can't have anything good in the
square or in five. All must be four or seven. You can't divide the
land in the square, she said. She made the whole landscape shift
and encircle me. She said the earth went far down and the whites
could only buy and deed the top. The earth waited, its fingers
clasped together like culms: she closed her brown fingers to show
the interlocking. She said that men and women were rooted, inter-
penetrating, turning to the center. She did not believe in hell or
heaven. She believed we were here now in this place. She said the

earth would give back a terrible holocaust to the white people for being assaulted, plowed up, and polluted. She said everything returned, everything was now, in this time. She said past, present, and future were invented by the white man.

But it was the grass, she said: Grass was one of the richest foods on earth and the prairie grass had salts and protein more than any other food. Before the plow, the plains grass could have fed nations of cattle — all the cattle in the world — just as it had fed the buffalo. They did not overgraze when there were no fences because they walked away as they ate. She said that now the earth-flesh was wrong side up and blowing away in the wind. The grass might never come back, the buffalo never return.

She said the government could not stop the Indians from prayer and the dances. They would take them underground with the unborn people. She swept her sacred feather around the horizon, to show the open fan of the wilderness and how it all returned: mortgaged land, broken treaties — all opened among the gleaming feathers like a warm-breasted bird turning into the turning light of moon and sun, with the grandmother earth turning and turning. What turns, she said, returns. When she said this, I could believe it.

I knew the turning earth and woman would defend me. I saw the powerful strong women, and I was a small green girl with no breasts and hardly a bowel for anger, but gleaming among them, unused, naked as the land, learning anger, and turning to cauterize and protect the earth, to engender out of their rape and suffering a new race to teach the warriors not to tread the earth and women down. At their own peril!

I saw them, the circle like the prairie holding the children within the power of the grandmothers, receiving the returning warriors from all thievery, defeats, and wounds. The fierce and guerrilla strength of the puritan and Indian women seemed similar, unweighed, even unknown, the totemic power of birth and place, earth and flesh.

Their fierce embraces seemed to crush and terrorize my brothers and me. There was something of anguish in them. They had the bodies of the fiercest exiled heroines in fiction and history, pursued, enslaved. They listened to each other and the horrors of their tales — how the Iroquois fled the assassins of my grandmother's village, how she came down the Ohio and brought a melodeon. My mother told of her flight from Texas, across the border into Oklahoma, where women were given the rights to their children. The Indian woman Zona told how her mother was killed in 1890 at the Battle of Wounded Knee, running with her suckling child till the soldiers gunned her down and left the child to freeze at the breast. How her father waited for the Ghost Dance buffalo to come out of the rock and they never came. The three women sat bolt upright in the afternoon with high and noble faces and told these stories so much alike in a strange way. I put it down in my heart that they were so fierce and angry and tempestuous, so strong, because they were bound for the protection of all and had a fierce and terrible and awful passion for vindication and the payment of ransom and the mysterious rescue of something.

My grandmother learned the native herbs and grasses and their uses from Zona. How the different parts could be used and how some parts of many plants were poison at some time in the growth cycle. The dried roots of chokecherry could be made into a gum to put into wounds to stop bleeding. The chokecherry bark could be eaten in the spring for dysentery. From the chokecherry wood spoons were carved. And the berries were crushed in pemmican, which was cut into strips and dried for winter or for a long journey.

My grandmother made a place for these plants in the root cellar and marked them clearly and neatly. The high four-o'clock that came up in the summer in the meadow was a drugstore, a friend. Nobody took too much, leaving some for seed so that it would appear again the next year, as it always did. Bear grass was used to weave watertight bowls. There were plants for digging sticks, brooms, and fishnets, plants for incense, incantations, clothing, soap, oils and paints, tanning, and branding. My grandmother especially loved to know about bulbs, roots, and tubers, for she always prepared for poor crops, famine, fires, disease, and death. Fifty plants were labeled for use in green salads, meal, flour, and syrup; five for beverages; three for contraceptives, remedies for snake bite, antiseptics, and astringents. She had twenty-six plants for the treatment of winter and summer diseases and for use as poultices, tonics, salivants, and thirst preventers. There were poisonous things, and they were used for poison. The pasqueflower, she said, would make a deadly liquor for enemies. The great sunflower was ground and made into a cake for long journeys. Some obnoxious distilled liquor was made from a putrefied toad. There was nothing like a worthless weed. Nothing was of no use. Everything was loved and cared for. I still cannot tear anything from the earth without hearing its cry.

It was a balm to feel from Zona the benevolence of the entire cosmos. Once she took me to Mandan, outside of Bismarck, across the river, to show me the most beautiful living space I have ever seen — the great mounded grass-covered excavations with no windows except at the top where the smoke escaped and the light poured down as in a cathedral. She showed me how they lived in that circle of the cosmos and the earth's orbiting around the round and burning fire of the grandmothers. She taught me that violence is linear and love spherical.

One afternoon as we all sat on the porch in the summer shade, shredding cabbage for sauerkraut, Zona told us about the Ghost Dance. When the government made it illegal for Indians to meet together for the practice of their religion, that was the end, she said; even the blueberries became scarce. My grandmother and mother nodded, fully understanding the strangeness of men and the dreams they get, invoking power on slim threads of reality. Zona spoke sadly of the Ghost Dance, saying that she hadn't believed in it fully and that she had hurt the power of the buffalo to come out of the rock by not believing enough. But her husband went on a long journey to talk with the prophet Wovoka and was convinced that the white man's Jesus was going to help the Indians, that if they all danced together the buffalo and all the dead would return and they would have the land again. She told how he came back and said that he had seen in Oklahoma a huge brass bed, a shrine on the sand hills, surrounded by prayer sticks and sacred objects, where it was said Jesus came and slept every night after helping the Indian people.

I am the one who held him back, she said, I couldn't believe this could happen. The dead appear, but they do not really return to eat the returning buffalo. She said the only thing you could believe was that the land might come back to them. All the grasses could return in one season if the overgrazing would stop. She remembered the real grass that moved and changed like a sea of silk. It took one color from the north, other colors from the south and the east and the west, but now it was short and leached of nitrogen and had only one color. The old rippling, running prairies were gone, she said. She could remember when the Indians had stood and called the buffalo to them, asking for the sacrifice of their flesh, asking them to give their bodies for food. There was great power and love in the earth then, she said.

Then came the last buffalo dream. The grandmothers brought their medicine in sacred bundles to bring the buffalo out of the rock. They brought the old-time power-songs back. She made her husband a ghost shirt through which it was said bullets would not penetrate. He went on a long journey to Texas to find a fresh male buffalo skin and skull for the sacred tepee. It was the last attempt to recover the Indian shield power. It was good power. Wovoka had seen the white savior who hung on the sun cross.

On four nights after the fast and the sweat bath, they sang, watching the rock out of which the buffalo and the dead were to come from the underworld. She said she didn't have the right thoughts. Once she wondered if she could get out of the way if they did come thundering out, and she almost laughed. She said she thought it was no use that way. The past did return, but not that way. But she watched all night. Some said they heard rumbling underground. They danced till they dropped. My husband, she said, stood sweating, his face dirty, his hide painted. My power, she said, was loving and good but not strong enough. My husband said his power was good and strong, she said, and I loved him for it, bringing the ancestors back and the buffalo, the good grass, and the fresh water.

And then in the night he stood with his hands out and cried, this is the way it is ending. No, no, she had cried, the circle never ends. But he did not hear her. He didn't live long after that. He just withered away, wouldn't eat, came to nothing. That was the end of the wild plums, she said, and the old life. We starved and wandered and went down into the culm. But we are locked together underneath, and living will go on. We have to keep things alive for the children.

My grandmother and mother nodded. They knew this. They had made long treks to farms they lost to the same enemies. We will have to do it, my grandmother said — keep the beginning of the circle, the old and the new will meet. And she sang her own ceremonial song then, "We shall come rejoicing, bringing in the sheaves."

There was always this mothering in the night, the great female meadows, sacred and sustaining. I look out now along the bluffs of the Mississippi, where Zona's prophecies of pollution have been fulfilled in ways worse than she could dream. Be aware, she had cried once. Be afraid. Be careful. Be fierce. She had seen the female power of the earth, immense and angry, that could strike back at its polluters and conquerors.

The great richness of growing up in a northwest village was in the variety and the excitement of all the ethnic cultures. I was free to go into all of them, even singing in Norwegian choirs and dancing with Finnish dance groups. The rituals were remembered from the old country, the national holidays were still celebrated. There was even a bagpipe group that marched on St. Patrick's Day, all in green, and in the park I listened to a lawyer, three sheets in the wind, recite the last speech of Robert Emmet. I liked to sample the rich foods, too, and secretly found in myself a riotous temperament different from my grandmother's.

I especially loved the dances. They were so colorful and varied, and some were so sensual and beautiful. They freed me from severe puritan sexual rigidity, from relating pleasure to guilt and sin. I remember my first dance. I don't know how my mother and my grandmother let me go, but it was not without warnings, threats, and a terrible armor against sin and excess. My first party dress was white, although I would have preferred red or even yellow. But only the Polish whores wore those colors, my grandmother said. So I wore a white dress and shoes that had a thin stripe of red around them and little heels. I had rolled my hair on newspaper to have curls, which seemed to me the height of voluptuousness.

Jon came to pick me up in a surrey with a fringe on top, though it was harnessed to a plow horse. The harvest was just over, and his huge forearms were browned from the sun and gleaming. He smelled of chaff, even though he was scrubbed to within an inch of his life and his wild straw hair was slicked down with bear grease. He seemed strange and huge as he helped me onto the high step. We drove slowly through the aspens, which were gold around us. I smelled of talcum powder and so did he. I had rubbed wet red crepe paper on my cheeks and blackened my eyes with kitchen matches, passing my grandmother quickly so she couldn't see my whorish color.

The old horse turned, laughing, to see if we were there, we were so silent. In the grove wagons and carriages had stopped for spooning as it was early. I was glad we weren't going to do that. My grandmother had told me to drink nothing, just as Demeter told Persephone not to eat anything in Hades, though of course she did and was trapped by pomegranate seeds. She warned me that even grape punch could easily be tampered with. She meant spiked.

In the big empty hall everyone stood around kidding and waiting. The men seemed very tall and hung their heads. The girls seemed unbearably bright, each in her best bib and tucker, all laughing too loud and embracing each other to show how good it was to embrace.

But soon the bung was pulled from the beer barrel. Mugs were filled, and moonshine was nipped outside the door. But lips that touch liquor shall never touch mine. Besides, I was bold and spiced enough, going out with a boy, wearing almost high heels, and waiting to dance for the first time.

The fiddlers started warming up. An accordion joined them and we were off. I began to be tossed from one tall man to another. My feet hardly touched the ground, and the caller could have been speaking another language. I didn't need to know the dance, I just followed. I went from one great harvester to the other. They were laughing, some yelling and "feeling you up," as the girls said. Through the hours we were flying, sweating, pressed, tossed, stamping out the rhythms, whirling from embrace to embrace, touching — Hitch 'em up and hike 'em up a high tuckahaw, give me the dance of turkey in the straw. Sugar in the gourd, honey in the horn, I never was so happy since the day I was born.

As the night got deeper and the fiddlers hotter, we were flung into the men's arms, back and forth, a weave of human bodies. I couldn't tell one from the other. A girl took me outside with her. The girls lifted their skirts on one side of the field, and the boys stood with their backs to us on the other. I never heard such laughter or sensed such dangerous meaning in the night, in what took place in the woods, when the dancers returned with curious smiles and leaves in their hair. We seemed on the edge of some abysmal fire. But they seemed unafraid, plunging into the heat and the danger as if into a bonfire of roses.

I never was the same again.

My grandmother homesteaded a piece of land and built a house on it which was a simple pure expression of the Protestant needs of her severe religion, her graceless intensity of the good, thrifty, work-for-the-night-is-coming, dutiful labor. She came alone to the wilderness, hired stonemasons and carpenters, and demanded a design to match her dimensions and spirit. Did she make a drawing on a piece of paper, or did she spin it out of her memory, prudence, and frugality? It was a New England farmhouse with a summer kitchen, a birthing room on ground level, and a closed front parlor where one did not let the sun come. She probably did not consider that the house was squared off on an ancient land of mounds and pyramids and cones, on land that had not been plowed in a million years. Neither did she think the land had been monstrously taken from its native people. If she thought of it at all, she undoubtedly felt the Christian purposes of her Anglo-puritan world would bring only benefit and salvation to them.

The design and beauty of this house moved me then, and when I see its abandoned replica on the plains, I weep. It was a haven against the wild menace of the time, a structural intensity promising only barest warmth, a Doric hearth, and a rigid, austere, expectant growth.

On the day of the opening of homesteading she got a corner lot, a small parcel of land she could register, and she built her wooden democratic temple upon it. The lot ran to what became an alley when the village was formally platted. The outhouse was on this alley. She had two cellars dug the first thing. The root cellar was half under the house, and the cyclone cellar, prepared at all times for disaster with blankets, food, and water, was separate from it. Once during a forest fire the cyclone cellar saved us from the smoke. Her dream, which was common, was to have a piece of land, free of mortgage, with enough room for grapevines, gooseberries, strawberries, asparagus, and rhubarb (all of which would return every year), a garden, three peach trees, and an apple tree. We had one milk cow freshening once a year, and one pig bought from a spring litter. The pig would fatten on our leavings by fall, and we would butcher him, smoke the hams and bacon, and render the lard for the year's frying. Even in a bad year we were almost independent. We had to buy (or exchange work or produce for) only kerosene, wood, coffee, and flour, although we could make flour from acorns or our own corn or, like Zona, from the cattails that grew in the swamp. Zona also ate young cattail shoots in spring salad.

The basement was under only part of the house and was lined with river stone, which made a foot-high base for the house — the yellow sandstone, as I saw it years later, remained strong and faithful. The pine boards also were still aligned straight in their naive simplicity and symmetry, the center holding, the beams holding, the floor hardly warped or slanting. The house was earnestly made with a sturdy belief that it was built to last for a hundred years at the least and to give hearth and ceiling and walls for earnest, simple people who did not ask too much. It contained not one piece of wasted wood or embellishment; it was made to hold the weather out and to hold the faithful human for a century within its piney undecorated wood, straight-angled at the corners, the strong hide of wood stretched to its utmost to protect us. It displayed only two indulgences. One was a little bay window, not rich or ostentatious, projecting barely enough to permit a table or a desk in the alcove; from the window I could look down two streets. I had my desk there and wrote my first stories there. The other indulgence was the front door with its clusters of acorn carvings that had been painted black or had turned black.

The first front room was the parlor, which was used only for company. The blinds were always drawn in the parlor to keep the big red roses in the rug from fading, and on two easels were lithographs of my grandmother's father and mother. The room opening off the parlor was the sitting room, and from there the large kitchen extended under the peach trees. We mainly lived in the kitchen with its big wood-burning stove in front of which we took our Saturday night baths in the washtub. My brothers and I bathed in the same water because we had to carry it from the pump, which was outside, or from the rain barrel, which stood under the eaves. I envied those who had indoor cisterns in which the rain water could accumulate and be pumped directly into the sink.

Through a passageway half open to the weather was the summer kitchen and the little room called the birthing room. In the summer people who had the money to buy "Mr. Rockefeller's kerosene" cooked in their summer kitchen and did not have to heat up the house or waste wood. (My grandmother always said, "Mr. Rockefeller's kerosene has gone up two cents. If it goes up any more to add to his wealth, we'll have to use candles!") Another small room off the kitchen was the only bedroom. My brothers and I slept in the sitting room on couches.

Perhaps another small indulgence was the narrow wooden porch that went one-third of the way around the front of the house, upheld by small handmade wooden pillars. Later we had a sidewalk in front of the house.

This type of house, found all over the Midwest prairies, is a cultural wonder expressing the clean, rudimentary, sober symmetry of the pioneer's needs and speaking of the builders and their materials. Expressing the solid duty of worker and timber and time — earnest, rigid, no fooling, no laxness, spare as the puritan world. The extension of my grandmother's skeleton, of her needs: of her rebuke to the sensuality and wildness of the frontier, faithful to a vengeful god, severe but just; of her rebuke to the sensual stridency of violence and rowdiness. Single-handed in her long skirts and modesty — she never saw her own naked body bathing under that shift — she remarked in time and space of decency, uprightness, and duty. In her pure cabin she took the Ahabs back from their journeys. She cured the mad-drunk crew of beriberi and brought them back to the church altar and the brotherhood of Jesus.

Inside we had my aunt's mission furniture, a style that had been fashionable but then had given way to antiques, so that the poor relatives got the heavy chairs covered in imitation leather. In the spaces of that house I worshipped. I heard my first music in the evening as my grandmother sat at the little foot-pumped organ and sang the only songs she knew, in the homely voice the puritan women seemed to have, as if a joyful or immense tone might be excessive. At church the cords of their necks always swelled out painfully and the sound was painful, of sorrow and asking, and preparation to cross over the river Jordan into the heavenly land. Lead us home, take our hands and lead us out of the wilderness, let us rest in thee. Horrors were sung about rugged and lonely wilds: day after day I plod and moil, sorrow in my troubled glimmering breast, death shining in the dark mysteries beyond my dust, stars in gloomy graves glow and glitter, let me walk in the air of glory, this is where we were crucified, this tree, this agonizing light, and the flowers blanched by fear, poor I pine, what hidden place conceals thee? And she sang her only love song, "Jesus, Lover of My Soul, Let Me to Thy Bosom Fly."

Only through these songs did I know the depths of her sorrow, her terrible loneliness, her wish to die, her deep silence. Sometimes I heard her cry in the night, but I could not humiliate her by going to comfort her. In the day there would be no sign. In abrasive irony she would fulfill the duties inside the shell of her devotion, this fragile house flung up in tepee-curled light by the sound of hammers where a nail had not been known, this puritan citadel, fragile yet strong, a psychic mansion, a fragment of hope and despair. We crouched in an alien land under the weathers, tossing at night on this ancient sea, captained by women, minute against the great white whale.

These houses still gleam empty on the prairies, the same houses from the same puritan, democratic dream, lost and lost again as my grandmother's house was lost in the depression before World War I. They still live in the minds of those fled to the cities or to battlefields in strange villages. This small enduring white frame house is in nightmare and terrible dream proliferated, floating in the flood of time. Let yourself down, as if under water, into these lost walls, to hunt for treasure, to illuminate violence with meaning. Under sea-strange light these little houses glimmer in memory, powerful as radium.

In that little wooden nutmeg of a house my grandmother's mind was full of angels, the last supper, and Mary's ascension into heaven. We were together in the vengeful wilderness with a vengeful god. We read the psalms and the resurrection of Jesus and the women at the tomb that morning of his rising. She waited to go to heaven. She thought she would and so would all those she loved. This world was run by the devil.

The frontier was a hard place to hold up the Christian virtues single-handedly, in fichus of crochet, corsets, gloves, and hats and covered to the ankle by long skirts. She had a big iron rod up her spine and a small one in her curled ironic lip when she at last was released from hell at eighty-five.

After World War II I went out to the prairies to look for my grandmother's house. It was still there in the village that had changed to an industrial center. I followed the sun on my shoulder to find the street. The house still drew me with its light and shine. There was the wide street, the corner house. It had been painted white not long before by some faithful Protestant, and the little front porch was still supported by the undecorated pillars holding up the staunch and unslanting room. The bay window was still there. The back porch even had the same lattice, though the roses had died out. The faithful lilac bush was uncut, frowsy but still there, and the little irises still grew by the river stones that held up the house soberly and straight. The grape arbor had returned to wild grapes. One peach tree remained, spread out like an old matron, and I am sure in season bearing some kind of peaches. The people living in the house had had a hard time. The steps to the cellars were littered with whiskey bottles and coke bottles. A beheaded doll lay by the cyclone cellar. But repairs had been made, and a toilet had been added in one of the closets when the village had gotten water mains. The grass had held well, and I could even see some lilies of the valley near the back door.

When the front door was opened, I entered fearfully, the spaces of my girlhood still curving around me. Grandma's tall figure seemed to be about to appear in the doorway, her long arms under her apron. You see, she would be saying, I built a good house. Yes, I said, the floors even are not slanting: you built it solid.

The walls had been repapered time and again. It was wonderful and strange again to be inside the safe little square box. Not only the wood but the spirit of our flesh and all the harried flesh of a century now moved inside the snail shell, leaving the marks of movement intimate as marrow. I could see how the generations had made jelly from the grapes and had painted the good skeleton bright colors, the essential strength of my grandmother's being carrying her memory in this beautiful Doric shell.

Our fragility turns out to be strength. That sacred house seemed sunbonneted like my grandmother, spare and virginal. It had survived, as we have, the holocaust of our time, the human cyclone, and the hostilities of mid-America.

When we drove away, I didn't need to look back. That Pandora's box house had opened inside me, aswarm with apocalyptic light.

We lived from a frontier economy to the machine age in one generation. I saw the plundering of the wheat plains that impoverished thousands. The year I was born, despite antimonopoly laws passed by the Populist Party, there took place the first gigantic amalgamation of wealth by the Hill and Morgan dynasties for the benefit of their children's children, they said, into eternity. I am glad I saw and suffered the desolation, distress, and sorrow of my people.

We lived through bonanza farming, absentee ownership, colonial oppression, wars, taxes, high interest, and mortgages. I participated in the organization of irate workers and farmers, Davids with slingshots against the Goliaths of power.

After a spell in Kansas we came back to the North Country during the time of the great strikes and depression, before the betrayal into World War I. At the People's College in Fort Scott, Kansas, my mother met Arthur Le Sueur, who with Helen Keller, Eugene Debs, and Charles Steinmetz had founded the greatest workers' school in the country. Thousands of farmers and hillbilly men, miners, and other workers took correspondence courses in workers' law and workers' English and workers' history.

My mother helped found one of the most amazing publications in our country, the *Little Blue Books*. In her course she used quotations from Marx, Jefferson, and Tom Paine, and the workers would ask her where they came from. It was impossible to get cheap editions of their works. She designed a book the size of the overall pocket and selling for a nickel. Millions of *Little Blue Books* were carried into the wheat fields, boxcars, and factories.

Arthur and Marion Le Sueur would not have said they were unique because they were soldiers in a large army of heroic people who with great courage stood against the kings of power in the vast new empire. They lived through many progressive movements, gave their lives to them, and never called anything defeat. Until he died at eighty-five, Arthur was still fighting for a change of venue against death. And Marion at seventy-five ran for senator, stumping the state to say a last word against war.

Arthur came from a militant family from the isle of Jersey. They had rowed across the channel after the failure of the French Revolution and were joined by the exiled Victor Hugo. They came to Minnesota for free land and settled in the rich Minnesota Valley across from Hastings in Ignatius Donnelly's town, Nininger, which was to be the Athens of the Mississippi. They broke the potato market in Chicago the first year and got their first lesson in monopoly and control of distribution. After Arthur's mother's death the three boys and their sister, Anne, all had to work to keep the free land during the depressions.

Arthur went to court the first time when his father horse-whipped the banker who came to foreclose the mortgage on the farm. He decided then to be lawyer to defend the poor. His fare of oatmeal kept him short until he was sixteen, but he didn't get to school until he was too old to fit into the seats. By working in the harvest he got enough money to enroll in the law school at Ann Arbor, where he was called the bull of the woods. He bought an

old McCormick reaper and hired it out in the summer to make
enough money to finish law school. He opened an office in Minot,
North Dakota, and furnished it with a kitchen table, two chairs,
one law book, and a gun. He defended frontier justice and also
picked up a little ready cash as lawyer for Jim Hill.

In his youth he had argued about God with the famous Bishop
Whipple of St. Paul, who came to their farm. While he was plowing, only nine years old, he challenged God, asking him to make
himself known or to be quiet. Asking him to strike him dead.
There was no answer. He got his power when he left the fear and
guilt and supplication and became a tribunal for the people. At
night on the Mouse River he studied Marx and became a Socialist.
He was elected the Socialist mayor of Minot and was arrested on
his first day in office because he ordered the shackles taken off the
ankles of the prisoners and the balls and chains thrown into the
river. The city arrested him for destroying city property.

He loved the frontier way of life and missed it when it passed
away. He was a stocky man with a fighter's stance, Indian color
from prairie wind and sun, and a powerful plower's body. He had
a curious stubborn quality of stolid incorruptibility, a solidity of
responsibility, a devout social integrity. He believed in something
called character, which was what you had of the root, something
that could not be bought or sold or even dug out. What some men
have as hunters for prey he had as public defender of his people.
It was some kind of code of honor, of integrity and bravery. He
had rigorous patterns for himself and the people. In a fight in
court these strengths rose in him like a prizefighter's and he shone
with all the powers of the cunning of the law used in defense of
the oppressed. He stood on the soap box with the Industrial Workers of the World during the free speech fight and was arrested with
them. He refused to be released and defended them all in court.
When a banker was going to foreclose on a mortgaged herd of cattle, he brought the whole herd in to graze on the bank steps, saying, "Here is your herd!" Without a good fight he languished. He
saw the enemy clear and never underestimated its power or his
own.

He never drank, was chaste and shy, told a fantastic story to my
children about Johnny Hoppergrasss. He was full of frontier fan-

tasy and Bunyan stories. He loved the poetry of Robert Burns and told funny stories in dialect.

His power was in the earth and the people. Above all, he liked to teach. He believed that the people had only to understand. He believed that he learned from the masses. He went to small towns throughout the Dakotas and Minnesota in his old car with his roll-down map. I went with him to many villages and passed out leaf-lets on Minnesota's iron range. Often we worked in secret because the Pinkerton spies and the company goons were watching every minute and people were shot outright for selling radical papers. We went in the afternoon, got permission to use the schoolhouse in the evening, and passed out leaflets saying, "Hear how the Grain Exchange robs you by a stroke of the pencil!" Then we would stop at some friend's house for supper, if we knew anyone, or would eat sandwiches in the village square. At seven o'clock we would ring the school bell, light the swinging kerosene lamp that hung from the ceiling, and hang Arthur's charts on the wall.

The charts showed how the Grain Exchange graded down prime wheat to third grade, robbing the farmer of millions. Arthur showed what was bad but also what was good and how it could be made better. He had charts of John Wesley Powell's study of 1878, showing how the 160-acre homestead was bad for the plains. Farm-ers needed more land and cooperative use of the land. They needed communal grazing lands and control of the public domain and water rights. The study showed why plowing was bad, why dust storms would result, why floods would come if all the forests were destroyed. The last page showed how only a few men were al-lowed to exploit the public domain through the railroads and the wheat monopoly — for example, the Pillsburys and the Washburns, who the farmers said had a congressional frank stamped on their buttocks at birth to assure them a seat in Congress.

The seldom discouraging word was being heard from orators in barns, at huge picnics where whole families and villages came in buckboards, the women setting out a rich feast and singing, "The Farmer Is the Man That Feeds Us All," "The Battle Hymn of the Republic," and sometimes "The People's Flag Is Deepest Red, It Waves above Our Martyred Dead." If you never heard the people singing together when you were a young person, shaking like an as-pen in the thunder of history, then you can't imagine these political bacchanals in the cottonwood groves or in the open fields with guards staked out to spot the enemy at fifty or a hundred miles on a clear day.

The last chart bore Ignatius Donnelly's cry: To your tents, O Israel! Return the land to the American people, rescue the rich earth from predatory plutocrats, transfer the American people from pawns and automatons in the hand of monopoly to principals with a voice in their own lives and their country's life. The party of the common people, the child, is come, and it is a giant at birth. The blood is circulating in ten million hearts from which the people cry out for a better life. Its sledgehammer swings with the muscle of the toiling army. This is your party. The thrones of the despots are trembling. Get into the fight.

A great wind of talk was stirred up. Visions excited the men and women of the farms who lived a hundred miles from each other. They were of different ancestry and languages but were at last moving together with their planners, orators, and organizers. At last they were pointing out the charismatic leaders who were stealing their grain and the homestead itself. They asked themselves why, out of the rich humus and the protean grasses, they could not make a living, why machinery was so expensive, whether fences had ruined the land.

The bloody strike on the range broke out. I saw that workers could be killed if they asked for an eight-hour day. Bill Haywood was arrested on the range. The miners struck against low wages and long hours. Thousands of gunmen were imported, and scabs were recruited in the Minneapolis Gateway, the largest hiring street in the northwest. A company gunman killed Litvala, a peddler. And all the radical leaders for twenty miles around were arrested. The unarmed miners were charged with the murder. And the IWW leaders were arrested.

Arthur was one of the founders of the IWW at the 1905 convention. He went to the defense of the miners at Ludlow when the women and children were murdered by Rockefeller mining interests. He defended Wild Bill Haywood. He defended members of the IWW and objectors against the war.

Nowadays everyone seems to recognize and to be shocked at

the insult and injury perpetrated against the IWW, the Socialists, and the conscientious objectors early in the century. It was different to know it then. Our family was not only isolated for our stand against the war, but we were shot at, our books were rifled and burned in our front yard on Dayton Avenue in St. Paul, rocks with obscene messages were thrown through our windows. Organizers for the Non-Partisan League were beaten and tarred and feathered. Tar is very hard to get off. I spent days with victims of beatings trying to get the tar off the skin without taking the skin as well. Minnesota had a vigilante committee, a state fascist organization with unlimited powers and headed by Governor Burnquist; it was called the Minnesota Commission of Public Safety.

Charles Lindbergh, Sr., was pursued from a parade in Red Wing, Minnesota, where the cars were covered with red paint. The participants in the parade drove to a farmer's field and the crowd followed them. The farmer's barn had been painted yellow. Lindbergh probably would have been tarred and feathered had not a train come across the meadow that happened to have at the throttle an antiwar engineer who stopped the train and hoisted the running Lindbergh into the cab and outran the pursuing vigilantes.

The Socialist Party was split in 1916 at the St. Louis convention on the question of the war. Arthur and Marion Le Sueur voted against the war. La Follette from Wisconsin stood alone in the Senate and voted against it. His picture in the statehouse in Madison was turned to the wall, and people spat upon him in the street.

Frank Little, a member of the IWW who had worked on the iron range, had gone to join the fight of the miners in Butte. He had broken his leg but was taken out of his rooming house and was hanged on a Butte bridge. He was protesting the fate of 163 miners who had burned to death in an Anaconda mine explosion.

The years of the war were terrible years. Most of the young men I went to high school with never returned. As a family we were like underground exiles. We hardly dared to go to school. But the Non-Partisan League in North Dakota elected a socialist government in 1918. For one year they had the governorship and a majority in the legislature. They expropriated the grain elevators, the mines, and the newspapers. Arthur, with other lawyers and farmers, created the first legislation for workers and farmers. They included laws on social security, unemployment compensation, the legal takeover of monopoly, and the recall of elected officials. These laws were later made into national laws under the New Deal.

The amazing thing about the radicals of that day was their indomitable optimism. Arthur went through many periods when the struggles and organizations were betrayed, smashed down, destroyed, and sent underground into what appeared to be silence. The leaders and followers were blacklisted, threatened, and sometimes killed. Arthur was plowed under but never destroyed. He knew the people would rise again. He was nominated as a municipal judge when he was sixty, but he lost the election when moneys were put up to defeat him. He had only the poor. When he was over eighty and half blind, without many cases, he defended prisoners in Stillwater who he believed had been unjustly jailed.

In this landscape of linear violence I grew in many climates. I was fortunate in a moment of cataclysm to see the geological and sociological base of our roots. I saw we were not walking on air. I was in a place and a time when people were coming out of illusion. I saw that the earth and its people were moving and real and that we could love them.

I went to the best college. I lived in a unique place of immense geological upheavals and social tracery. Here as in the climate there were fierce oppositions, set down in the wilderness. The pendulum swings were visible and extreme. The immigrants, the native people, the exiles from revolutions were as militant and explosive as the soil or the landscape and the cyclonic weather. We moved in a forest carpeted with humus laid down during the million years since the river channels and the Great Lakes were formed. About five hundred million years before that the Mississippi Valley had been alternately inundated by seas and subjected to volcanic activity. We moved in a glacial drift, a terrain that burned, exploded, lay fallow, and burst upward into crops. The land lay above the iron, copper, nickel, and gold deposited four and a half billion years ago. The snow became radioactive in my time and the soil was poisoned by strontium 90. The lichen pointed in strange directions. Powerful men arose from these queer collisions. Return here from other space and you will see the deep roots and the turmoiled earth.

It is not unusual here that four or five generations have stayed where they were, being dissidents, radicals, mavericks, abolitionists, red republicans, and antimonopolists. These movements have deep and meandering roots like alfalfa.

I was nourished by this place and time and people. Through our house on Dayton Avenue there came the dissidents, the brave exploded root, the radicle. I think the IWWs had the greatest influence on me: They believed that only from the working class could come the poets and the singers, the prophets, the heroes, and the martyrs. They rode the trains with their red membership cards and gathered wherever there was an attack upon their fellow workers. When they came to our house to recuperate, eat, and take a bath, they told hair-raising tales about riding the freights, the wheat fields, the docks of San Diego, the timber workers, the free speech fights in Seattle. They knew which were the best prisons to stay in all winter to learn, read, and eat till spring.

Charles Ashleigh, the son of an English lord, carried a cane and a volume of poetry and walked the wheat fields, teaching and reciting poetry. Joe Hill, tall and blond with amazing blue eyes, sang in the Gateway and at the meetings in Smith and Rice parks in St. Paul, where classes were taught from a soapbox. The teachers were often interrupted by the police and given a night in jail.

They carried in their pockets poetry, the Little Red Song Book that also fitted the pocket, and leaflets of poetry and songs. They carried the *Appeal to Reason* and distributed a million copies of one edition of the paper. They would save the money they earned during the harvest and open a school on lower Hennepin Avenue or on the river flats and study the class struggle all winter. They prepared for prison by learning poetry and how to teach without books. They were transistors, conveyors of lightning.

Kate Richards O'Hare, a tall Irish woman, was arrested in North Dakota for opposing the war and came to our house before the trial. She had taken a children's march to Washington after their fathers were arrested in Oklahoma for what came to be known as the Green Corn Rebellion. They had hidden with their hunting rifles in the tall corn rather than go to the war, until the militia shot them out when the corn withered. She walked with these children across the country, fed by the farmers on the way. To the horror of President Wilson they stood before the White House in their hunger and rags and asked for amnesty for their fathers.

Our house was not large, an extension of my grandmother's puritan white house with an upstairs and a stairway upon which fifty people could sit. We heard the Colorado miners, a lean and terrible sight. Lincoln Steffens, his papers seized by Wilson, secretly came to tell the people of what had happened in Russia.

Bill Haywood, the one-eyed giant of the miners, hid out there. He talked to us and paced back and forth in the little wooden rooms. He was out on bail and he told us how you had to fight your weakness to be a fighter for the working class. He said he liked to drink and sometimes went on a spree, lurching in and out of saloons, brawling, taking on enemies, and reciting poetry. And then he would hole up and discipline himself for the working class, his class, and study Darwin and Morgan and London and Marx. Above all, he loved Shakespeare and could recite whole scenes. Sometimes, he said, he strengthened himself by fasts.

Haywood said his first school was with the miners. Each one would have a book and they would pass them around, and there was always a student, a scholar, among them who went around teaching. From such a scholar he first heard the slogan "an injury to one is an injury to all." He told how he had first been impressed by the Haymarket martyrs. He felt that a great light shone from them. He seemed to me to have grown out of the mines and the gloom and terror like some giant plant, fed by the lives of the miners. He would tell about their maiming toil and about the color of the lead miners, a deathly ashen gray, for they were dying of lead poisoning. He mourned them all and fought for them all. I had never before seen a man like that.

Clarence Darrow spoke eleven hours at Haywood's trial, and fifty thousand people marched in Boston alone. Roosevelt said Darrow was an undesirable citizen, so we all wore placards saying, "I am an undesirable citizen." Darrow said, "I speak for the poor, for the weak, for the weary, for that long line of men, who in darkness and despair, have borne the labors of the human race." The whole world waited and the jury found Haywood not guilty. He is buried in the Kremlin wall.

But Eugene Debs was a man the likes of which I had never seen before or since. He was a man who expressed love boldly. He loved and kissed the people. Kissing was not common on the puritan prairies, but he kissed comrades and children and women. He couldn't have been made anywhere else but in the Midwest. He knew poetry and the IWW preamble and all the people's expressions. It seemed to me that his growth actually came from the people, his growth forced upon him by their needs, and he returned to them the image.

He was fed, matured, and consumed by the struggles of his time. He loved the American earth and its people. He would sit in our kitchen and recite the death speech of John Brown. He believed in oratory and poetry and love. He was a lanky, tall man, who moved, like so many farm boys, as if the shy body receded backward, hung on the bones; his delicate face and bald head and his whole being were full of a kind of tenderness. He also liked to drink in a bar with the workers and recite poetry, orations, and stories and to listen to theirs.

He was a marvelous speaker. In the time of no amplifiers his delicate message rang like a bell, as if his whole being became a resonance. He walked back and forth lifting his long arms and spoke like a lover and a teacher. Arthur had traveled with him on the "Red Special" in the 1908 presidential election. They spoke every hour from the train platform; the farmers stood in the fields to listen, and the workers came down to hear him at the station.

It was a tradition that the young girls, when he spoke, should present him with a bouquet of red roses. We wore white dresses and each carried a bouquet of red roses, the sign of the blood of the workers. We each could say something to him, and he leaned his tall frame down tenderly. I'll never forget the tears coming to my eyes, and I said to him a quote from his own speech, "All we want is the earth for the people." He took the flowers and leaned down and kissed each one of us. The audience was crying, too. It was a new kind of tenderness. I met an old man in Seattle once who after fifty years remembered the sunny day in the park and the exact words of Debs, and he cried, too, telling me about it.

I heard Debs tell with wonder how he confronted Jim Hill at the foot of Fourth Street in St. Paul, after he had held up Hill's trains in the Pullman strike of 1896 and how the big cyclops had said that not a man would go out on strike, that he knew every man who worked on his railroad (and he probably did). But they followed Debs and they won the strike, and Debs told how when the train pulled out of the St. Paul station, thousands of railroad workers stood silent and bare-headed beside the track. The greatest tribute ever paid him, he said, was when they stood with their shovels and with happiness radiating from their faces, yet with tears in their eyes, their tribute more precious than all the bouquets in the world. These prairie agrarian prophets, these sagas of the people, still rise in the nitrogen of the roots, still live in the protein.

HARRISON E. SALISBURY

The Victorian City in the Midwest

by Harrison E. Salisbury

I was born into a Victorian family and spent my early years in a Victorian house in what was essentially a Victorian city, although, to be sure, Queen Victoria had been dead for some years and the new century, the twentieth, was well underway. The first cartoon I can remember was the famous one in *Punch* in which the middle-aged Prince of Wales, Edward VII-to-be, stands beside a great window looking out at the London downpour, saying: "My, what a long reign!"

Thus, inevitably, I suppose, I was myself a Victorian child, looking inward and backward at life rather than outward and forward, and this tendency was strengthened not only by my family, which was firmly rooted in the attitudes of Victoria's time, but by the house in which I lived, which was pure Victorian Gothic — a house of attics, back staircases, hidden closets, nooks under the eaves, fireplaces, gingerbread, crannies, and crankiness. It was a most uncomfortable house in which to live. I thought it was heaven.

This house was set on a street of similar houses, shaded by great elms which met over the gentle curve of the avenue. The street, of course, was unpaved, and in summer the sprinkling wagons twice a day gentled down the dust, and barefoot children like myself ran behind in delight, wetness, and a good deal of mud.

Every house in this little enclave set among tiny parks, two small

49

lakes, and a rather lively creek was of a piece — broad verandas, sparkling green lawns, pergolas, improbable second-floor and third-floor balconies, mansard roofs, and copper gutters and drains. On the Fourth of July and Decoration Day — the only two public holidays we really celebrated — flags flew from the windows of every house. Nothing thrilled me more.

Before I went to school I was given a large atlas which had belonged to my father. It contained a double-page map of the world. The British Empire was marked in red, and I could see, at a glance, how true it was that the sun never set upon it. Everywhere great splotches of red dominated the map — most of Africa, the huge expanse of Canada, India, Australia, New Zealand — and almost all of the islands of the world. Beside the glory of England's far-flung possessions the green patch of the continental United States, the green daub of Alaska, and the pinpoints of Hawaii and the Philippines seemed almost trivial. I longed for empire.

I grew up in Minnesota, but I never thought of it in that way while I was growing up. I don't think I had much feeling of *state*. I had a strong feeling of nationality mixed, I now know, with a national inferiority feeling. To be American was the best thing in the world. But, of course, England was *the* power. Not only was England the biggest, strongest, most important country, England was the seat of culture, of knowledge. It was where the *real* authors wrote — Dickens and Thackeray and Macaulay, and I knew who the real authors were because their works lined the cherry bookshelves of our library. Each room in our house was finished in a different kind of wood. Cherry in the library and in my parents' bedroom, which once had been Grandfather Salisbury's medical office. Oak in the front hall and the upstairs hall. Ash in the dining room. White-painted pine in the front parlor. Each of the upstairs bedrooms had trim of a different wood as well. But you could not always tell what it had been because the bedrooms had been done over and the woodwork covered with paint.

Certainly Minneapolis was a Victorian city in the early years of my life. The truth is that the nineteenth century did not come to an end in 1900. Not in Minnesota and not, I think, in the United States. It ran well into the twentieth century and only after World War I did it gradually die away in the glitter of the Jazz Age, Prohibition, the shimmy, the Charleston, and all of those evocative signs of the New Culture which, in truth, had no relationship to the Old Culture of my childhood. Or, if it did, it took someone like F. Scott Fitzgerald, who was growing up an age ahead of me in St. Paul, to find it.

Minneapolis was then a granite-and-sandstone city, dominated by great castles — the old Public Library, the Lumber Exchange, the Masonic Temple building, the West Hotel, and the gray cut-stone buildings like the old Pillsbury "A" Mill, the Washburn-Crosby Mills, and the old Exposition Building — and the massive fortresses of the warehouses belonging to Butler Brothers and the others. Of these temples of nineteenth-century wealth and grandeur almost none but the Courthouse remains in its original magnificence.

If I reserved my boyhood patriotism for my country rather than my state (and in speaking of my country I invariably called it "the United States" and never "America" because the latter for some reason seemed not quite *patriotic*), I had a plentiful supply left over for my native city which in all things seemed to me not only fairer, but more civilized, more grandiose, more metropolitan, and just plain niftier than St. Paul, which I understood to be little more than a haunt and a dive, populated, in large part, by politicians (a very lowly breed indeed), Democrats (even more lowly), Irish (another step down), and drunks. Drunkenness, I believed, was the normal condition of the wretched St. Paulites. What a pity the beautiful Capitol with its golden dome, second in beauty only to that in Washington, should by some mischance have been located in this dismal town, this sink of iniquity which even had the brass to boast of itself as a "twin" of Minneapolis! I thought I could detect the difference as soon as we crossed the boundary line riding the beautiful golden trolley cars which Tom Lowry so beneficently permitted to serve not only Minneapolis but the lower depths of St. Paul. To my boy's eye, once the magic line between the two cities was crossed, one entered (in St. Paul) a region of dismal slums, alien people, narrow streets, saloons, and God-alone-knew-what evils. On recrossing into Minneapolis, I breathed freely once more and noticed how bright the sun shone and how pleasant were the streets and the people.

This was a peculiarly narrow and inbred chauvinism. The first page-one newspaper headline I ever got I won for a story in the old *Minneapolis Journal* revealing that the St. Paul Municipal Airport was under water. It had been flooded by the spring Mississippi freshets, and the St. Paul authorities had deliberately kept this shameful secret from becoming known. One of the great shocks of my boyhood was learning that my St. Paul uncle (his St. Paul-ness was made up for by the miraculous fact of his being a locomotive engineer) not only was a Democrat but intended to cast his vote for Woodrow Wilson in the election of 1916. In my Teddy Roosevelt Republican family Democrats equated with town drunks, and Woodrow Wilson was "a yellow dog" who had kept us out of war and proposed to do it for another four years. How could this wonderful uncle whom I had seen at the throttle of his great engine — indeed, he had invited me to ride with him but I was too frightened — vote for the man who had refused to go to the aid of bleeding Belgium with its Dogs of War, ravaged Louvain, its nuns used as bell clappers, its Edith Cavell — the whole terrible litany of crimes inflicted by the *Boche*! The contradiction was beyond my understanding.

I had, as I say, little feeling of citizenship in Minnesota. My world was much smaller — my family, including my mother and father and sister, the old uncle who lived with us (my father's uncle), and my aunt and uncle and cousin who from the time I went to school shared our house, living in the vast precincts of upstairs. This was my world. Its outer perimeters were the broad lawn that flowed down to the curving street, the jungle of the vacant lot next door, the huge and mysterious Victorian barn or coach house which shouldered almost up to our kitchen door, and the house itself — every rambling floor of it from the dark, dangerous, ghost-haunted cellar to the endless corridors and passages of the attic, freezing in winter, blazing in summer, but so packed with treasure that I was always certain if I looked hard and long enough I would find the magic powder that made you invisible, drops that made you small as a dwarf or huge as a giant, and certainly the door which led to the back of the north wind. All of these were there and much much more — if one only were persistent, if one had enough time, if only Mother did not call, "Children! Time for supper!" or time for a nap, or whatever it was time for — the time that always seemed to come just at the worst possible moment.

I think every detail of that house from the depths of the most cobwebby closet to the dank, dark, windowless room behind the furnace, where my great-uncle year after year with persistence and total lack of success tried to grow mushrooms, is etched indelibly in my mind. And well it is. Not a matchstick of the house remains. Gone the Gothic gables. Gone the great front lawn where we tumbled in grass piles in the summer twilights. Gone the old backyard oak tree, the coach house, and the manure pile, gone the thorn apple hedge and the arbor vitae tree which my grandfather planted with my Aunt Sue helping him (and my father taking their picture). Gone the gas lamp at the front of the lawn and the lamplighter whom I used to watch summer and winter with his long pole, setting the soft white mantle aglow. Gone, too, the arc light which replaced the gas lamp — replaced it with a sizzling and sputtering and the smell of ozone given off by the carbon arc. Gone the cedar-block pavement which replaced the well-trodden earth of my earliest memories. Gone the fire engine which raced around the slow corner, smoke belching from the boiler and three good great grays pulling it along. Gone the endless procession of heavy sledges with their burdens of coal, of lumber, of hay, of God-knows-what kind of supplies — and gone, too, the children who followed along picking up the spits and dribbles of coal and taking them home to fire their sputtering round-stoves.

Yes. All of it gone. Not only the era — twice gone — but the whole milieu. Not a stick of the house. Not a blade of the grass. Not a single thorn apple. Not even the dirty box elder we used to climb. Gone not only our house but all the houses. Gone the street — indeed, the whole network of streets. Vanished as though they had never been. As though Oak Lake Addition had never existed. Gone from memories. Gone from maps. And in its place acres of blacktop and concrete. Blocks of buildings, military and rectangular.

Gone the slum that grew year by year with the days of my boyhood. Gone Royalston Avenue, Highland Avenue, Sixth Avenue North. Oak Lake itself — dried up, vanished, drained. I don't know what happened to it. It was gone before I went to Sumner School.

Gone Sumner School with its sooty yellow brick and its sweat-and-floor-polish smells. Gone Rappaport's grocery store with its frost-patterned windows, its hanging banana bunches, day after day turning blacker and blacker, its salt-glazed glass jar of pickles, its wooden boxes of salt herring and prunes, its small barrels of soda crackers, its nickel milk and nickel bread, its winter smell of asafetida and rotten potatoes. Gone with the hot-ironed tailor shop next door where cloth always seemed to be scorching and the smell of steam and sweat took your breath away. Gone the old paper-box factory and the small pond beside it. Gone within a few years of my birth—Bassett's Creek, corseted into an underground sewer and compelled to flow in these strict bonds into the Mississippi.

Well, they say, it's progress. We can't live eternally with the past. New times. New needs. The area was run-down. A slum. High crime area. Unsanitary. Unsightly. Bring in the bulldozers and the concrete pourers.

So it was done. Indeed, it began happening so long ago that it was well underway before I even left Minneapolis. This was progress. So I understood it as a youngster. So we all believed. I don't suppose there was anywhere that the doctrine of progress was worshipped with greater awe. Hadn't Minneapolis been built in the name of progress? Hadn't those great old New England families — the Pillsburys, the Washburns, the Crosbys, the Ameses, the Lorings, and the rest come west and reared up this city on the Mississippi in the name of the great god Progress? To be certain. Progress was growth. Growth meant tearing down the old, putting up the new. This was surely the theology of the Victorian era. It was the philosophy of Minneapolis, as true a Victorian city as could be found on the continent. I breathed in this philosophy with the prairie winds and there still was a prairie when I was growing up. But I gloried to see that prairie blazing with golden wheat. I gloried to see the iron rails cut across its endless expanse, the water towers and the grain elevators like monuments on the horizon — monuments of progress.

No one in those growing-up days worried about growth. What worried people was the slowing of growth. Minneapolis did not grow as rapidly from 1890 to 1900 as in the previous decade. It slowed down more between 1900 and 1910 and still more between 1910 and 1920. That was what worried people. Some people were pulling out and moving to the new horizon — Seattle and Portland or California. More people were jumping over the Midwest and heading straight for the Pacific Coast. That was what was worrying. Maybe Minneapolis was beginning to get *old*. And what could be worse? This was a young country. This was the frontier. This was where things happened. Fortunes were made (and sometimes lost). But by the time I was growing up those great fortunes in lumber, in flour, in ore, in railroads, and in land all had been made. Jim Hill sat in his great Gothic mansion on Summit Avenue and awaited the end. He had spanned the continent with his railroads and the trains roared back and forth through the night, the jewels of the Northwest. The mills stood at St. Anthony Falls in their corona of flour dust like blockhouses guarding the rapids of the river. The grain poured in from Montana, the Dakotas, the Red River Valley. It poured into the Minneapolis mills, and the flour in its cotton sacks and its great jute cloaks filled countless red freight cars and poured out over the country and over the world. The lumber . . . well, it was gone, or almost gone. But there still stands in my nostrils the fresh smell of pungent pine that hung over north Minneapolis, the acrid smell of the sawdust fires, and the terrifying sight of the lumber drives, when the river from shore to shore was a mass of logs and men with peaveys and spiked boots leaping across the logs like mountain goats, frightening in their size, their red-and-purple colors, their iron implements. But now the lumber was gone. It had all been stolen. That was the legend. Everyone bragged of the timber barons and their exploits, and I grew up to the raw smell of the forest fires — Moose Lake, Cloquet — the smoke covering the city at noon so thickly it seemed the sun was setting and hanging in the air for one or two weeks, bitter, irritating our lungs and making us cough. It was frightening — who could say whether the fires might not leap down to the city itself? — and birds and animals fleeing the smoke and the flames took refuge in the city. An owl, blind and staring, sat in our backyard oak, and deer were seen at the city outskirts. Yes, the timber was gone — slashed, burned, logged, cut away — and northern Minnesota (and northern Wisconsin and upper Michigan as well) were left an ugly desert. But no one, I think, was shocked. It was Progress. The trees were there to be cut. And the city savored the tales of the timber barons and how they had made their millions.

All of this was in the great Victorian tradition — go out into the world and make a fortune. Build a mill, erect a city, plow the prairie, dig the riches from the bowels of the earth. This was, as I understood it, man's right. No, man's duty. He was not placed on earth simply to contemplate nature and its beauties. He was placed on earth to do his duty. To improve his own condition (and that of the world along with it). And if this meant that one must dam the pure waters of the rivers, slash down the proud Norway spruce, rip the rich cover from the prairie and sow it to wheat — well, this was what man was put on earth to do. Life was real, life was earnest. One must do one's duty.

And yet. My father told me of going to the Dakotas when he was a boy with his father, my grandfather. In those days the buffalo hunters rode the open ranges. The buffalo hides were stacked at the prairie stations of the Great Northern and the Burlington lines like cordwood. Thousands and thousands of them. My father had seen the buffalo on the prairie. There was no sight like it in the world, so he said. The great herds stretched to the horizon. They moved slowly over the rich prairie, grazing as they went. And there was no cloud of dust as they passed because the prairie was so rich, so thick, the turf so heavy that the buffalo passed by and did not tear it. Now they were gone. My father was sad and puzzled by this. "I don't know how it happened," he said. "The buffalo filled the prairies and then suddenly before you could imagine it they were gone." There were a few kept in a pasture at Fort Snelling, and there were a few here and there over the country. But the great herds were gone.

The prairie was gone, too, and no one understood that. Certainly I did not understand it as a boy in Minnesota nor did I, really, until fairly recent years. My mother, who had come to Minneapolis from Ohio at the start of the 1880s, remembered the prairie very well. It had begun right outside the house where she first lived on Bloomington Avenue, south of Lake Street. The prairie began there and ran on to infinity. She walked on the prairie as a child and picked pasqueflowers, the first flowers of spring. They came even before cowslips and long before violets. There was nothing like the prairie, she said. The freshness of its smell, the compound of a thousand grasses and a thousand flowers, and you could walk on it forever. In summer the grass in some of the wallows came up to your waist, and the buffalo seemed to swim through it. The turf was so heavy a plow could hardly cut a furrow.

The prairie was just beyond the horizon in my growing up. I never really knew it. I knew it was there, but the prairie I saw had been put to the plow. It was wheat or barley or oats. Never corn, of course. Minnesota was too far north for corn. But up in the Red River country they were beginning to grow potatoes. That was something new.

They say small prairie preserves still exist in some places in the West — small islands of the original grassland which for some curious reason have survived. But I think that is very much like the sad and mangy herds of buffalo which I used to see as a boy. It was hard to connect those decrepit creatures with the noble herds that reached to the far horizon. I venture that it is even harder to connect the preserved patches of prairie to those seas of grass which once filled the continent from the Mississippi west to the Rockies.

I was conscious of one natural tragedy as a youngster — the disappearance of the passenger pigeon. I think the passenger pigeon may have vanished in the first years of my life or just before. I never saw one, but I heard much of them in school, and I think their extinction was the first natural tragedy to arouse me. For years I never went into the forest, never traveled along the roads and highways without hoping that I would see a passenger pigeon. My discovery would make headlines from one end of the country to the other. But all I saw were mourning doves. Beautiful birds. I was fond of them. But they were a source of endless disappointment.

My concern over the passenger pigeon and my mild puzzlement at the vanishing of the buffalo were but the most trivial punctuation marks in my basic Victorian conviction that the role of man was to "improve" the earth, that is, to appreciate it and to use it for his own material good and betterment. It never occurred to me when I was growing up that it might be wrong for a public utility to put up a high dam at St. Croix Falls and thus change the whole ambiance of the St. Croix rapids. In fact, I clung to my father's hand, looking at that gigantic structure with a profound mixture of terror (the swirling waters, the dashing spray, the great heights) and pride at man's ability to erect so remarkable a creation. And the same with the building of the High Dam on the Mississippi. That this dam turned the river from St. Anthony Falls to the dam into a stagnant pool of nauseous sewage was a simple fact — neither bad nor good. What could one do about it? It never occurred to me that something *should* be done about it. Nor did it seem wrong that the open sewers of Minneapolis poured into the river. Why not? What were rivers for? And later the construction of the Chicago drainage canal to divert water from Lake Michigan to convey Chicago's titanic sewage effluent into the Illinois River struck me as a magical kind of super-engineering rather than a rape of nature.

Can one be a chauvinist at the age of six? A believer in manifest destiny and the white man's burden? I think so. In our household the name of Theodore Roosevelt was a holy name. I had heard of the Great White Fleet before I went to school. And the Rough Riders and San Juan Hill. I was sorry that we had not kept Cuba. Then it, too, could be colored green on the map along with Hawaii and the Philippines. And when I heard of Pancho Villa and Vera Cruz, I did not think of freedom and revolution. I thought of that map and how wonderful it would be if now the green might extend down all the way to Central America and, after all, why not to the Canal Zone? There were times when I took out my father's atlas and looked very contemplatively at the western hemisphere and North America. If only Canada were green, too, the whole continent could be one color — American. And the stars and stripes would fly over it all.

This chauvinism was not really very pure. It was mixed with other things. For instance, I was a violent partisan for the Allied cause. My great-uncle Jim (with some help from my father and mother) taught me to read the newspaper headlines so that I could follow the progress of the Allies. I cut out maps of the western front and invented strategy for Haig and Foch, and a year or two after the war started — actually it was after we entered the war in 1917 — I embarked upon my first (and for a long time only) literary effort — a history of the war, biased, vindictive, and prejudiced, in which the English, the French, and the Belgians emerged as shining heroes and the Germans as cowardly criminals. The Russians got little attention in my history (I imagine the *Minneapolis Journal* did not cover the Russian front in detail), but when the revolution came, the boy soldiers of whom I read captured my imagination. In the cold and snowy November of 1917 I remember shouldering my homemade wooden rifle and tramping sentry duty on our lawn as dusk fell and a raw wind blew, looking at my long silhouette, black on the snow, and imagining that it was the same as those of the boy soldiers of Petrograd, the peak of my stocking cap an identical black shadow of the Russian felt helmets which later became known as Budënny helmets.

I now know that Minnesota was a hotbed of progressive socialist thought in those times. There was a strong movement in the state against the war, against American involvement in it, and against the influence of the "big interests," Wall Street, and the eastern financiers who were presumed to be running the country and the economy for their own benefit and not for the benefit of agrarian, rural Minnesota. I now know that in those years there was raging unrest in the West — violent agrarian movements, the rise of the anarchistic philosophy of the IWW (the Industrial Workers of the World), and the solid and principled Socialism that was brought to Minnesota by Swedish, Norwegian, Danish, and German emigrants from the turbulent Europe of the 1840s.

But not until I reached the University of Minnesota in the last years before the Great Depression did any of this begin to penetrate my consciousness. I had heard of the IWWs, probably during World War I, as I-Won't-Work because that was the way my good Victorian father referred to them. When I first saw the initials IWW chalked on an alley fence, there ran through me a little thrill of fright — who could have scrawled those dread letters on a fence in the back alley which led from our house through the middle of the block and emerged just before the intersection of Sixth Avenue North and Lyndale? There was a kind of delicious horror in imagining who might have done it — certainly no schoolboy of my age would have been so daring. Certainly none of the solid burghers whose houses backed up to the alley. It must, I realized, have been done by a stableboy or a coachman or someone like that — for at this time most of the sheds and barns opening onto the alley housed horses, not automobiles, just as ours did until halfway into World War I.

In a way the back alley was a more vital part of my life than Royalston Avenue, Highland Avenue, and the city streets. Here was the real life of the neighborhood. Half of our neighbors kept chickens and the cry of the cock awakened me all through my boyhood. The clatter of horses and carts on the rough cobble of the alley formed a counterpoint to the softer trot of horses on the avenues.

We read of the great cries of the city of London and we forget or perhaps we never knew of the cries of the city of Minneapolis and all of the other Victorian cities. There was, of course, the ragpicker's cry, "Rags, rags, old rags, anyone," and the bell which hung just under his cart and jangled as he progressed up the rough stones of the alley. Not, of course, just one ragpicker. A succession of them. And perhaps not one every day. But it sometimes seemed that way during World War I when everything had a value — old copper sinks, discarded after endless soldering; newspapers — twenty-five cents a hundred pounds; magazines — forty cents for fifty pounds (we ripped out and sold all of the advertising sections from the stacks of *Scribner's*, *Harper's*, and *The Atlantic* in the attic); old bottles; iron of every kind; rubber; tinfoil in great round balls; cotton and wool rags (but not, I think, silk rags). Sometimes, the ragpicker would come right into the basement where these treasures were stored and offer to buy the whole contents for, let's say, three dollars. He had a small spring scale which he held up in his hand when weighing the paper, and he paid his money out of a purse with a nickel clasp. The purse smelled of money. Well, maybe it didn't smell of money, but it was a strong smell, something like leather, but not exactly. I still think of it as the smell of money. He counted the money in "bits" — one bit, two bits, three bits, four bits — and he always paid in silver dimes, quarters, half-dollars, and cartwheel dollars with the Liberty cap on them. (The Victory head came out during World War I, and everyone was excited by it.) Other tradesmen also sold their wares and services in the alley. The Italian vegetable merchant (from whom we bought regularly) and other "wild" vegetable men — who knows where they came from? Did they buy their fruit and vegetables at the big open market across the railroad tracks? Or were they farmers? Perhaps both. And there was the milkman with his patient horse and rattling baskets — if the rooster did not awaken us, the milkman did. And fish men and meat men (we never traded with them).

Some street vendors plied their trade on the avenue. The scissors grinders, for instance. One who had his own wagon with a jangling bell came down the curve from Highland Avenue. Others pushed or pulled their grinding machines along the sidewalk while the characteristic bells tinkled intelligence of their arrival.

The most wonderful phenomenon, to be sure, was the waffle man. Not the popcorn man who came just at dusk with his gas-lighted, glass-enclosed wagon, popcorn heaped up to the window level, constantly shaking his popper over the blue flames of the burner. The popcorn man was splendid — the way he picked up the tin pitcher of liquid butter and the grandiose gesture as he spilled it over the corn, and the gleaming white paper bags, butter already oiling their walls, that he handed out for a nickel — but he was as nothing compared to the waffle man. The waffle man seldom came, once or twice a year at most. (Where did he spend the rest of his days — crisscrossing the entire city?) Long before he came around the far bend of the avenue you heard the silver bugle he blew as his wagon slowly proceeded down the street. The bugle hung on a blue cord attached to the ceiling of his wagon so that he need use only one hand to put it to his lips and let forth a loud tattoo. No one could mistake it. You heard it three or four times before his wagon made its majestic appearance at the curve and slowly, ever so slowly, moved down the street, the crowd of youngsters steadily growing until the waffle man came to a full stop just before getting to our house. Here he handed out the crisp pale-yellow waffles — not covered with maple syrup as ours at home were, but steeped in butter and sprinkled with powdered sugar from a polished tin like a great pepper shaker. Waffles were not cheap. They cost — can my memory be right? — twenty-five cents! A genuine luxury. But the waffle man was magnificent in a white chef's apron and a tall chef's cap, and his wagon itself had an air of luxury about it — polished wood, possibly mahogany. He was not just a casual street vendor, he was the elite. I imagined that he was French, I don't know why. He was so elegant that he could not be just a plain American.

There was a life and activity on the street which you could hardly tear away from. I spent my first years with my nose pushed against the plate glass of our big bay window which looked out on the avenue. I watched everything that came along — the peddlers, the great horse-drawn wagons, the sprinklers, the iceman with his cold-dripping water and the slivers and chips of ice which youngsters clambered onto the rear of the wagon to "steal," the spring-water man (not many people used the city water for drinking in those days), the smart enameled delivery wagons of the department stores — Dayton's and Donaldson's and Powers; the traps, the carriages, and the buggies. And, occasionally, just occasionally, an automobile (although with World War I the automobile very rapidly began to proliferate).

I have said enough, I think, to make clear that the world into which I was born was essentially a world of the past. To be sure, change went forward constantly, but as a small child I did not perceive change. The world in which I lived seemed immutable. I did not go to school until the autumn just before I was seven. I came home from my first day at class and told my mother there were seven "Sullivans" in the first grade. She was gently skeptical. With good reason. The seven Sullivans were, in fact, seven Solomons. The well-to-do, upper-middle-class enclave which we inhabited was swiftly changing. Indeed, it had already changed, although of this I was not aware. Formerly the home of the Hookers, the Dericksons, and the Anglo-Saxon stalwarts, Oak Lake was now the home of the Solomons — a wave of Russian Jewish emigration in the pre-war and early war years had quickly overwhelmed the neighborhood. The old Victorian houses were hacked and cut into "light housekeeping" apartments, rooming houses, and the like, and many of the solid bourgeois owners fled to the newer developments near Lake of the Isles, Lake Calhoun, and beyond. This had no real meaning to me. Nor did my mother's gentle correction of the Sullivans into Solomons. For, in fact, I had no more notion of the meaning of the words Jew and Gentile than my Aunt Mary, who a few years earlier had been told by a friend that a young man she was going out with was a Jew. "I don't understand what you mean," she said. "Is that some kind of disease?"

Perhaps because I was so much a schoolboy chauvinist I was weak on national distinctions and national characteristics. I had a music-hall notion of the Irish. They drank and sang comic ballads. I knew about Swedes because in those early days we had maids, cooks, nursemaids, and cleaning ladies, and they were invariably Swedish — blonde and large and strong and cheerful. That fixed my picture of the Swedes. The other national group I knew something about was the Germans and this image was set by World War I. There was nothing good about Germans. I could not even understand how or why my father could have studied German in school, and it seemed wholly right and proper that the teaching of this disgusting language was banned in the Minneapolis schools in 1917. And it was not until some years later that I realized how shameful it had been that Emil Oberhoffer had been harassed as conductor of the Minneapolis Symphony Orchestra because he was German. We no longer ate sauerkraut at our house — it was Liberty cabbage — and when my sister and I got ill, it was with Liberty measles. We knew a family which had changed its name from Schmidt to Smith, and this was fine and patriotic but one couldn't help but wonder, could one, how deep the change really went.

Far worse than the Germans (who after all could easily be identified by their names and watched and guarded against) were the "pros" — that is, the pro-Germans. And the pros might by anyone. Your next-door neighbor, for instance, who cleverly concealed his sympathies but whom you suspected of harboring disloyal thoughts. These enemies, the "pros," could be anywhere, and who could know what they might be up to — destroying the grain crops with bacteria and rot, sabotaging the flour mills, or even, it was whispered, planning to blow up the shell factory on University Avenue which was working twenty-four hours a day turning out shells for the French and the English. Oh, the "pros" were clever, all right, but sometimes they betrayed themselves. They didn't always give to the Red Cross (and so you kept an eye out to see who didn't have a Red Cross sticker in the window). Or they refused to subscribe to the Liberty Loans and the Victory Loans, and so you tested them out by asking them to contribute somewhat more than others might give. Or, in school, they might not buy savings stamps. Of course, there were many poor children in Sumner School, but at least they should be able to afford twenty-five cents a week in savings stamps. I was *very* suspicious of one schoolmate who bought no savings stamps. Moreover, when the class chose songs to sing, he never picked "Over There" or "Good-bye, Broadway." He always asked for "The Worst Is Yet to Come."

It was in this period that Congressman Lindbergh, the father of Charles A. Lindbergh, was defeated for reelection in Minnesota in a scandalous campaign in which he was pelted with rotten eggs and tomatoes and on at least one occasion was driven out of a small central Minnesota town and nearly lynched. I knew nothing of this until my first years as a cub reporter when I happened to go to Alexandria on a story and was told of the incident with great glee by the local residents. It was apparent that, far from feeling any shame about the incident, they would gladly have done it again. By this time I had outgrown enough of my childhood chauvinism to understand how wrong all of this had been. But I am afraid if I had been taken to one of Congressman Lindbergh's meetings as a child, when I knew him to be a pacifist and opposed to the war, I would have enthusiastically joined in the rotten-egging.

Perhaps I am overemphasizing the primitive racism of my boyhood. Of course, it didn't seem like racism to me, and I would not have known what racism was if I had been asked. My father was, I believe, the most gentle man I have ever known, probably far too gentle for his own good. I cannot believe he would have deliberately caused pain to anyone, and he had been taught compassion by his doctor father. He once told me, "Always be kind to women. You just do not understand the pain and suffering they endure in life." Only once or twice in his life did he ever raise his voice to me – God knows he should have done it often. I don't recall that he ever lost his temper with my mother – again, God knows he should have. Yet, this gentle, quiet, sensitive man customarily spoke of poor Jews as "sheenies" and made a distinction in his mind between Jews who were "sheenies" and those whom he called "white men." I did not know what this distinction was when I was a child and it was a long time before I knew to whom he was referring as sheenies, but I finally got it clear. These were the poor Jews, the peddlers, the proprietors of the small notion stores on Sixth Avenue North, the immigrants who had not yet learned the language. The "white men" were the Jewish business-men, the white-collar Jews. I don't know how he adjusted these at-titudes to the fact that all of my childhood friends were Jews and that they were in and out of the house constantly. I don't think he made a correlation.

We are always expecting people to be logical, but they seldom are in their prejudices. They simply fit them into their lives, and let the contradictions go hang. My father, for instance, was indis-criminate in his prejudices. He worked all his life in a firm of Scots businessmen who had come from Dundee to Minneapolis in the '80s, and there probably was no nationality which he disliked more — possibly for that reason. He regarded the Scots as mean, grasping, clannish, unpleasant, hard people. He felt (I think quite accurately) that since he was not a Scot but half English and half Welsh he was always kept outside their inner confidence and was never given the preference which was reserved for the latest young cousin to arrive from Dundee. He called blacks "niggers" but in-herited from his Unionist father and uncles a staunch, almost aboli-tionist support for Negro rights and the Negro cause. Although he was half Welsh (as was my mother), he had no use for the Welsh — he thought them a sniveling kind of people, not so much a nation-ality as an itinerant race of beggars and ne'er-do-wells. I suppose the sociologists would call him an "old American," and this was, indeed, his real identity. He was cranky over his rights (a police-man had to save him from being beaten up when he insisted on go-ing to the offices of the *Minneapolis Journal* and purchasing his copy of the newspaper during a newsboys' strike) and very hostile toward organized religion of all kinds, but especially toward Methodism, the Baptist church, and Christian Science. I remember the childish glee with which he once placed in my hands Tom Paine's atheistic tract when I happened to ask him some questions about a Sunday School lesson.

I suppose this is why I grew up with a skeptical attitude toward religion even though I faithfully attended Sunday School at the Church of the Redeemer, the First Universalist church. As the pa-rishioners gradually moved to new homes around or beyond the lakes, they were not deemed strong enough in their faith to make a Sunday drive of fifteen or twenty minutes to Second Avenue and Eighth Street in the downtown section — although it seemed to me that this wouldn't be too terrible a burden, even for old ladies in their electrics — and the splendid gray stone building eventually was sold to the Catholics.

Religion played little role in my growing up. I was brought up to be hostile to Roman Catholicism, but I could not tell you why on pain of my life. I never heard any specific faults attributed to the Catholics: they did not, so far as I knew, commit any crimes; they were, as I could myself see, perfectly ordinary working men and women — usually Irish or Polish but sometimes German. The only specific prejudice which I can recall hearing was that they always managed to build their churches on the highest hill in town so the steeple could be seen for miles around. The only Roman Catholic priest I can remember meeting (or even seeing) was a wonderful man at St. Bonifacius who kept bees. We often went there to buy honey from him. My father was very fond of him, and they usually had long talks over the honey purchases. I can't imagine what about.

The religion which interested me most, by far, was the Jewish religion. Almost all of my schoolmates and friends were Jewish. On Jewish holidays Sumner School stayed open, but there were seldom more than four or five children in a class. I thought it most unfair. My classmates took all the other holidays plus their own. But I had to go to school. The bitterness was slightly assuaged when someone would appear from the Orthodox Temple at the corner of Sixth Avenue and Lyndale and ask for two or three youngsters to come to the temple to write down the names and the pledges — since writing was forbidden to the Orthodox on the high holidays. This was a fascinating occupation, and you were paid a dollar. I also enjoyed earning ten cents from two or three old Orthodox ladies, all dressed in black, who paid me to light their stoves so they could get the cooking started before the end of the holiday at sundown. My great frustration was the fact that all of my friends went to *keder* (Hebrew school), as soon as we were let out at Sumner School, and I had to wander on home, alone and with nothing to do, until they were released an hour later. I didn't see why I shouldn't go to *keder* too, and my friends felt the same way about it. This grew to such an issue that finally my mother did make inquiries, but it was quite apparent that the presence of *goyim* at the orthodox institution would not exactly be welcome. Later on I came to treasure this growing up experience, for I realized that I had quite reversed the usual pattern. Ordinarily, it was the Jews who grew up as a minority with all the slights and pains which that implied. But in my childhood I was in the minority, on the outside looking in, unbidden to the seders, making do with Easter eggs instead of participating in Passover.

It is true that in these years the small Victorian enclave in which I was born did change, did start its downhill progress into a slum. That was the meaning of the arrival of the Jews, poor Jews, the newest wave of immigration, who came to Minneapolis in large measure through Winnipeg, Canada, the last wave to get out of Russia before World War I, the wave touched off by the terrible pogroms of Kishinev in 1903 and Odessa and Kiev in 1905, and by the intolerable conditions of military service in the czar's army. You might as well lose a boy altogether as give him up to service in the czar's army. So it was that I learned about revolution, Russia, the czar, the Bolsheviks, and Petrograd at first hand, as it were, or at very close second hand, sitting in the furniture-jammed kitchen of my friend Ruben's house across the street from our broad green lawn, listening to his father talk, his brown eyes gleaming fiercely as he drank tea from a glass (I had never seen that) and hearing what it was like in the Old Country and how he had smuggled himself across the frontier under a load of hay in a peasant's cart and had made his way into Germany where his wife already awaited him and how they had come in steerage across the Atlantic to Montreal and then by train to Winnipeg (where they had relatives) and then on to Minneapolis when 1914 made them fear they had traveled thousands of miles to evade the czar's army only to fall into that of King George. If I could not understand the rationale for running away from King George's army, I at least was captured by the drama of the escape, the terror of life under the czar, and the imminence and need for revolution. I was not quite certain what revolution was, but I knew that we had had our own revolution in the United States. Obviously, what was good for the

United States would be good for Russia. I was automatically on the side of the revolutionaries.

It was these Russian Jewish refugees from the autocratic rule of the czar who first began to open a bit wider the narrow doors of my Victorian world. They lived in a milieu of ideas, of culture, of philosophy, of literature, of mores which I did not know existed. They did not eat their meals at regular hours. They did not get up from the table after eating and go to a living room. They sat right at the kitchen table where they ate and talked and talked and talked. I never heard the end of an argument or the conclusion of a discussion. I always had to go home while it was still in progress (but this seemed to make little difference because the same argument would be going on the next day). Nor was there anything authoritarian about these arguments. Everyone took part and my opinion (if I had one) seemed to count as much as that of anyone else. It was a window on a different world and sometimes I was shocked by it, unexpectedly, when, for example, I asked the question of a Child of Plenty to a youngster across the street: "What are you having for Christmas dinner?" And she complacently replied, "Cheese sandwiches."

Cheese sandwiches for Christmas. Well . . . Christmas was the event of the year for me. I don't know how old my sister and I were before we broke the custom of getting into one or the other's bed together trying to keep ourselves awake all night long on Christmas Eve, telling endless stories and waiting for the noises of the adults behind the closed door of the bedroom finally to cease so that we might silently slip out, hand in hand, through the mysterious heavy-scented darkness, through the dining room with its dimly gleaming silver and porcelain, through the living room where stockings hung bulging at the fireplace, and into the parlor — now a place of strange shapes and imponderable riddles, a Christmas tree silhouetted against the bay window , the scent of spruce mixed somehow with other fragrances — then tiptoeing back to bed, promising each other not to take another peek until the loud-ticking cuckoo clock struck three; probably sinking back into sleep and not awakening again until — horrors! — six o'clock, time to tumble into our parents' bedroom and wheedle them into staggering up, heavy-lidded, to set the fires going in the fireplaces, to shake up the furnace so that hot air began to billow up through the open registers and then, but only then, in heavy woolen bathrobes and fleece-lined bedroom slippers, to begin the ritual of the presents.

Yes, Christmas was *the* day of my childhood — a private day, really. Just the family. My aunt and uncle and cousin. Sometimes another aunt and uncle and cousin — if they were in Minneapolis. A day of excitement, of joy. Usually either my sister or I got sick. Sometimes both.

For weeks we had been building up to it. The anticipation started immediately after my birthday in mid-November. There were not-too-subtle warnings that Santa Claus was observing the conduct of young children with special care. And if one wanted his full attention and kind response, one had best give him no cause for displeasure — that is, eat your meals quietly and leave nothing on the plate, no joking or playing at the table; go to bed swiftly at the appointed hour, no "five minutes more"; do your chores without being told; pick up your boots, don't leave them strewn about the kitchen; see that your toys are in their places in the cupboard or the window seat, and don't leave the building blocks scattered around; and don't complain about errands to the basement and the woodshed.

Well, there were many more admonitions and they changed a bit, year by year, but that was the start of Christmas. Then came the composition of the letter to Santa Claus, a serious occupation which required much thought. One should not ask for too much — that would certainly cause him to think he was dealing with a greedy child. But, on the other hand, one should try to remember to put on the list the things one really wanted — otherwise how could he know what presents were the most essential? The list was usually completed just after Thanksgiving Day. Then the pace began to quicken. There were visits downtown, perhaps to Donaldson's Glass Block, the nearest thing to Brighton which Minneapolis boasted. A sight of Santa Claus with his bell and his chimney (soliciting alms for the Salvation Army or the Volunteers of America). Sometimes — heavens — two Santa Clauses were spotted and that required a bit of explanation. But the climax of the pre-Christmas activity was the visit to Holtzermann's store. I don't know how I managed to square this most wonderful of institutions with my deep-seated germanophobia. Holtzermann's was the most German of German stores. It had been transported direct from the Black Forest. It was crammed from top to bottom with German toys (and there *were* no other toys in the years coming up to World War I). Somehow, possibly through Captain von Boy-Ed and his U-boat, or more likely by prudent advance buying, the stock of German toys, the mechanized animals, the Anchor blocks, the miniature trees, the small chimes which played "Stille Nacht," the lebkuchen, the pfeffernüsse, the gilded angels, the shepherds, the golden stars, and the crimson ornaments with German Christmas mottoes on them did not vanish in 1914. They went on through 1915 and 1916. Only in 1917 did Holtzermann's become more of a ghost than a store, with Japanese trinkets replacing the Black Forest music boxes and cuckoo clocks, but, miracle of miracles, the great basement bins of Dutch wooden shoes were somehow still filled to the brim. But no tin soldiers, no Prussian horsemen with their lances, no small leaden cannons, no banners and flags of grenadier regiments, no flaxen-haired dolls with slow-closing blue eyes, no stuffed animals with genuine leather hides. I did not cry on that wartime visit to Holtzermann's. I was too big a boy. But I felt like it. It was a dream vanished. A world that was never to return.

I don't suppose I ever thought of myself as being from Minnesota until I was thirteen or fourteen years old and then only when I left the state for the first time. Oh, I had been out of the state before that, of course. To Wisconsin. But that was not really away. Wisconsin and Minnesota were a bit like Minneapolis and St. Paul. If you were a youngster, you could see tremendous differences. If you were a bit older, it was hard to find any at all. But that was not like going to Washington and New York and Boston. That was really away. And when you got to New York and someone asked you where you were from, you said Minnesota and more than once their faces remained blank and you knew they simply had no idea of where Minnesota might be or whether it was a state or a city or what. Once, on top of the Woolworth Building (the Empire State Building did not yet exist), a man asked my mother what it was that lay beyond the Hudson. She said New Jersey. "Oh, yes," he said. "Well, I've never been west of the Hudson." How to explain Minnesota — not only west of the Hudson but west of the Mississippi? It was not easy. New Yorkers didn't seem to understand the difference between Minneapolis and Indianapolis. And even when I explained they didn't seem to think it really made a difference. I knew that New Yorkers were very sophisticated people. In fact, I was ashamed of coming from a place way out west where, as I understood the New York view, no one really lived and certainly no one from New York ever ventured. I felt very gawky, very provincial. But then, after I had spent a month or so in New York, I began to think of myself as a New Yorker, too, and when I went back to Minneapolis I felt very superior. I knew how to do things in the New York way. So I felt. That was the way New York was then — and still is.

But there was more to this. I certainly didn't think there was anything to be proud of in coming from Minnesota and that feeling persisted for a long long time. Not until I had been long away from the country and had lived in many places and then came back to the United States did I suddenly find myself saying with a good bit of pride that I came from Minnesota.

And I say that today. I say it not really for the Victorian life I was born into and the Victorian life I led as a child. Nor for the special circumstances of growing up *in* but not really *of* a slum. Nor for the remarkable good luck of living in a Jewish community, a Russian emigrant community at that. Although all of that is part of it. What I think of as the Minnesota contribution to my growing up is the spirit which I acquired at the University of Minnesota, and this, I think, was not to be found at the other neighboring universities and the neighboring states of that day. It was a spirit of particular independence and even crochety thinking. A heels-dug-in attitude toward the world, not accepting beliefs or doctrines or movements simply on their credentials but subjecting them to a skeptical kind of scrutiny. I suppose it was (and is) a kind of "aginism." A little like that old I'm-from-Missouri attitude. But in Minnesota it took a more social form. It was not so individualistic as the Missouri image. The Minnesota way was more thoughtful — the long hard look, the deliberately provoked argument to see what each side had to say, the determined search not for just two sides of a question but a third or even a fourth side; an independence from political clichés and a determination not to be bound by the past or by any stereotype of the future. I am an enrolled member of the Republican party. This is partly the chance of inheritance and partly, I suppose, a kind of crankiness. But in Minnesota Republicans have always insisted on the right to be what they wanted to be, regardless of national policy or individual candidates. And, if the party proved too restrictive, no Minnesota Republican thought anything of breaking the party ties and fitting on another label. All of the great progressive and agrarian movements of that part of the world had their origins in the Republican party, a breeding ground of Bull Moose-ism, mugwumpism, and I don't know how many other aberrant and radical doctrines which then and now are calculated to send shivers down the backs of the respectable and conservative GOP of Wall Street and Big Business.

But that was not the politics of my childhood. The politics of my childhood was button-oriented and straight-party-line. I wore a Hughes button in 1916 (although my secret passion was for Teddy Roosevelt), a Harding button — God help me! — in 1920 (although my personal favorite was Blackjack Pershing), and I was all for Coolidge in 1924. My party moorings began to waver in 1928. I wore a button for Hoover, but I was strongly attracted to Al Smith, and in 1932 when I voted for the first time as a registered Republican I voted for FDR for president and Floyd Olson, the Farmer-Labor candidate, for governor. I don't know which Republican I voted for, but I did vote for one. I was proud of the fact that I crossed my ballot so completely that I voted for one candidate of almost every party except the Prohibitionist ticket.

When the boom burst in 1929, I was at the university. It did not seem at first that the Wall Street crash would have much effect on Minnesota. I had been raised in sharp memory of earlier busts. I knew of the crash of 1893 because several Minneapolis banks had failed and most of my grandfather's money had been lost in them. I knew about the crash of 1907 because it was close to my childhood and my father spoke of its effect on business. It probably took some of his savings, but I don't know about that. And, of course, everyone in Minnesota knew of the postwar crash. This was a special crash which didn't seem to affect the rest of the country but which affected us very much. In World War I the price of wheat went up to $2.50 a bushel. It had been selling, I think, at less than a dollar. This remarkable price rise spurred a tremendous boom in land values, in farming, and in business. My father worked for what was then the Northern Bag Company, which made bags for the flour mills. The boom in wheat meant enormous prosperity for the flour business and, naturally, the bag business. But after the war the price tumbled. Production had overexpanded. It was hard times for the farmers, for the milling business, for the bag business, for Minneapolis, for Minnesota and the Dakotas, and for our family. While the rest of the country roared into the 1920s, we limped along. It was typical of my father that he almost never referred to his financial straits. In fact, he felt, as I came to understand, deeply guilty because he was unable to keep up his family in the style which he felt was proper. I remember him coming home on Saturday afternoons — everyone worked at least half a day on Saturdays then — after lunch. Twice a month he brought two things to my mother. His pay envelope, a small brown tough-paper packet tied with red string. She would strip it open and topple out on the table a small stream of golden coins — twenty-dollar gold pieces — ten of them, I believe. This was how salaried employees of the firm were paid. The factory workers, the hourly workers, were paid once a week but in paper and silver, not gold. The second present was a box of chocolates from Ivey's on Nicollet Avenue, a miraculous box covered in green pebbled paper flecked with gold and stamped in red. The box was always opened immediately and unless I had committed some particularly serious crime in the immediate past I was allowed to pick the first piece. I always chose the largest.

This cosy Victorian affluence of gold and chocolates long since had come to an end. Chocolates, if we had them, came from one of the new "wholesale-retail" stores which sprang up on Seventh Street after World War I. The gold had been transmuted into monthly checks which tended to diminish. Maids and cooks and even cleaning ladies had vanished, We children, my sister and myself, did household chores (twenty-five cents for scrubbing the kitchen floor on Saturday mornings). By the time I was ready to go to college, there simply was no money for it although my father carefully and typically concealed this fact. I should — like most of my classmates — have stayed out of school and earned enough to get started at the university. But this was glossed over. Although he feared and hated debt, my father secretly borrowed on his insurance to raise the money for my education. No one knew this, least of all myself. Nor, I think, would it have made any difference. It was, he felt, his duty to look after his family. He would have been hurt and angry had anyone discovered the exact nature of his straits. A year or two later I discovered to my horror that he had sold practically all of the small stock of men's jewelry he possessed (most of it his father's) — a few pairs of cuff links, some gold tiepins — and had pawned his watch in order to buy the "big" present which he traditionally got as a surprise for the whole family at Christmas. I don't remember what it was — a new victrola or record player, possibly a radio — something we could and should have done without. I never knew what to do about this, but I did have sense enough to understand that the worst thing was to let him know that I shared his secret. I did make one resolution — to earn as much money as I could in my spare time to pay my own expenses and to help out with the household in any way I could. I kept that resolution — not brilliantly, but fairly well.

Thus it was that neither I nor my classmates at the university took the Great Crash seriously. Nor, I think, did many in Minneapolis. Our crash had already come nearly ten years earlier, and it seemed to me that the rest of the country was now just going to catch up. I could not have been more wrong. I began to think rather grimly of my old schoolmate's favorite World War I song, "The Worst Is Yet to Come." My class at the university graduated to a world of no jobs. I was the fortunate one. I had a newspaper job, working at the United Press. I had been lucky enough to get it before I finished school. My friends had no jobs. That summer they rode the rods because no one had money to travel and there were no jobs in Minneapolis. Perhaps there would be jobs in Chicago, New York, or Seattle. Or maybe you could ship on a freighter and find something in Shanghai. It was a help, if you rode the rods, to carry a "red card," an IWW card. The fraternity of the "boes" — the itinerant, migrant workers — was still strong. A card would get you a place at the slumgullion can in the Hoovervilles that began to spring up near the railroad junction points and the big freight yards. A card admitted you to the fraternity of the wandering jobless, a fraternity which looked after its own and protected its members against the enemies — hunger, cold, and the railroad police. I never got my red card, but that autumn of 1930 I went down to the IWW hall and wrote a story about the new members who were flocking from the ranks of the proliferating unemployed. The story almost cost me my job—articles about IWWs, unemployment, and lack of jobs would, the Minneapolis paper complained, give the city a bad name. People would begin to think the city was in trouble. What was needed in these times, the editors said, was good news, not the kind of news that would frighten people and make them think there was a depression in Minneapolis.

Yes. The world had changed. The Victorian era into which I was born had ended, sharply, suddenly, finally. We had moved away from the old house on Royalston Avenue. The old neighborhood was gone. The old Victorian safety and comfort were gone. A new social era had dawned, one with harsher edges, a tendency to call things by their right names, one in which the soft layers were scraped off and the fundamental mechanisms of society were beginning to be exposed. I had grown up in Minnesota. Now it was time to move on, to see what kind of a life might be built on these foundations. Soon I too would be leaving — not riding the rods, but taking the night coach to Chicago (eight dollars one way). Leaving Minnesota, but never really leaving it, after all, for what is in one's life stays there to the end of one's days.

GERALD VIZENOR

Chronology

I Know What You Mean, Erdupps MacChurbbs: Autobiographical Myths and Metaphors

by Gerald Vizenor

1936 *Measuring My Blood*

My Anishinabe grandmother told me that my young father was a trickster, a compassionate trickster, who was not mindful of the sinister tribal stories about the great evil gambler when he left the White Earth Reservation.

"The land you intend to visit is infested with many evil spirits ..." the legendary tribal grandmother of the woodland people once told her brave grandchildren. "No one who has ever been within their power has ever been known to return."

Clement William Vizenor, one of six sons born to Henry Vizenor and Alice Beaulieu, did not return. Smiling and laughing most of his life, he came to Minneapolis a painter and paperhanger and bled to death in a downtown alley three years later.

A story dated June 30, 1936, on the front page of the *Minneapolis Journal* reported that "police sought a giant negro to compare his fingerprints with those on the rifled purse of Clement Vizenor, a twenty-six-year-old half-breed Indian ... found slain yesterday with his head nearly cut off by an eight-inch throat slash ... He was the second member of his family to die under mysterious circumstances within a month. His brother, Truman Vizenor, was found in the Mississippi river, after he had fallen from a railroad bridge ..."

In a later story the *Minneapolis Journal* reported that "the arrest of a Minneapolis negro in Chicago promised to give Minneapolis police a valuable clue to the murder of Clement Vizenor . . . Three half-breed Indians were being held by police for questioning as a part of the investigation . . . Seven negroes were questioned and then given the option of getting out of town . . . Captain Paradeau said he was convinced Clement had been murdered but that robbery was not the motive. The slain youth was reported to have been mild tempered and not in the habit of picking fights. Police learned that he had no debts, and, as far as they could ascertain, no enemies."

Family Photograph

among trees
my father was a spruce

corded for tribal pulp
he left the white earth reservation
colonial genealogies
taking up the city at twenty-three

telling stories
sharing dreams from a mason jar
running
low through the stumps at night
was his line

at twenty-three
he waited with the old men
colorless
dressed in their last uniforms
reeling on the nicollet island bridge

arm bands adrift
wooden limbs
men too civilized by war
thrown back to evangelists and charity

no reservation superintendents there
no indian agents
pacing off allotments twenty acres short
only family photographs ashore

no catholics on the wire
tying treaty money to confirmations

in the city
my father was an immigrant
hanging paper flowers
painting ceilings white for a union boss
disguising saint louis park

his weekend women
listened to him measuring my blood at night

downtown rooms were cold
half truths
peeling like blisters of history
two sizes too small

he smiles
holding me in a photograph then
the new spruce
half white
half immigrant
taking up the city and losing at cards

Clement Vizenor was survived by his mother, his wife, three brothers, two sisters, and his son Gerald Robert Vizenor, one year and eight months old.

When my father was murdered, I was living with my Anishinabe grandmother and aunts and uncles in a small cold-water apartment near downtown Minneapolis. The only personal memory I have from then is my grandmother hiding my nursing bottle, which, she said, I carried around all day clenched between my front teeth. When I was older, she told me between pinches of snuff that she stopped hiding my bottle when I learned the game and started hiding her bottles of whiskey. When she laughed, her round brown cheeks shook and her jumbo stomach jumped up and down under her dress of printed flowers.

Twenty-five years after the death of my father I met with police officials to examine the records of their investigation. Several people had been questioned, and the case was closed as an unsolved homicide. The chief of detectives, who was surprised to remember that he was the first officer called to investigate the crime, defended his superficial report: "We never spent much time on winos and derelicts in those days . . . who knows, one Indian vagrant kills another."

"Clement Vizenor is my father!"

"Maybe your father was a wino then," he said, looking at his watch. "Look kid, that was a long time ago, take it on the chin, you know what I mean?"

1938   *Crossing the Wires*

When I was four years old, my mother claimed me from my Anishinabe grandmother for the beginning of a new life. We moved into a cold two-room apartment above a trunk manufacturing plant located on Washington Avenue in north Minneapolis. One warm spring morning I awakened early, climbed up on the cupboard, and searched the shelves for something to eat. I found only a box of soft prunes. Leaning from the kitchen window, I ate the whole box of prunes and one by one spit the pits like bombs at empty whiskey bottles in the oil and mud on the ground below.

My mother found a job as a waitress, but her salary was little more than the cost of our rent. Her eyes were always filled with tears, especially during birthdays and holidays. The electricity was terminated for nonpayment the day after she had trimmed a small Christmas tree with one threadbare string of lights. She was so distant and alone then. We sat in the dark; she cried and retold the tragedies of her twenty-two years of life. She confessed her deepest fears and guilt and stared at me through her tears before withdrawing into a depressive silence. Then it was time for me to melt the ice floating on the window or follow in silence a new crack in the flooring from one room to the next. I scraped the dirt from the cracks in even rows and then plowed it back again. During the night she summoned all her courage and broke the seal on the electricity meter, crossed the wires, and called me awake to see a lighted tree. She was so happy. The tree with one string of lights was her symbolic triumph over poverty and loneliness. She was crying again, but this time she touched me and hugged me and kissed me and told me her dreams and fantasies of a happy life for us sometime in the future. We were both so young.

During the next five years of my life I was placed with three different foster families, all of whom lived in poverty and had their electricity terminated for nonpayment, while my mother worked very hard for our future and suffered with her growing guilt. From my small places in the world then I learned how to recognize the sounds of poverty and the smell of brackish water in the city.

1941   Apples from the Evangelist

The old man had a deep white frown across his forehead and a shriveled unnerving arm and hand which he would swing from the shoulder to beat his biological son. He was my first foster father. We lived near Pierce elementary school in northeast Minneapolis, next door to a soft-spoken and cold-fingered evangelist who was building his first church on the narrow lot in front of his small house. After school he would invite the neighborhood children in to sing and listen to his religious stories. None were worth remembering, but when his bare-breasted wife nursed her child in front of us, and when he offered us free apples once a day for helping him help the Lord build his church of concrete blocks, we sang high and mocked his strange stories. For months we hauled blocks to the wall, and when the blocks were set in concrete by the evangelist, who wagged his tongue and pinched his lips over his work, we would stuff newspapers in the holes for insulation. When my foster parents objected to their children seeing a bare breast, the woman and her child were hidden from us when we came to sing and work. We never saw her again.

When war was declared, we were all instilled with racial hate. The assumption was that the racism and hate of children at home would help defeat the evil enemy in Asia. The evangelist enlisted for the war. There were no more apples, the church was never finished, and the foster father became more obsessed with his disability — he beat his biological son all the more. When he caught me stealing food or wandering off for hours along the railroad tracks playing war without permission, he would never beat me but only stare at me with one hand on his hip — the other hand hanging limp — and turn away in silence. I never felt like his son because he never hit me with that shriveled arm. My fosterage was only for the money.

His wife, my first foster mother, was very gentle and kind. She would smile for us and plan things with her daughter, but when her husband was home she would seldom speak. He became more abusive and started drinking and staying away from home, which delighted and animated us, but soon his wife joined him and they would both come home drunk.

He lost his job and we looked after ourselves. One night when the electricity was terminated and the space heater ran out of fuel, we fell asleep waiting by the window in our winter coats for him and his wife to come home from drinking. Everyone contributed something to the war which lasted so long at night.

1943   Silence in the Third Grade

My mother married Elmer Petesch, a burly and balding man who left the security of a successful farm family to become an insecure, hard-drinking stationary engineer for a millworking company in the city. He carved his thick curling toenails with a broken pocketknife, ate large bowls of boiled cabbage, carried a pocketful of farmer matches to burn off the effluvial odor of his stomach gas, and was slow to show his love for people.

We lived in a small one-bedroom double bungalow in north Minneapolis across the street from an undeveloped cemetery where I spent most of my time alone with my dog. I built dugouts covered with woven grass and forts in the trees to watch for the evil gamblers of the city.

I entered the third grade at Hamilton elementary school and do not remember speaking an audible word for the whole school year. I had created a life of benign demons and little people from the woodland of love in my head. There was no reason then to leave my fantasies for academic prisons and cold rooms, which, until then, had been peopled with violence and promises and parental guilt. I sat at my little desk seven rows back, never gesturing for recognition or uttering a word. It was a peaceful time. By the end of the school year I had earned the affectionate reputation of being a very well behaved slow learner. At night, in a secret corner of the basement I would sit reading parables to my dog.

During the summer my cemetery territory was overrun and occupied by the enemy who became my friends: Myron Game, whom we called The Frog because he lost his breath on every other word when he was excited; Randolf Mullins, whom we called Black Foot Broth because he was so big and stupid and unclean; Wilbur Wannum, who owned his own real gun. These and others invaded my shelter, rebuilt my esthetic woven fortresses, competed for the loyal affection of my dog, and taught me the good times and places to peep in bathroom windows for a glimpse at naked female bodies.

The leaders of the cemetery legion were always the biggest and toughest but never the witless. Black Foot Broth never had a chance at leadership — we only used him as a servant. For my new place among new friends I practiced the roles of dutiful follower for favors, the daredevil trickster and clown, and as a last resort the intellectual, but I was never successful enough at any role to command the attention of my new friends for more than ten minutes at a time.

The following school year, my second in the third grade, I protested the arbitrary demands of authority — since I had been identified the year before as the well-behaved slow learner, my efforts to be the daredevil intellectual were not convincing — and wandered in my own fantasy of time, defining my own free space. I often skipped school with The Frog to explore the sewers and woods along the river. I was free and guiltless until a very savvy art teacher told me I was a brilliant painter. She displayed my watercolor paintings of setting suns over peaceful lakes, birch trees and moss, canoes, and jumping deer, while brainwashing me with the need for personal discipline. For a time, in the slow course of therapeutic art on the third-grade level, she was very successful. She told me, with an affectionate pat on the head, that I would be famous some day if I worked hard and obeyed the rules.

1946   *Petunias in Juvenile Court*

Come in, Zero Three, this is Zero Four. Suspects have just removed cartoon films from department of children and are proceeding to the escalator near aisle seven, over.

This is Zero Three. Have visual contact with suspects, one in brown winter coat with matching fake fur collar and the other suspect in surplus blue parka . . . will pursue on escalator.

Check, Zero Three. Zero Two will intercept next floor. Believe suspects are destined for winter mittens and sports department, over.

Check, Zero Four.

Silence.

Zero Four, suspects are leaving winter sports department with ski poles and mittens, advise Zero One immediate interception on elevator and notify police, over.

Check, Zero Two.

Main floor, please.

"We made it, Wannum," I said.

"The mittens are mine," he demanded.

"But I thought you wanted the ski poles. Idiot, I wanted the mittens, you already have a pair and I don't," I argued. Looking over my shoulder, I noticed a gray-haired man holding a portable shortwave radio.

"Let's get another pair then," said Wannum, flashing his solid-gold-capped front tooth.

"Never mind, dummy."

Zero One grabbed us by the coat collars. "I see you boys have been shopping for ski poles and mittens," he said. "Have you stolen anything else today?"

"Oh shit . . . you asshole Vizenor," yelled Wannum, backing away from me. "This wasn't my idea, I didn't take a thing," he pleaded as we were dragged from the elevator to a Big Zero office.

My first shudder of fear, having nothing to do with knowing right from wrong or my public image, was the thought of my step-father Elmer stumbling at me with his big hairy arms and jerking my body and beating me until he was breathing so hard he could not swing again.

"Hey mister, I'll do anything, anything," I pleaded to the man in his Zero One office, "but please, do you have to tell my father, do you have to tell him?"

"Are you ashamed for what you have done?" Zero One asked, leaning back in his executive chair behind his desk.

"No, I mean yes, but do you have to tell my father?" I pleaded a second time. "You don't know what he will do to me when he finds out about this."

"Well, I don't think it is my place to tell your father what to do or not to do," Zero One said in dictation tones. "At any rate, we are pleased with your confessions and when the police come along any minute now the whole matter will be out of my hands."

Four two-hundred-pound police officers came puffing into the Zero One office. Zero One gave them the facts while they looked us up and down. We were dragged to a police car and driven in silence to the courthouse.

In a dark room juvenile officers questioned us about other crimes, while we confessed again and again to the shoplifting and then they called our parents. About an hour later burly Elmer picked me up for the long ride home. He smelled of boiled cabbage and sulfur from burning matches.

Silence.

Turn right, turn left, next corner, but we were not going home. Elmer was taking me out to dinner and a man-to-man talk, he said. His kindness was a new form of torture because I could only measure the long seconds to the beating when we got home.

"Are you going to hit me?" I pleaded.

"No, not this time, and you know I don't like doing that any more than you like getting it," said my stepfather.

"You won't beat me?"

"No."

"Ever again?"

"Well, there might be a time when you'll need it again, but you're old enough now to talk about things man to man."

"When?" I asked, telling myself that I was always old enough to talk about things in place of a beating.

"You just eat now and let's just talk about tonight before I lose my temper and change my mind," he said, beating the bottom of a ketchup bottle. "You and that kid you were with have to appear in juvenile court and that will be punishment enough for stealing. The judge will be tough, but you need the lesson."

We were well dressed for the event in juvenile court. Wannum was even wearing a new necktie his mother bought for the occasion. We waited for the judge to sentence us for our crimes. He looked down from his cruddy bench and said it was not the first time we had stolen something. We fell for the bait and confessed everything we had ever even thought about lifting.

"Do you want to grow up to be criminals and spend the rest of your natural lives in prison . . . do you?" he asked, but never waited for an answer. "Let me tell you this, young man," he said leaning over the bench and pointing at me, "and you too, young Wannum; if it was not true that our two juvenile training schools were filled I would send you both there in a minute for your crimes . . . you deserve no less . . . but because Glen Lake and Red Wing are filled, I am giving you a chance to do good by placing you both on probation for six months . . . and if during that time you ever steal, or do anything wrong again, I will let someone out just to make room to put you in. Do you understand what I have just said?"

We looked at each other, nodded, and listened again. We were scared and knew the judge was very serious, but we did not understand what he said about institutions and probation.

"You will report to your probation officer every Monday afternoon for six months . . . and you will tell the principal of your school that you are on probation for stealing and he will permit you to leave early to report to your probation officer. Do you understand what I have just told you?"

"Yes sir . . . sir."

"Have you learned your lesson?"

"Yes sir . . . sir."

Wannum's parents blamed me for influencing their son in the evil life of crime, and my mother blamed me first and then Wannum for leading me into a life of crime. But both parents agreed on one thing: we were never to see each other again. Close your eyes, they said, and turn the other way when you see each other in school or on the street. We listened, nodded, and went on looking at each other and playing together in the cemetery. We were always together on Monday afternoon when we went to see our probation officer at the courthouse.

There were no more than two or three probation officers for the whole city of juvenile criminals on probation. Every Monday every juvenile on probation would line up at the same time in the courthouse waiting to report. We were petunias on the low road in the juvenile world of crime. Shoplifting was no crime at all compared to the things the northeast bandits boasted about: rape, armed robbery, extortion, burglary, and car theft. The Frog and I had been kidnapped the summer before by the northeast toughs and hauled across the river where we were stripped and tortured. Being the smallest and petunia criminals, we waited in line the longest while the northeast bandits came late and took their places at the head of the line to see the probation officer.

His face was cracked like old yellow paste.

"Did you go to church?" the probation officer asked. He waited for my answer with his head down and his pencil poised to enter my answer on a large yellow card.

"Yup."

"Attending school every day?"

"Yup."

I never saw his legs behind the desk.

"Staying away from other known criminals and juveniles on probation?" he asked, rubbing his forearm on the edge of the desk. Behind me was another probation officer asking the same questions.

"Yup."

He could be a cripple without legs.

"Very good, Gerald . . . you are making very good progress and I think in a month or so, if you behave yourself and stay out of mischief and follow the rules, we may release you from probation early."

"Really?"

"Yes, but don't forget to attend church every week," he said. He flashed a one-second smile and told me to send in the next boy. "Keep you nose clean, kid, you know what I mean . . ."

I looked under the desk before I left to see if he had legs. He did, but he could still be a cripple.

1947   Trustworthy and Brave But Not Stupid

Many Point Scout Camp
Sunday

Dear Mother,
   You never told me when I left for camp that they were sending me back to the reservation. You should have said something. My father grew up here you know, everybody knows that, we are on the White Earth Reservation.

There are animals and birds everywhere, but I don't like the people very much here. Everybody is always telling me what to do all the time. They think they own this place. I can't even swim when I feel like it, everything is on time, go here and go there, and I am hungry.

I am living in a tent with another scout and he eats sardines all the time and leaves the cans in the tent. He said he can do it because he is a Norwegian. He smells like a fish in the tent. He never gave me any either.

One of the scout leaders started a fire in the big fireplace in the main lodge with his mouth. I was fooled at first but then I saw the gasoline he drank and spit at a match he was holding in front of the logs. But don't worry because he told us never to drink gasoline.

Yesterday they killed a whole pig and roasted it over a fire outside. I didn't eat any because it smelled awful.

Everybody tells us to work all the time. We wanted to explore around the lake but nobody would let us. One kid has all the merit badges they make. He's an eagle scout and everything, but he looks dumb with his thick glasses. He walks like Black Foot Broth — you know, my dumb friend across the alley.

We learned about canoeing and life saving and fire building. In the morning they give us cold toast and cold eggs. They gave us time after church today to write to you.

Your Loving Son,
Jerry

Wednesday

Dear Mother,

You won't believe this but they took us away from the camp yesterday to find our way back with a compass, but we went for a walk around the lake and they said we were lost. The kid with the thick glasses said he hoped we would get lost for the day on purpose. We had a great time. Nobody told us what to do all day. We circled the camp and walked around the lake until dark. We saw a nest of bald eagles. We knew where we were and didn't need a compass. Nobody could get lost walking around a lake anyway. It was really wild.

When we came back they thought we were lost so now we have to stay here all the time. The kid with the thick glasses laughs at us all the time. Nobody believes we were not lost. Another dumb thing here is the order of the arrow when all the scouts pretend they are Indians. Tell The Frog I will be home next weekend.

Love,
Your Son, Jerry

Envoi: The Many Point Scout Camp Reservation is operated on twenty-four thousand acres of valuable wilderness tribal land on the White Earth Reservation by the Viking Council of the Boy Scouts of America. Few loyal and trustworthy scouts are aware of how the land was obtained from tribal people.

1948   *Jaunty Pirates on Green Lake*

Mean Nettles was born a squatter. He played high school football without practicing, drank hard booze from a jar, smoked two packs of cigarettes a day, had sex with older women before he was fifteen, and owned his own lake below a concrete block factory on the shores of the Mississippi River. He was very quiet and very mean, so mean that even the great river mosquitoes circled beyond his reach.

The Frog and I were enchanted by the river woods in the summer. We were small and quick and took pleasure in the excitement of tormenting giants like Mean Nettles. We waited in the brush pinching blood from mosquitoes and watched the mean giant build his sailboat. He hauled oil drums, deck joists, and boxcar siding to his dockyard on Green Lake. The lake, once a huge gravel pit near the river, was filled with limewater waste from the concrete block factory up the hill. The lake was chartreuse in color with a fuzzy gray bottom that turned yellowish at dusk. The water was thick and clear like cough medicine. We tried it as a mosquito repellent, but it only turned our skin into fine white wrinkles. Mean Nettles once threatened to baptize his enemies there.

The six cross-eyed Pitcher brothers squatted in the house next to Nettles about a mile below the bridge in north Minneapolis. Unlike Mean Nettles, the Pitchers talked all the time — talking twice as much about what they saw with double vision — and they were always together like a pack of hungry reservation tribal dogs. The Pitchers had equal rights as squatters, but they were not welcome at Green Lake. Mean Nettles ruled the lake.

In the evening before dark when Mean Nettles was away drinking and having sex with the river sirens, we entered the dockyard and sabotaged the construction of his sailboat. We punched holes in the drums and set them afloat on the thick chartreuse water. The giant had nailed a book, opened to a schematic drawing of a schooner, to a boxelder tree near the dockyard. His oil drum sailing vessel was a rectangle about six feet long. We wrote obscene phrases about giants on the book.

Next day Mean Nettles rescued his drums and with the help of the Pitcher brothers set a trap for Vizenor and Game. They dug a six-foot hole on the running path along the river and covered it with a thin layer of earth and leaves. In the morning the little Pitcher was placed as a scout on the bridge to signal our arrival. Once we were on the river path, the three biggest Pitchers jumped from the brush and chased us along the path. Two more Pitchers joined in the chase. At a curve in the path we both dropped into the pit. When the dust settled, we looked up and saw Mean Nettles straddling the hole and heard him grinding his teeth. It was the only sound he made. Then six faces with crossed eyes looked into the hole.

"Let's just bury 'em," said the little Pitcher, out of breath. He kicked dirt at us in the hole.

Mean Nettles ground his teeth again.

"No," said another Pitcher, who covered his mouth when he spoke to hide his rotting front teeth. "Let's strip 'em, Nettles, and dump 'em in the lake."

"Badtize 'em, badtize 'em . . ." the others chanted.

"Hey, come on, you guys, you know us," I said with a graceful hand gesture. "We didn't do nothing . . . let us out of here."

Mean Nettles ground his teeth again.

"You sonnofabiches," said Game, losing his voice, "goddamit, you sonnofabiches, open this hole and let me out of here!"

"Throw it up," said Mean Nettles.

"Throw what up?" we asked.

"Throw it up," he repeated, grinding his teeth.

"Throw what?" The little Pitcher kicked dirt into my mouth and stumbled away in hysterical laughter.

We knew what to throw up, but we protested as long as possible, hoping that what we would throw up would spare us from a beating or a baptismal ceremony in Green Lake.

"Throw it up."

"My uncle is a cop and he gave me this knife," said Game, holding his hunting knife out and losing his voice again on every other word.

"Throw it up, assholes, throw it up like we said," said the little Pitcher, kicking more dirt on our heads in the hole.

"My brother in the army overseas sent me this watch," I said in protest.

"What brother?" Game asked.

"What brother . . . what brother . . ." I snarled at Game, "the same one as your uncle cop, you idiot, give up your goddam hunting knife! Hey, Nettles, how about it, let me keep the watch, just the watch."

"Throw it up."

We threw up our hunting knives, the watch, billfolds, coins, rings, belts, sacred stones, and a pair of pigskin climbing gloves.

The Pitchers grabbed everything and ran off fighting over the booty while Mean Nettles, still straddling the hole and grinding his teeth, unbuttoned his pants, pulled out his giant penis, and, while we protested and waved our hands, urinated on our heads.

When he left, we dug our way out of the hole and plunged into the river, scrubbing the urine of the giant from our hair and clothes. We had tormented the giant and got caught, but we knew with careful planning we could outwit him and his cross-eyed followers. We applied our abstract movie-matinee knowledge of piracy on the high seas and planned to plunder his dockyard and capture his sailboat.

Weeks later when the sailboat was built, we staged our assault on the dockyard. Our strategy was to capture the sailboat about noon, sail back and forth across the lake tiring the giant, who we knew would chase along the shore after us, and then, when the giant was near exhaustion, we knew he would run to the house of the Pitcher brothers for help.

He did everything according to plan. We knew he would not jump into the limewater lake after us, but twice he almost caught us near shore. We had never sailed before and forgot to reef at a turn at one end of the lake and almost capsized. The second time he almost caught us in a doldrum with only a small board to paddle the heavy four-drum vessel into deeper water. We yelled at him as he ran back and forth around the lake and gave him the finger and other obscene high signs. He went for help when we said things about his mother and his riverfront breeding.

We ran the sailboat ashore according to plan. Rather than running for the bridge and the security of home, which later proved to be our only mistake, we climbed to the top of two boxelder trees which we had selected earlier along the river path, believing that the giant and his cross-eyed followers would think we were hiding deep in the woods. I waited like a crow in the top of the tree holding my breath and laughter, listening to the Pitcher brothers plunging through the thick brush below.

Pounding through the brush, they yelled at us and threatened to baptize us in the lake, whip the bottom of our feet until they bled, drive soft sumac stakes into our armpits, pound shit in our mouths and ears, and pull our eyelashes out.

We waited in the top of the trees, swaying peacefully in the afternoon sunlight. The katydids sounded, the leaves rattled on the breeze, and my foot fell asleep. I was dreaming of soaring as a crow or an eagle. I rubbed my wings against the limbs and sent my eyes above the trees.

Mean Nettles was a silent squatter, but we discovered he was not stupid. While the cross-eyed Pitcher brothers were searching deep in the woods, the giant walked down the the river path looking for signs of our escape. He stopped beneath us and examined the scuff marks on the soft bark. He called for his followers, and with their hunting knives, which were once ours, they chopped us down. When we swung to the ground, the cross-eyed brothers grabbed us. I was beaten and kicked until I felt as numb as a bird with broken wings.

The little Pitcher kept spitting at us while our hands were tied behind our backs. With ropes around our necks we were led like animals to the dockyard where the giant, smoking cigarette after cigarette and drinking from a jar, told us he was holding a trial to find us guilty of messing with his sailboat. Point by point, Mean Nettles listed the evidence against us. We denied everything at first — it was a case of mistaken identity because we had been in the trees all day — but then we admitted to the theft of the sailboat only as a practical joke. "Have you lost your sense of humor?" we pleaded.

The cross-eyed jury found us guilty and the giant sentenced us to be stripped, whipped with leather thongs, and banished to an island in the river for the rest of our lives.

The stripping was embarrassing, because between The Frog and me we had a total of no more than a dozen dark pubic hairs. The whipping was painful but less frightening than the hand of my stepfather, and the banishment was far better than being baptized in the limewater of Green Lake. We were transported to the island on a raft and left naked with our hands and feet tied to trees.

It was late in the afternoon. Hot and humid. Blackflies bit the top of my head. The giant river mosquitoes, too bloated with our blood to fly, just fell from our bodies into the moist grass and crawled away.

We loosened the ropes just before dark and swam down the river to the bridge. The cool dark water soothed the welts on our bodies. Naked, we ran home through the alleys. My dog was waiting for me in the basement. He listened to me curse the evil giants of the world and praise the courage of the little people.

1949   Every Threshold an Internal Fire

The benign demons and little woodland people of love who lived in my thoughts and fantasies during my year of silence in the third grade came to life as real people with real names.

They are the stature of the people and images in my dreams, moving through my head at night, nudging me in daydreams along the river and leading my visions through boring and repetitious rhythms of controlled learning in school. They are the little people who raise the banners of imagination on assembly lines and at cold bus stops in winter. They marched with me in the service and kept me awake with humor on duty as a military guard. The little people sat with me in baronial ornamental classrooms and kept me alive and believable under the death blows of important languages.

The little people told me stories when I cracked my elbow, cut my wrist to the bone, and stood in line waiting to report to my probation officer and when I was shot in the lower lip during a real quick-draw gunfight on a dusty road with The Frog. The little people know how to distract me with humor when I am desperate enough to become a spiritual victim and to make promises to religious warlocks offering to change my life for the better again.

The little people came to life this year under velvet throws in the loft of a garage where I was hiding on a summer afternoon. The world around me was buzzing with the energy of little lives. Old trees from the woodland swayed and creaked as beams and joists and shiplap siding in the haunting memory of the wind. Insects etched their vibrations on wings and millions of little feet through cosmic space and violet visions of the sun. The little people told me they make themselves known when there is trust in knowing the world through different visions. Terminal believers, those believing only in one vision of the world, are never known to the little people. Terminal believers are too important to laugh at themselves.

Erdupps MacChurbbs walked across the red velvet throw and introduced himself to me. "We have been traveling together in dreams for a long time, and now we are one and know our names as little people. You are me, and I am you. You have become a little person and I have become you," MacChurbbs told me, knitting the fingers of his little hands and bowing in mockery of the terminal belief in proper manners and high social breeding.

"But I am not a little person," I said, moving my fingers and toes to validate the great space between them.

"You are when you free yourself from the customs of civilized measurement," he told me, extending his arms. "We are so big, and so little at the same time. You have learned only one way to measure the world. Little people disappear when civilization and terminal beliefs surround them. Imagination and humor expire and people grow too big for their eyes when they seek cultural perfection through the exalted structures of the past. Civilization is a burnished skull for those who will never know the space between dreams . . . I will show you." Standing on my shoulder with his head cocked in front of my left eye, he continued to speak. He said we were flowers and birds and at times only numbers. "I am in your eye and you are in mine, and I see you back again as a little person. I will disappear when you think about what you will be in the future, but are not now, by the measures of the past. What will you be when you grow up? What civilized attention will you demand from the world? Who will you be?"

"Just me."

"But whose skull will you be?"

"A famous writer . . ."

Erdupps MacChurbbs snapped into dust before my eyes. I searched the velvet throws calling his name. I felt large and mechanical. My hands were numbers, massive and improper, as I patted the red velvet folds for his little body. He was gone. I had been tricked by my own thoughts and felt stupid. I laughed at myself. I was nervous. Who cares what I will be? I said to myself. I will be nothing, no matter who I think I will be.

I leaned back and changed my mind again. The window in the loft was open. On the breeze of warm air great flowers of dust floated through the pillars of sunlight. I was dust when a dragonfly hovered at the opening of the window. Her shadow reached to the floor at my feet and examined every ridge and crater on the wood. When the dragonfly entered the loft closer to her shadow, I took up warm wings and watched my shadow move across time and space. I could only feel my eyes as the loft turned in shadowless circles of marbling greens and violets. In spiral space I saw Mac-Churbbs and other little people a hundred times my size. They were everywhere the same as if my vision had crossed and crossed without end. I bounced with my wings on the sunlight and listened to my eyes.

Bishop Bartholomew Baragga, a little old world missionary and linguist dressed in a scarlet gown and a black satin hat with a ragged tassle and carrying a sprig of white pine, moved across my eyes a hundred times with his head swung backward reciting a strange litany that no one answered. Then he stopped and stared at me in silence. Hundreds of bushy eyebrows moved with his wide lips. He explained that he carried white pine because bald eagles always have a fresh sprig in their nests.

"There are so many of you," I said, trying to blink away the many images of his stern face. "Which one of you is real?"

"The one you see."

"But I see you everywhere."

"Then you must be everyone to see me everywhere."

"Did you come through the window?"

"Yes, always through the windows of the world," the bishop chanted with his elbow resting in his hand. "You see, I am burdened with five glorious centuries of terminal belief in celibacy and the virgin birth and I am not able to pass through time and cross thresholds . . . My life is waiting at the edge of time in the past. I can only move as a spirit through windows.

"But you could fly across thresholds."

"Only windows."

"Why?"

"Every threshold is a fire."

"Would you burn up if you crossed?"

"No, but the internal fires would go out."

MacChurbbs appeared a hundred times in my eyes of the dragonfly with a beautiful dark-skinned woman dressed in leather and white linen. Her dark hair was drawn back with silver and turquoise jewelry. Her skin was soft and moist. On her left hand she wore a gold ring with tiny bells. Sophia Libertina, who first met MacChurbbs when he was wandering in the mountains seeking the mystery of translation, touched my face with her fingers and I felt warm and clean. I saw her everywhere, and the sound of the tiny bells on her ring made us all smile and laugh a hundred times in my eyes.

"Famous writers spend too much time alone perfecting the style of their experiences from the past. No one has ever lived a life of humor and love in blank verse," MacChurbbs told me, poised on a rafter in the loft with one eye closed. "Love and passion are never left to the dull men who create history from all the words they have read. Some people put things together, some people take things apart, but little people float between words and dreams."

I found my shadow, and the little people in the loft came back to my eyes one by one. Leaning on my elbow in the velvet throws, I listened to the bishop move his eyebrows telling me that MacChurbbs was a wise clown, a cosmic jester who was never tricked even by believing in his own humor. He drew his humor from a moment of knowing the contradictions between passion and reason, between the terminal beliefs of men and women, between cats and dogs, between night and day, between up and down, between words and dreams. He tells fathers they are sons, criminals they are victims, women they are men, saints they are sinners, and he turns the visions and cultural measures of the world around to share the humor of little people floating through their own shadows.

Bishop Baragga blessed himself, and we all joined hands and danced across the rafters and flew home before dark. The little people have been with me ever since, and I always remember to leave a window open for those who cannot cross thresholds for fear of extinguishing their internal fires.

1950   Masturbation Papers on the Double

I lied about my age to enlist as a private in the Minnesota National Guard. For two hours once a week I learned how to march, with hundreds of older men, back and forth in the Minneapolis Armory. After six months of marching and memorizing the mechanical parts of my rifle I was ready for two weeks of summer training at Fort Ripley near Little Falls in northern Minnesota.

"Private Vizenor," the loudspeaker rang out one Sunday morning at summer camp. "Private Vizenor . . . get your ass to the orderly room on the double."

I was there on the double.

"Vizenor, I have been going through your service file," the sergeant said with disdain, "and I have not found your masturbation papers."

"My what, sir?"

"Your masturbation papers, soldier."

"Sorry sir, but . . ."

"Well, get your sweet ass over to headquarters and get them right now, soldier," said the sergeant. "On the double, soldier."

"Yes sir," I said, not knowing about masturbation papers but worried that I had failed to do my duty to my country as a proud and brave soldier in the Minnesota National Guard.

"Private Vizenor, sir, reporting for my masturbation papers," I told the sergeant at headquarters.

"Where the hell have you been, soldier? Your masturbation papers are at the command post! Get your skinny ass up there and ask for the colonel."

"Yes sir," I said and double-timed from the headquarters tent to the command tent about two blocks away.

"Sir, Private Vizenor requests permission to see the colonel, sir," I said.

"At ease, soldier," he said, returning my salute. "What is so urgent that you must see the colonel, soldier?"

"My masturbation papers, sir."

"Your what?"

"Masturbation papers, sir."

"Who sent you here?"

"My company sergeant, sir."

"Just a minute, soldier, I think the colonel will want to talk with you about this," he said, cranking the field telephone to call the colonel. When the colonel entered the command tent, I snapped to attention and saluted. I knew I was in for real trouble when he frowned and returned my salute with a nubby swagger stick.

"Private Vizenor, sir, reporting for my masturbation papers, sir," I said in a loud and strong voice which I had learned by calling marching commands in the armory.

"Yes, where did you lose your papers?"

"I don't know, sir."

"Do you know what masturbation means?"

"No sir."

"Then how can you find your papers?"

"I don't know, sir."

"Do you know what jacking off means?"

"Yes, sir."

"Masturbation means the same thing, soldier. You can pick up your jacking off papers from your company sergeant," the colonel said. "You tell him I sent you."

"Yes sir."

"Hang in there, soldier."

"Yes sir."

"You know what I mean, soldier?"

"Yes sir."

"Carry on."

"Yes, sir!"

The company sergeant was not pleased when he learned that I had told the colonel who had sent me looking for my masturbation papers so he ordered me to clean the urinals for three days. Two weeks at summer camp as a soldier had taught me what masturbation meant, how to march in the sand, how to wire a field telephone, how to field-strip a machine gun, and how to keep the urinals clean.

1951   *We Both Need a Good Home*

Elmer Petesch returned from the mill right on schedule and found a short note from his wife of eight years. She told him she was moving on to a warmer climate and a better life, leaving him with the mortgage, a secondhand piano, and some old wedding gifts, and as a parting gesture of ironic affection she also left behind her only son. Elmer did not appreciate the reminder. A few months after the departure of my mother I also rejected his authority and violence and left his house.

We had just finished another boiled dinner with ring bologna when he struck me on the back while I was washing the dishes. He cursed me for my mother and hit me again. I left his house in silence determined never to return.

Elmer was alone for four days, and on the fifth day he began searching for me. He left thoughtful messages around the neighborhood that he wanted me to return. I ignored his rapprochement and peddled my own defensive stories about his violence to my friends and their parents. The Frog invited me to stay at his house, which pleased me because his father told great stories about his adventures in the wilderness and drank whiskey like a man — winking at us when his wife complained. We were willing listeners and eager conspirators of his boyhood memories.

The old man was convincing because he had a bullet hole in his leg from a gunfight at a mining camp in the mountains. He even had the gun he said he took away from the man who shot him.

We were playing basketball in the backyard of the Game house when Elmer found me. I told him to leave because I would never listen to him again.

"Let's just talk it over," he said. Before he left, he told my friends to tell me that he would be back the next night to talk again. It gave me a feeling of personal power to have him on the defensive.

On the sixth night he met me in the alley with my friends. We first agreed that he would stand across the alley and that we would listen to each other without interruptions. He was the first to speak.

"Please believe me . . . I am very sorry. I know you want to be with your friends now, but I want you to know how sorry I am for taking your mother out on you. I have been very lonely since you left and I know it was wrong to hit you. It was not your fault, but sometimes we hurt the people we love the most. You know what I mean? I want you to come back home. We need each other now. I have never had a good home and you have never had a good home either, now we need to make one together."

He was crying. Tears were running down his fat cheeks. He took his glasses off and pleaded to me with his hands. I felt like reaching out to him, but I had been hurt too many times in the past to yield only to tears and a stand-up promise. My thoughts were over-burdened with his violence. My friends were embarrassed because we had all been taught to believe that tears were a sign of weakness in a man.

"I wish I could take back all the times I have hurt you," he said. "Leaving home was the best thing for you to do and I have no right to expect you to trust me now and come back home . . . but I do want you to believe me this time." He blew his nose.

"I don't believe you," I said in a cold voice. "You have said all those things before. Go take it out on my mother, not me. Go away."

"Can we talk tomorrow again?"

"Maybe."

I would not yield. As a visitor I had fantasized my ideal place as a new son in the Game family, in which I was at least free of the fear of physical abuse. But visitors are visitors, and that night I was encouraged to return home.

The next night in the alley Elmer faced not only my friends but their parents and other neighbors who had learned from gossip about the negotiations in the alley. The women stood behind their children with their arms folded over their breasts. The men stood in the shadows of open garage doors chewing toothpicks and looking down. I was silent. The audience was tense.

"I will come every night to tell you I want you to come home, but not the way it used to be. I promise you, and you have your friends here listening, that I will never again mistreat you. We both need a good home. Please come home."

"Let me think about it," I said.

Elmer turned and walked down the alley toward his home. The neighbors and friends looked at each other, husbands and wives walked home with their children between them. Screen doors banged closed. Kitchen lights went on. I could smell the young trees and the moist leaves. Fireflies blinked and disappeared in the dark grass. The apples and plums were still green. My hands were swollen from clenching my fists. I was alone.

Watching the summer sky and listening to my uneven breath, I walked toward the river. That night I slept beneath the bridge with the little people and fell between dreams of flight over the woodland.

The house was cool and smelled of mold and dust. My ears buzzed with excitement. I walked through the house touching things like a stranger, putting thoughts from the past to rest, and was overwhelmed with a good feeling. I cleaned the house, washed the dishes, cut the grass, and baked a blueberry pie, his favorite, and waited in the kitchen for him to return from the mill. He walked in without speaking, took my hand, pulled me out of the chair, and embraced me. It was the first time he had touched me with affection. We both wept and never spoke of the past.

We lived together as equals, sharing our time and space without rules. We both became sons and fathers and brothers and friends at the same time. If I had not had the will to trust him again, I would not have known that Elmer was a very compassionate and loving man.

Five months after our negotiations in the alley, Elmer fell two stories down an elevator shaft while working at the mill. His pelvis was crushed, and he died three days later in the hospital. He was buried in the cemetery across the street from the house.

1952   *Is the Little Man Ready?*

We stopped a crowd of boys playing baseball in the street and asked them directions to 314 John Street. They looked at each other and then burst into laughter. The pitcher for the team, slapping a ball in his mitt and snapping his gum, asked us what we wanted there.

"Just a friend," I replied, squeezing the steering wheel of my 1934 Ford with a crank-out front window to flex my triceps in his face. He backed away from the car and extended his arm and mitt to the west and yelled the directions: "Two blocks that way! Down and at 'em, boys!" The team laughed. I raced the eight-cylinder engine, which burned a quart of oil every fifty miles, and peeled rubber on bald tires, heading for the first real live sex purchase of my life.

At 314 John Street, an address we had heard for two years in high school, was a house, or rather a duplex, of prostitution that looked like any other house on the block. It was painted white with black shutters and had a front porch and a swing. We had expected at least some sign or symbol advertising the business of sex.

We drove by the duplex three times and parked several blocks away. We hid our billfolds, rings, and watches in the car and took only folding money with us. Matthew Bridge, my friend from high school who was called The Candidate because he talked and laughed like a politician, took five dollars and I took three.

The Candidate knocked at the door of the duplex of prostitution. The shades were drawn. We waited. A boy and his dog ran down the street. Two cars stopped at the end of the block. The palms of my hands were sweating. He knocked again. The door opened and we were greeted by a sweet grandmother in a print dress and apron. I knew we were at the wrong place.

"May I help you, boys?" she asked.

"Well . . ." The Candidate said, hesitating and scratching his arms, which I knew was a sign of great anxiety.

"Are you collecting for the paper?"

"No," said The Candidate, "we were wondering if you by chance had any propositions . . . you know what I mean?"

"Propositions?"

I was ready to run. The Candidate scratched his arms and jerked his head back and forth looking at the street and her face and then her feet. She was wearing pink slippers.

"How old are you boys?"

"Twenty-five," said The Candidate.

"Twenty-three."

"I see," the sweet grandmother said. "Well, come in now, but be sure not to get your noses out of joint."

We followed her into a room where there was a wide ascending stairway. She told us to sit down and wait and to obey the rules of the house. The rules were to pay in advance, enter by one door and leave by another, and to stay out of the hallway when the red light was on, which meant that someone was leaving who did not wish to be seen. We sat in leather chairs facing the stairway and waited our turn. The Candidate scratched his arms. I picked at a blackhead in my ear.

"How much will it cost?"

"Five dollars," said The Candidate.

"I only have three."

"You can hold hands for that."

"Propositions . . . who told you that word?"

"Do they come for us?"

"She said from the stairway."

"This is it," The Candidate said, jumping out of his chair and bounding up the steps to meet a big blond woman with large breasts. They walked up the stairs laughing. A door closed. I was alone. My wet hands squeaked on the arm of the leather chair.

"Are you waiting for me?" she asked, standing at the foot of the stairs dressed in a pink strapless high-school-prom formal evening gown. She was tall with long brown hair and small breasts, and she spoke with a southern accent.

"Well, yes, but . . ."

"But what?"

"Nothing . . . which way do we go?"

She led me into a small room with a window overlooking the backyard, three pink plastic flamingoes, and the alley. The room was very warm and smelled sweet from lilacs and roses. When I turned from the window to tell her about the three dollars, she was standing naked by the bed.

"Do you want to talk or play?" she asked, mounting the brass frame bed and rolling over on her back. I watched her naked body as I undressed. The leg of my trouser caught on my shoe and the lace on one shoe was knotted. When I was undressed, I sat next to her on the bed. She touched me, and I asked her how much.

"How much am I worth?"

"Three dollars?"

"We better hurry then," she said, running her fingers across my back and humming. Everything was so distracting. Every odor, every sound, every touch, everything was distracting me from the thought of sex. I wanted to look and talk for a while the way we did in the back seat of the car by the river. I could not stop talking and thinking. Everything was so easy.

"How did a nice girl like you end up in a place like this?" I asked with interest and affection.

"No words," she said, touching my lips with her fingers. They were sticky and smelled sweet. I said so. Then she ran her hand through my hair and told me to come down on the bed next to her. When she kissed my ear, the one with a blackhead in it, I jerked my head around to look into her big brown eyes.

"Is the little man ready?" she whispered.

1956   *In a Low Voice without Words*

A good game hunter is never competitive. Hunting with friends turns the hunt into a passionless and destructive contest. The instincts of a survival hunter are measured best when he is alone in the woods. In groups, people depend on each other for identity and security, but alone the hunter must depend on his own instincts of survival and must move with the energy of the woodland.

I walked into the woods alone and found a place in the sun

against a tree. The animals and birds were waiting in silence for me to pass. They felt my coming from the lifeless energy of mechanical things. They knew my evil thoughts, the thoughts of a cunning killer. Falling asleep brought my mind and energy in touch with the life around me. When I opened my eyes, after a short rest, the birds were singing and the squirrels were eating without fear and jumping from tree to tree. I was jumping with them but against them as the hunter.

I raised my rifle, took aim, and fired at a large red squirrel running across an oak bough. He fell to the ground near the trunk of the tree, bounced once, and started to climb the tree again. The bullet passed through his shoulder, shattering the bone. His right front leg hung limp from torn skin. He fell to the ground and tried to climb the tree again. He instinctively reached up with his shattered paw, but it was not there to hold him. He fell again and watched me watching him. Blood was spreading across his body. He tried to climb the tree again and again to escape from me.

He was a survivor. He knew when and where to hide from the hunters who came in groups to kill — their harsh energies were burned in the memories of his animal tribe. I was alone. My presence and my intention to kill squirrels were disguised by sleep and camouflaged by my gentle movements in the woods. I did not then know the secret language of squirrels. I did not know their suffering in the brutal world of hunters.

The overbearing hunter learns not to let an animal suffer. As if the hunter were living up to some moral code of tribal warfare, wounded animals must be put out of their miseries.

When the squirrel started to climb the tree again, I fired one shot at his head. The bullet tore the flesh and fur away from the top of his skull. He fell to the ground still looking at me. In his eyes he wanted to live more than anything I have ever known. I fired a second time at his head. The bullet tore his lower jaw away, exposing his teeth. He looked at me and moved toward the tree again. Blood bubbled from his nostrils when he breathed. I fired again. The bullet shattered his forehead and burst through his left eye. He fell from the tree and watched me with one eye. His breath was slower. In his last eye he wanted to live again, to run free, to hide from me. I knelt beside him, my face next to his bloody head, my eye close to his eye, and begged him to forgive me before he died. I looked around the woods. I felt strange. I was alone. The blood bubbles from his nose grew smaller and disappeared. I moved closer to his eye. Please forgive me, I pleaded in tears. Please live again, I begged him again and again.

He blinked at me. His eye was still alive. Did his blinking eye mean that he had forgiven me? Please forgive me, I moaned again and again, until my self-pity fell silent in the woods. Not a bird was singing. The leaves were silent. He blinked again. I moved closer to him, stretching my body out on the ground next to him, and ran my hand across his back. The blood was still warm. I wept and watched the last of his good life pass through me in his one remaining eye. I sang a slow death song in a low voice without words until it was dark.

1972   We Came Here to Die

Thirteen armed leaders of the American Indian Movement, including Russell Means and Dennis Banks, filed into the tribal Headstart classroom on the Leech Lake Reservation and took their seats on little-people chairs. They sat with their knees tucked under their chins, dressed in diverse combinations of Western cowboy clothes and traditional tribal vestments from the turn of the last century. Dennis Banks, who was a charismatic wanderer then, was wearing his fur-trimmed mountain man outfit. Most of the leaders of the militant organization were from urban centers.

Simon Howard, then president of the Minnesota Chippewa Tribe, entered the classroom, took his little seat, and twirled his thumbs beneath his heavy stomach while the leaders argued about their places in the chain of command — who would stand next to whom at the next television press conference. Howard wore a nylon bowling jacket and a floral print fishing hat in contrast to the renascence of traditional vestments worn by the militants. Howard was born on the reservation and had lived there all his life. He was at the meeting as an elected tribal official to keep peace between white people and the militants. The militants were there for an armed confrontation with white people on the opening day of fishing. I was there as a press officer for the tribal government to modulate threats and rumors at scheduled press conferences. The militants were not happy, and the press was not happy, but Howard avoided a confrontation.

"All right boys, quiet down now and take your seats again," Howard said. The tribal leaders and militants had agreed to meet twice a day with each other and then with the press. "Now, I don't know everyone here, so let's go around the room and introduce ourselves," Howard said. "Let's start with you over there. Stand up and introduce yourself."

The man stood up, dragging his feet forward and swinging his rifle. "My name is Delano Western, and I am from Kansas," he said in a trembling voice. Western, leaning forward and looking down like a shy school child, was dressed in a wide-brimmed black hat with an imitation silver headband, dark green sunglasses with large round lenses, a sweatshirt with "Indian Power" printed on the front, two bandoliers of heavy ammunition, none of which matched the bore of his rifle, a black motorcycle jacket with military colonel's wings on the epaulets, "Red Power" and "Custer Had It Coming" patches, and a large military bayonet strapped to his body next to his revolver.

"We came here to die," Western said in a loud voice and sat down. He and about six hundred militant followers had come to Cass Lake on the Leech Lake Reservation to fight for treaty rights to hunt and fish on the reservation, which had already been won by reservation tribal officials in federal court.

When white officials from Cass Lake had refused to pay the money demanded by the militants, who were camping on treaty land given over to a church group by the federal government for a summer camp, the leaders held a press conference on a rifle range to scare the public.

Means, smiling for television cameras, was plinking with his small-caliber "white people shooter," as he called his pistol, while Banks, my hero then, was preparing for fast-draw target practice. Dressed in a black velvet shirt with ribbon appliqué, he stood before a collection of empty food cans placed like the faces of white racist fishermen, dropped to one knee, and attempted to draw his small-gauge sawed-off shotgun. It stuck on the rope holder attached to his belt. Banks stood up and tried again, but it still stuck.

Then he untied the rope, walked away embarrassed and angry, and never carried his shotgun-pistol again. Banks, a new hipshooter from the city, was out of the running for a lead role in my imaginary hall of fame for fast-draw heroes.

"We came here to die defending our red brothers and sisters from those white racist fishermen," blared the loudspeaker voice across the church camp headquarters. "Dinner will be served in one hour, and there will be a dance contest tonight. We need volunteers to help out in the kitchen, and some brothers and sisters who know how to hunt deer . . . make that just the brothers for now."

The television newscast had reported the indiscriminate slaughter of deer on the reservation by militant hunters in violation of state laws. In fact, the brothers out hunting for two days missed every deer they shot at. One deer, pictured on television being dressed by militants at the church camp, had been killed in an accident with an automobile and was delivered to the encampment by the local game warden, who knew the militants needed food. While the militants were "shining" deer one night, they fired seven rounds at the big brown eyes of a cow. The owner of the cow fired back, and the militant hunters scrambled a fast retreat to the church camp, declaring that they were under attack by white racist fishermen.

My boyhood dream, after good food and a dentist to plug up the black holes in my front teeth, was to have in my employ a good listening chauffeur — someone to take the place of my dog and move me in peace through heavy traffic. The impossible dream was to be an unemployed radical and to have a chauffeur. My hero Dennis Banks had a chauffeur during his one-week administration of the militant encampment. The chauffeur was a good listener employed by the community relations service of the United States Department of Justice.

Two burly and bare-chested brown militant tribal guards stopped me at the entrance of the church camp because of my light skin color.

"No whites allowed, honky. This is a sovereign camp now," said one bandit with a shotgun leveled at my neck.

"Back this heap out of here, honky," said the other charming bandit. He had a self-styled tattoo recognizing his mother on his arm and wore reflecting sunglasses. Somewhere behind the mirrors over his eyes I knew he was aiming his buffalo gun at my head.

"Drop the color shit," I said with an aggressive snarl. "Since when do all tribal people look like you two? Put the guns down before you lose your chance for a press conference."

"Who are you, honky?"

"I am the new little mixed-blood press chauffeur for Dennis Banks, now put your guns down and open the goddamn gate, please..." My bluff and blood pressure, measured by the little people at the cosmic laboratory of human relations and survival, rang the right bells and the gate opened. Inside I parked my car like a good chauffeur for the little people.

"Vizenor!" Erdupps MacChurbbs called from the back seat. "You have given too much thought in your life to the violence of terminal believers! Show more humor and give yourself more time for the little people and compassionate trickery... remember you are over the hump and holding, you know what I mean?"

"I know what you mean, Erdupps MacChurbbs."

KEITH GUNDERSON

Dedicated to the memory of Earl Gunderson
and to his wife Gladys

Author's Note

My two oldest boys, Christopher and Jonathan, now age twelve and ten, respectively, when younger often acted like field anthropologists intent on weaseling out of me ever a bit more data on the primitive generation to which I belonged. It was their tireless interviewing of me with respect to "how it was" growing up with my mother, father, sisters, other relatives, and friends that led me to conceive of a long sequence of prose poems dealing with childhood from a child's point of view. Some of the prose poems from the sequence are included at the end of "A Portrait of My State as a Dogless Young Boy's Apartment."

The narrative that precedes the prose poems provides a general look back at the micro-Minnesota in which I spent much of my Minneapolis childhood. It is designed to chink those memory-gaps which even the completed poem sequence would leave unfilled.

"The Little King" and "Grape Flavored Ice Cream Sodas" were first published in *3142 Lyndale Ave. So., Apt. 24 — Prose Poems (20 Selections)* (Minnesota Writers' Publishing House, 1975). "The Delicious Gravy" has appeared in *Epoch*, and "When the Lights Go On Again All Over the World" and "Playing Worm" have appeared in the *Chicago Review*. "The Milky Way strings out in a/traffic jam of stars" and "Las Vegas" are from *A Continual Interest in the Sun and Sea & Inland Missing the Sea* (Nodin Press, 1975) and *To See a Thing* (Nodin Press, 1976).

A Portrait of My State
As a Dogless Young Boy's Apartment

by Keith Gunderson

When I try to remember what the Minnesota I grew up in looked like, I don't for the most part think of its lakes or rivers, pines, birches, wheat fields, cows, horses, barns, silos, white frame houses, or much of anything else that could contribute to what we'd call a landscape. Instead I think of the hallscape of The Upland Apartments at 3142 Lyndale Avenue South in Minneapolis and the immediate environs: a cement back porch where tenants would hang their washing out to dry; an alley where I played kick-the-can, stickball, and flashlight tag and kept an eye out for (nonexistent) black widow spiders; and the outside front steps of the building where I'd sit and guzzle pop and compete with my peers at identifying the makes and years of the cars driving by on Lyndale Avenue. My father, who had (and has) a richly imaginative sense of proportion, told me that Lyndale Avenue was probably the longest avenue in the world, so I felt lucky to be able to name cars speeding past on an avenue like that.

The hallscape itself was simple. Each of the three residential floors and the front steps and landings connecting them were covered with a dark maroon carpeting. The woodwork was also dark, and combined with the carpet color and the enfeebled artificial lighting it produced a continuous dusklike effect. My father said it was better that the halls were dark, because that way we couldn't see everything that was out there. We did on occasion, however, see a bat or a confused bird, and now and then a nonchalant rat which we knew had a comfortable home near the storage spaces and boiler room in the basement, although the landlord would always claim it had wandered in from somewhere up the alley.

There were eight apartments on each of the three floors of the building, a little basement store, and two or more other places to live in the basement, the exact number shrinking or expanding with the remodeling whims of each new owner. Each of the three main floors could, in principle, be divided in two by huge heavy fire doors which if shut (by *very* strong people) in an emergency would keep half of the apartments from burning up. The presence of the fire doors gave me a somewhat exaggerated fear of fires and of being trapped on the second floor with nowhere to go but out the window. But the fear turned out to be somewhat abstract, for on those occasions – three during fourteen years – when a fire actually occurred, I felt only bug-eyed wonder as I was being hustled out of the building while observing at close range the firemen who ran up and down the halls dragging their long hoses over the maroon carpeting.

Much of what the Minnesota I grew up in looked like, then, looked like what the inside of The Upland Apartments at 3142 Lyndale looked like; and much of what the inside of The Upland Apartments looked like, I am sure, was in no way typically or peculiarly or characteristically Minnesotan. Nevertheless, as I grew up living, moving, and having my being in this apartment building, I carried with me a distinct sense of there being a strikingly different kind of Minnesota where most Minnesotans grew up and that however it was they grew up, it was probably quite different from the way in which I would grow up. Perhaps the only thing typically Minnesotan about growing up in an apartment building in the 1940s was that it was so untypical. But I never felt that the way in which I was growing up in an apartment in Minneapolis was remotely like what it was like to be growing up in an apartment in New York City. Whenever I would watch movies about kids growing up in New York City, I would think that that was the worst possible place to grow up. To grow up in The Upland Apartments with houses on every side was just fine; to grow up in some giant-size version of dozens of Upland Apartments all squashed together struck me as horrible.

By the age of eight I had a firmly fixed view of what the part of Minnesota was like which was not located in the hallways of my apartment building or the immediate neighborhood. The only important places I knew about in this comparatively unimportant residue of the state were New Ulm, Zumbrota, South St. Paul, Powderhorn Park in Minneapolis, and the North Shore of Lake Superior.

New Ulm initially seemed to me to be a significant part of the state simply because I was born there in 1935. I then learned that New Ulm was also an important town because everyone knew that an Indian massacre had taken place there in eighteen something-something, and the only surviving whites were those who'd hid in the basement of a bakery. Thereafter New Ulm seemed to me to be a significant part of the state because I was born in New Ulm in 1935 *where* an Indian massacre took place and the only survivors hid in the basement of a bakery. (At that time, of course, "massacre" unambiguously meant something that Indians did to innocent white people.) After my assimilation at an early age of the aforementioned alleged facts, my knowledge of New Ulm peaked. It is only those ever-to-be-encountered "DATE _____" and "PLACE OF BIRTH _____" places on application forms that keep this knowledge close to the surface of my consciousness. And even so, I only make use of part of it. For I've yet to write "PLACE OF BIRTH: New Ulm, *where* an Indian massacre . . ."

My understanding of the North Shore of Lake Superior was only somewhat more richly textured than my knowledge of New Ulm and consisted entirely of self-selected highlights of the one driving trip of any distance or duration our family took together. I was nearly five and my sister Janice almost ten during the summer I absorbed the following formidable facts about our state's most scenic drive. First and foremost there was a live bear on a long chain in a pen beside a gas station somewhere near Duluth that would drink as much pop as you cared to buy for him. All you had to do was pay the owner of the gas station for the pop and he would place it on a little table in the bear's pen. The bear would waddle up to the table, sit down on his big rump, pick up the pop bottle with his forepaws, and finish the drink in a couple of gulps. Then he'd toss the bottle away and waddle off to some other part of the pen. He was willing to drink any kind of pop anyone bought for him, but he liked grape soda best.

Because they were so large I also enjoyed looking at Lake Superior and the iron ore barges in the Duluth harbor. But they weren't nearly as interesting to see as the bear drinking pop was. Later on, after Pearl Harbor, the iron ore barges seemed a little more interesting to me than they had when I'd seen them in Duluth. For I was told that the ore and some of the scrap iron they were carrying had been on its way to Japan where it had been used to make weapons and ammunition to kill Americans with. That was interesting to know, but it didn't mean to me that the barges were as interesting to see as a bear drinking pop was.

I also saw a lot of rushing rivers which my mother said made her so dizzy she had to hang on to my father, and I picked up pine cones and acorns to take back to Minneapolis with me. But I didn't understand how the rivers could make my mother dizzy, or why I picked up the pine cones and acorns to take back to Minneapolis with me, though I knew that if Janice hadn't picked up pine cones and acorns, I wouldn't have either.

The only other experience I had on our trip to the North Shore which even came close to rivaling seeing a bear drinking pop was seeing the inside of a souvenir shop for the first time. I thought it was wonderful that there were so many different things you might buy to remind you of your trip to the North Shore, and my parents let me pick out a little piece of pine wood which was shellacked and shiny and had a colored photograph of a gray squirrel on it. I kept it for a long time and liked looking at it and being reminded of our trip to the North Shore.

Except for Minneapolis, Zumbrota was for me the most important place in Minnesota. It assumed a prominence in my kid-consciousness of the state mostly because the only grandparent I ever came to know and love, my father's father, Gunder Gunderson, lived there, as did Earl, my favorite uncle.

My parents had grown up in or near Zumbrota, gone to high school, married, and lived there for a short time after I was born. Much of what I came to know about Zumbrota I learned through listening to my parents talk about it and from listening to my father read to my mother whatever paragraphs in the most recent *Zumbrota News* most amused him. I am still able to keep abreast of the changes in Zumbrota by visiting my parents, who now live in Orange, California. For they still subscribe to the *Zumbrota News*, and my father still reads to my mother whatever paragraphs in the most recent edition most amuse him. I have learned much more about how to read poetry out loud from listening to my father read the *Zumbrota News* out loud than I have learned from listening to recordings of Dylan Thomas reading Dylan Thomas's poetry out loud. But that was, of course, only an accidental side benefit of learning about Zumbrota.

I knew, then, through listening to my parents, that there was the *Zumbrota News* before I knew there were Minneapolis newspapers. I knew that Zumbrota High School's athletic teams were all called the Tigers, and that my father played for most of them, before I'd even heard about the Minnesota Gophers, Bernie Bierman, and the great All-American halfback Bruce Smith. I also knew by heart by the age of five one of the cheers used to spur the Tigers on to victory. It went:

> Ki Yi, Ki Yi,
> Ker flippety bin!
> Come out of the woods,
> Sandpaper your chin!
> We're wild, we're woolly,
> We're rough as a saw!
> ZUMBROTA HIGH SCHOOL,
> RAH! RAH! RAH!

Whether or not this rural Minnesotan equivalent of a Pindaric ode is still part of the Tigers' oral tradition, I couldn't say; and whether or not my mastery of its meter has influenced my own poetic rhythms I wouldn't say.

The rest of my mental portrait of Zumbrota, and, hence, for me, of Minnesota small-town life, was dabbed in as a result of the three or four trips our family would take there each year until my grandfather died. My father would either borrow a friend's car or our family would pile into a car already filled with relatives and drive down on a Friday evening or Saturday or Sunday morning to spend a day or two visiting my grandfather and Uncle Earl. My grandfather was a semi-retired and then retired tinsmith by the time I started being included in the pilgrimages to Zumbrota. Earl was working as a plumber. My grandfather's parents came to Minnesota from Oslo when he was eight, but about them I knew and know almost nothing.

My relationship with my grandfather was a very simple one and a very happy one. From an early age it involved sitting on his lap or being bounced on his knee and being allowed to listen to his shiny gold South Bend pocket watch, which has now had to settle for the role of informing me when I have overlectured the students in my philosophy courses, or when other poets I've been giving public readings with have overread and poached some of my own allotted time. Later my grandfather taught me how to play checkers, and by the time I was seven I could beat him and everyone else I knew with the exception of Uncle Earl, whose strange strategy of settling for rapid piece-for-piece exchanges during the early parts of the game left me baffled and disoriented. I was pretty much dominated by the view that if I can't get two of yours for one of mine the move isn't worth making.

After I became old enough to mimic an appreciation of money, and responsible enough to run errands involving it, my grandfather would ask me, each visit to Minneapolis, to run up to Dean's Drugs and purchase him three White Owl cigars. Upon my return I'd be given a new silver dollar, which I always saw as being in small part a reward for my effortless errand and in large part a reward for being with even less strain on my part his grandson. Four colored circles are thus associated with my childhood memories of my grandfather: his gold watch, red checkers, black checkers, and silver dollars.

The rest of my knowledge of Zumbrota was learned through my experiencing it as a child, and what I experienced was roughly this: there was a drugstore where one of my parents would buy me some colored pencils and a pad of paper and maybe a connect-the-dots book. I think it was only in Zumbrota that I connected lots of dots, and remembrance of that kidhood pleasure eased into my imagery many years later in my book *A Continual Interest in the Sun and Sea*, when I wrote:

The Milky Way strings out in a
traffic jam of stars.

Constellations cartwheel across
the screen of the sky

loose change of our galaxy.

Men have drawn lines connecting the stars
with each other
and trace out the shapes of animals
or cooking utensils:

bear.   teakettle.   dog.   dipper.

In this way the stars
grow familiar
like things in a forest down here
or a kitchen.

In a typical translation
Kant would be said to have said
we make them to "fall under our
concepts"
meaning:

now we've got a grip
on stars.

(Cf. A kid's book
of connect-the-dots.)

But stars are just stars

and the lines disappear
as you lift your eyes
from the star chart

to the sky:

stars.   stars.   stars.   stars.

There was also a cafe in Zumbrota which was the only place in the world I believed you could purchase a chocolate cone with vanilla ice cream covered with chocolate and nuts and called a drumstick. (I had my first drumstick at the same time I was certain a tornado would blow Zumbrota away, and because the shape of the treat reminded me of a funnel-shaped cloud, it did not taste as good as it could; but because it tasted as good as it did, I did not feel as frightened as I could.) I was also allowed in a bar where my father and uncle and their friends would drink beer and where I discovered cream soda. Occasionally I would see my grandfather working by the shed where he worked as a tinsmith and visit the plumbing shop where Earl worked.

When I was very young, the most striking recurrent perceptual experiences I had when visiting Zumbrota were of a fire truck that was white and of cars parked at angles to the curb instead of parallel to it. Throughout my childhood no one in the town ever bothered to try to correct the falsely painted fire trucks and wrongly parked cars. For all I know this permissiveness persists in the southern part of our state.

For me, all roads in Minnesota starting from Minneapolis led to Zumbrota, the North Shore, or South St. Paul. South St. Paul had a dot in my mental cartography because when most of the people we knew in Zumbrota came up to the Twin Cities, they would stop in at Flo and Harry's 440 Club in South St. Paul. Harry was another of my uncles, because, as was explained to me, he was another of my father's brothers. It was interesting to me to learn that uncles are not quantitatively restricted in the way that mothers and fathers are. Harry was quantitatively unrestricted in another way as well. For he weighed almost as much as the number of the club which he and my Aunt Flo owned. I liked visiting Flo and Harry's 440 Club just in order to look at Harry. He was to people what Lake Superior was to lakes, but he could also do an impressively nimble Charleston, the sight of which made him for me just about as interesting as the bear drinking pop at the gas station near Duluth.

Besides being able to look at Harry, I could have free pop and potato chips and be allowed to play the slot machine whenever we visited the 440 Club. Harry would always give me a few slugs for the machine and let me cash in for nickels and dimes whatever extra slugs would come down the chute after I pulled down the lever. Sometimes, however, too many extra slugs would come down the chute and someone at the bar would yell "Jackpot!" and Harry would have to fix the machine by taking the back of it off and putting all the slugs back in where they belonged.

Almost twenty years later, Harry, the 440 Club, and the rhythms of the slot machine came back to me when I was trying to write a poem about Las Vegas. Quite possibly I saw my lack of success against the slot machine at Harry's club mirrored in the lack of success of the patrons of the Las Vegas casinos.

The only thing I didn't like about visiting the 440 Club was that to get to it you had to drive through the part of South St. Paul which smelled of the stockyards. Maybe there wasn't any part of South St. Paul that didn't smell of the stockyards. Apart from knowing that the stockyards smelled, and that Janice and I would have to hold our noses for a couple of miles before we got to the 440 Club, I also knew that they were the largest stockyards in the world except for those in Chicago and maybe Kansas City, and that another of my uncles, my mother's brother Paul, worked there. I never understood why my Uncle Paul wanted to work at the stockyards, because he was a very nice uncle and not at all unusual, and I never understood how he could work there without holding his nose, which I was told he didn't have to do. I guessed he was like a lot of other people I saw at the Minnesota State Fair, who could walk through the animal barns without holding their noses. The animal barns at the fair were to me like the part of South St. Paul that smelled of the stockyards, and the midway with its rides and pinball machines was like the 440 Club. Whenever we visited the state fair, we would go through the animal barns before we got to the midway, so it was awful but worth it.

Between the ages of two and six I lived in south Minneapolis across from Powderhorn Park on Fourteenth Avenue. During the summers there would be band concerts, and families would rub themselves with mosquito repellent and bring blankets and picnic suppers and sit on the hillsides listening to that remarkable music you can only hear at band concerts. Sometimes the audience would sing along with the music and everyone would applaud for every-

Las Vegas

presto

pear lemon bell $ another quarter $ lemon pear pear $ another quarter $ lemon lemon bell $ well another quarter $ orange bell pear $ and the jabber of the jazz $ moving money for the House $ putting rhythms in the air $ in the arms $ pulling down the arms $ of the slots $ with the little windows $ showing pear bell pear $ so another quarter $ or a half $ or a dollar $ and a prayer $ and another prayer $ to the little windows $ showing orange orange pear $ so another dollar $ and a mother with her pennies $ and her kids $ and her pennies $ and her pulling $ and her staring for the $ bell bell bell $ where the $ pear bell pear $ reappears $ so another penny $ moneychangers everywhere $ swapping slot-fitting money $ for the making of the money $ off the man passing through $ or the systematic sucker $ with his pencil and his pad $ and his probably improbable probabilities $ and the rancher and the star $ and the singer on a fling $ and a small-time monarch $ where the cards flutter in $ King of Hearts $ 4 of Spades $ so a hit me $ again $ and a miss $ and a win $ for the all-the-luck House $ at the money-green table $ where the green money falls $ disappearing as it falls $ and the spinning of the wheel $ clicking red black red black $ red black $ and red $ and black $ and and red $ so another spinning $ and the losing and the winning $ and the winning $ of the House $ as the girlies glitter in $ sipping Singapore Slings $ with their week-end men $ or another diamond ring $ for a marriage anytime anyplace anyone $ to a rich man $ poor man $ beggar man $ thief $ to a moth hooked on neon $ in the middle of a desert $

one else after the number was over. Each park which had band concerts during the summer would be rated for audience participation,
and at the end of the season one park would be proclaimed the
audience participation champion, and the results would be published in the paper.

The morning after a band concert Janice and I would get up
especially early and comb the hillsides near the bandstand for lost
change. We always found at least as much as whatever it was we
were then getting for our weekly allowances. We added even more
to our summer incomes by employing the same search strategy
after the Fourth of July and the Southside picnic.

Every summer Powderhorn was the host park for what was called
the Southside picnic, a two-or-three-day miscellany of games, contests, concerts, concession stands, and the like. A traveling carnival
would set up rides and shows, and once each summer my father
would try to trick me into not being afraid to ride on the merry-
go-round horses that went up and down on their poles. But he
never succeeded, and either I'd yell and jump off the merry-go-
round or hug and stay on one of the little horses you could trust
not to move up and down on its pole and which was so safe you
could hold a baby on it. My father probably made the mistake of
thinking that just because I wanted to own a real pony and liked
to ride on my broom horse Neigh-Neigh all over Powderhorn, I'd
like to risk breaking my neck on an up-and-down-going merry-go-
round horse. But I was already five or six and too old to take a
chance like that.

There were all kinds of things you could buy to eat and drink
at the Southside picnic, and I especially liked eating fresh popcorn
and drinking Coca-Cola. The Coca-Cola stand was one of my favorite places to go at the picnic, because they'd give kids free tiny
Coca-Cola bottles filled with real coke. If you went to different
sides of the Coca-Cola stand at different times of the day, you
could get lots of free tiny Coca-Cola bottles if you were a kid.
Janice and I had almost a case each of Lilliputian Coca-Cola bottles. We liked filling them up again with coke from the ordinary-
sized bottles, and sometimes at night, before we'd fall asleep, we'd
use them for making shadows on the walls of our bedroom.

I didn't care too much for the contests at the Southside picnic and never entered any. And I got tired of hearing how famous Janice was because she once took second prize in a doll buggy decorating contest. I wasn't sure if she won her prize in Zumbrota or at Powderhorn and didn't bother to find out, though I did ask what the *first*-place doll buggy looked like. Every year when the Southside picnic rolled around and someone would mention that someone on the block was entering the doll buggy decorating contest, a big picture of famous Janice and her famous *second*-place doll buggy would be dragged out and everyone would force me to stare at it.

The summer I turned seven our family moved into Apartment 24 at 3142 Lyndale Avenue South. It was not until 1955 that we left those three and a half rooms and a bath to move into the first house of our own, which was located in the Minneapolis suburb known as Richfield. Even though I was by that time a student in college (Macalester), it was like being shot to the moon, without having been trained to be an astronaut: a giddiness in the face of new spaces and new proportions — a front yard, a back yard, a room which I did not have to share with even one sister, much less three sisters. (My younger sisters, Nancy and Judy, had spent all of their respective nine and seven years in Apartment 24 and had shared the bedroom, which my father referred to as the barracks, with Janice and me. My parents slept on a rollaway in the living room.) To explain further the initial disorientation I felt upon moving from Minneapolis to a house in the suburbs, it's necessary to say something more about the sense of inner-space mobility I felt in Apartment 24 between 1941 and 1955. I do so at some length, for it touched on virtually every aspect of my life.

Apart from the habitual summer fishing I did, and still do, in the beautiful chain of lakes in Minneapolis located about a mile west of 3142 Lyndale Avenue South, most of my childhood adventures, traumas, and so on were enjoyed or endured within a three-block radius of The Upland Apartments. I felt pretty uncomfortable wandering anywhere very far beyond the area of that circle. I suspect that by living in the apartment and its building during a fair length of time I acquired and developed survival tactics best suited for close-quarters confrontations. Whatever skills were involved were geared to coping with very familiar people and very familiar things seldom more than a hallway-length away and often much closer. The once or twice I was taken to visit the relative of a friend who owned a farm, I was hardly inclined to explore the woods or fields or to feel "free at last to roam," but instead I shrank into myself and wished only to return to good old over-crowded Apartment 24, where I'd again be safe and comfortable.

Because of the all-too-condensed area within which I felt secure, summer camp was always a threat, mitigated only by my knowledge that it might be a bit too expensive, and my firm resolve each June to make clear to my parents as politely as possible that nothing on heaven or earth could ever drag me off to camp. Only once was this resolve somewhat compromised, which was when I was tricked into visiting my mother's brother Herb's resort, the Milwaukee Inn, near Hayward, Wisconsin, where my father told me (correctly) there was the best muskie fishing in the world. That two-week trip was not really like what I imagined going to camp would have been, but it was a *little* bit like it, so I always thought my parents were lucky that it worked out so well and that I came back to 3142 Lyndale happy as well as safe. (I also returned with a trophy: a semifrozen two-and-a-half-pound smallmouth bass that I had caught on a minnow. It was the first fish I had ever hooked that broke from the water in such a way as to make the covers of *Field and Stream* look believable to me.)

Not only did I face the problem of what to do within large unfamiliar spaces whenever I was unfortunate enough to end up in them but also the problem of needing to carve out some minimal private life for myself within the confines of Apartment 24, as the inhabitants increased from four to five and then to six in number. For the first few years at least, I had the following spaces all to myself: two shelves in the closet off the bedroom where Janice and I slept in twin beds, and a corner of that closet where I kept a large cardboard box; also my bed, together with the gap between the bed and the wall and the radiator which prevented the bed from being flush with the wall. On one of my closet shelves I kept all my *National Geographic* magazines, which a great-aunt-and-

uncle had given me a continuing subscription to at an early age because of my fondness for the pictures. (I remember that the first
story in the first issue I received in the mail was about a famous
sailing ship named the *Yankee Clipper* and the adventures of its
crew as they sailed around the world very far from The Upland
Apartments.) On the other shelf I kept most of my smaller and
less prominent stuffed animals — the B-squad — and in the box in
the back of the closet I kept my collection of comic books, which
in its heyday numbered around three hundred issues and was
topped only by Henry Willigalle's. Henry, who lived in a house up
the block, had a collection probably three times the size of mine.
But like the dinosaurs it was suffering from oversize. It was hard
for him to keep track of which comics he owned and which he
didn't, and the bulk of his archives was settling into the tar-pit-
dark corners of his cellar where his mother stashed them in order
to keep them from messing up the house. My collection, spilling
over the brim of the large box in the closet, was far more accessible.
I, and all the kids I traded with, knew its contents in detail, and
my complete up-to-date pile of *Classic Comics* functioned as a
kind of open stack, to be used in writing desperate last-minute
book reports from seventh grade through senior high school. In
the gap between the bed and the wall I kept the varsity squad of
my stuffed animals. At night I'd sleep with all of them plus one or
two lucky B-squaders.

My privately controlled spaces were as efficiently used as was
possible. But they didn't add up to quite enough room *just for me*,
which is why, I think, I had to look elsewhere as well; and about
the only unthreatening elsewhere I could find was inside my own
head. It was there, in my own mental spaces, that I could knock
around however I liked, confronting and coping with strange people, places, and things; taking risks, sailing with my favorite animals
through my own construals of scenes depicted in the *National
Geographic*. (I knew, of course, that even my own father would
sometimes travel great distances and come back alive. Still, I was
always greatly relieved when he would return from a plumbers'
convention in Chicago, and I was always delighted with the tokens
of his travels that he'd bring back to me: tiny bars of soap and little tubes of toothpaste, and sometimes a glass or a towel with the

name of a hotel on it. When I'd read my *Classic Comics* about the adventures of Marco Polo and how he brought back spices and silks from China to hand out to his pals who had stayed in Europe, I'd think of my father coming back from the plumbers' convention and bringing me tiny bars of soap and little tubes of toothpaste.)

Apart from the lilacs, honeysuckle, and spirea that grew on bushes in the neighborhood and formed a blossomy border for the small park I liked to play in — Bryant Square, a safe block away — I was much better acquainted with the floral patterns on the maroon carpeting in the apartment building hallway than I was with any of the typical Minnesota flora. So too, because I had little opportunity to observe Minnesota's wildlife, with the exception of one captive bear, a few rats from the boiler room, and gray squirrels, I developed rather intense relationships with a wide variety of idiosyncratically selected stuffed fauna. I loved animals, but in Apartment 24 I had to make do with stuffed ones. As surrogates, they were altogether successful — to the point, I think, of alarming my parents. Not only were my animals things to play and sleep with, dress up, and so on, I also imposed their personalities on my real world in somewhat bizarre ways. Unbeknown to the owner or manager of the Minneapolis Millers — the American Association baseball team which was to Minneapolitans what the Yankees were to New Yorkers — I clandestinely identified each of my favorite animals with one of the starters on the Millers team and most of my less liked animals with aging or recently acquired bunglers. (Only my great childhood buddy, Jack Hemken, knew about this, and only I knew that his teddy bear, Teddy, also played on the team.) I remember a small lamb made out of an old dishtowel and stitched with pink thread which I constructed myself by trying to follow a pattern from *Good Housekeeping* and which didn't turn out right. Each time some player on the Millers sank to new depths in his batting average or was ready to be sent back to St. Cloud (in the Northern League) — a town I gratuitously disliked — the ill-bestitched lamb would suddenly, for me, become that player. Whenever I'd sneak into a Millers game at Nicollet Ball Park, I'd *see* my animals — the best and the worst of them — compete with the Milwaukee Brewers, the Toledo Mudhens, or the St. Paul Saints.

My favorite animal — Dumbo, an elephant with gray fur and polka-dotted trim — was in my head Babe Barna, the cleanup slugger for the Millers. Barna usually struck out, popped up, or hit a home run. He was rumored to like beer a lot and even drink it sometimes in between doubleheaders. But I didn't mind, I got his autograph a half dozen times and saw him as my elephant. It was somewhat shocking to me, then, when his son enrolled at my grade school — Lyndale — for he didn't appear to me to be stuffed or in the least way elephantine, though he was, like his father, a bit chunky.

Growing up with three sisters, I very much liked what I saw, and I doubt if my desire for female companionship, which was in bloom by the age of six, could ever have been allayed by stuffed surrogates. When we first moved into the apartment, three girls about my age were already there, which was to my mind more than enough compensation for my loss of Powderhorn Park. We'd flirt with each other up and down the halls of the building, or out on the back porch, and I'd fall in love with first the one, then another, then the third, then the cousin of the first one visiting for part of the summer. I usually failed to fall in love with the right one at the right time, though, and the one loving me seldom coincided with the one being loved by me. All too soon, however, through sheer chance or diabolical cosmic design, The Upland Apartments became depopulated of girls my age and was never appropriately resettled. This meant that for romance I had to venture beyond the safe spaces of my address. School was the next safest place, because it was a kind of apartment building away from my apartment building, and, besides, I had to go there anyway. So by the age of eight I was in love with Ann Bamby, a brown-haired third grader, and so much in love that I was willing on two occasions to risk life and limb by walking all the way to her house on Thirty-Sixth and Pillsbury — nine blocks distant and at least six blocks beyond the borders of my security. Fortunately, there was always the possibility of letters, though even these, as the prose poem "I Love You Very Mush" will show, were not completely safe.

Because of the tree, the presents, and visiting friends and relatives, the Christmas season together with New Year's was always an exceptionally crowded, though very happy, time within Apartment 24. My father would make bowl after bowl of Tom and Jerry batter and invite anyone he could find in the apartment building in for a drink. I liked to drink my Tom and Jerry without spoiling it with whiskey and boiling water. But everyone else except my sisters seemed to like theirs spoiled that way. Tom and Jerrys were only one of the things my father liked to mix up for you to pour down your throat. He liked to cook period, and he also liked to sew and often made clothes for my little sisters. He'd come along when his parents were expecting a girl, so they just named him Luverne and turned a lot of the housework over to him at an early age. He never seemed to regret that that had happened, and if it hadn't he might not have been so famous for his Tom and Jerrys. Sometimes he got overconfident, though, and tried to cook things that only my mother could prepare right, such as Swiss steak or fried chicken and gravy. My mother never dared try to make Tom and Jerrys.

Whenever Tom and Jerrys were around, so were friends from Zumbrota and my grandfather. My mother would make lefse and bake a ham and do whatever you have to do to prepare lutefisk. I loved the lefse and ham but never tried the lutefisk which I could tell from the smell was a terrible mistake as food. Each Christmas Eve supper my father would explain to me that we had to have it because it was Norwegian and my grandfather was Norwegian. I knew they were both Norwegian, but I couldn't understand why we had to have them together. Besides, having so much lutefisk around seemed to me to be just another way of making the supper last longer so that I wouldn't be able to begin opening my presents.

The least happy Christmases in Apartment 24 were those during the war when my father was in the navy, stationed in Hawaii, and was unable to come home on leave to make Tom and Jerrys or anything else. He would always send us some big Christmas boxes full of presents, and we always got four boxes of Hershey chocolate bars — two of milk chocolate and two with almonds. These were highly prized and rationed out to us by my mother, because you could no longer buy them in stores, since they were needed to supply "our boys overseas" in order to keep their morale up. I was always glad my father's morale was being kept up overseas by his being able to buy boxes of Hershey bars to send home to us.

At Christmas and for my birthday I would often get a supply of genuine sailor hats, and whenever my father would come home on leave he'd check up on whether I was folding them just like they did in the navy. Because of the war and my father being in the navy I was willing to enlist in the Cub Scouts and go to den meetings which were held in a house far away from the apartment. Because the uniforms were blue, I could think of them as being sort of like the navy ones. But I didn't stay in Den 2, Pack 206, for much more than a year and was honorably self-discharged at the rank of Golden Bear. The one thing I didn't like about Cub Scout uniforms was that you couldn't wear sailor hats with them.

During the first part of World War II my father worked in a defense plant in New Brighton. Almost every kid's father and lots of kids' mothers seemed to work in defense plants, and if you lived in Minneapolis the defense plant they'd work in was either Honeywell or New Brighton. Wherever they worked, you became quite proud that they worked there and not at the other place. Because my father worked at New Brighton, I pitied kids whose fathers could only get a job at Honeywell. I don't think that many of us my age grew up with the knowledge that only a few years earlier most people couldn't get a job anywhere.

While the war was going on, Lyndale Grade School would sponsor scrap drives to help out with what was always called "the war effort." Kids would scrounge around looking for whatever thrown-away metal stuff they could find and take it to school for their room's collection on behalf of the war effort. It was hard to find much thrown-away metal stuff in the halls or incinerator rooms of 3142 Lyndale, but my father came to my rescue by lugging home for me a variety of half-completed casings for bullets, bombs, and so on, which I would in turn lug to school so they could be collected and turned over to defense plants such as New Brighton, where they could be used for making casings for bullets, bombs, and so on.

Much of the rest of what I learned or did while at Lyndale Grade School seemed to have something to do with the war effort: if our teachers weren't telling us why we should buy war stamps and bonds, they were teaching us a patriotic song or having us collect soap and toothpaste and washcloths to put in boxes to send to families in England. And whatever important news we had heard on the radio at home would be heard again at school during the current events period.

After my father was discharged from the navy, he took a job in downtown Minneapolis with American Standard Plumbing and Heating — a company which he'd worked for before his job at New Brighton. I was once again as content as I'd been before he'd joined the navy and felt that everything was safe and snug. But as the crowding increased, since at least the youngest three of us literally expanded in volume year by year, my father talked more and more of "moving out of the dump." At first I was very disturbed by what I took to be the implications of his mood, but as we lingered on in Apartment 24 my anxiety over being snatched away from the small corner of the universe I knew best subsided. It was not until my return to Minneapolis to settle, at the age of thirty-two, that I began to be acquainted in any detail with the *state* of Minnesota, most of which I only then came to realize existed outside of The Upland Apartments.

Neigh-Neigh Was a Good Old Horse

This old worn down broom my Mom gave me was really my horse Neigh-Neigh and I rode him all over Powderhorn Park and around the block and through the house and the sweeping part of Neigh-Neigh was his head and the handle part was his tail though Carl and Bobby had broom-horses with the sweeping part for the tail but if you made the sweeping part the tail it seemed like a horse with no head unless you tried to pretend the end of the broom handle was a head even though it was too smooth and shiny to be a good horse-head and would always be there in front of your eyes looking worse than a horse with no tail since you didn't have to look in back when you were riding and somewhere in the straw stuff of Neigh-Neigh's head there were ears and I'd talk into them a lot and say giddy-up Neigh-Neigh and once when I saw smoke coming out of a pile of leaves in our street I said giddy-up Neigh-Neigh we're going to a fire and he galloped me over to the leaves but I couldn't see any fire just only smoke coming up so I climbed down from Neigh-Neigh and looked hard at the leaf heap to see if I could see a fire but I couldn't so I poked around where the smoke was coming from with my broom and poked some more and swept around until all of a sudden lots more smoke came up and some fire too and when I pulled my broom out of the leaves I saw Neigh-Neigh's head on fire so I yelled and screamed and waved him around to put his head out but the more I waved it the more it burned so I just ran up the block yelling NEIGH-NEIGH'S BURNING NEIGH-NEIGH'S BURNING and a big fat man came running out of his house and grabbed Neigh-Neigh and crunched his head around in the street like my Dad did his cigarettes in an ashtray when he didn't want them anymore but I still wanted Neigh-Neigh so the man gave him back to me but had to say at me that I shouldn't be playing with fire and that he bet my Mother didn't know what I'd been doing but I was crying too much to make words and just ran home with Neigh-Neigh to wait for the police to come and get me for setting a fire like that because I knew the police came and got people who set fires and when I got home I yelled at my Mom what I'd done and asked her when the police would come but she said she didn't think they would and not to cry and maybe I'd like to help her make some cookies and I said I would but how Neigh-Neigh's head was all burned and she said I could have her sweeping broom and she'd get a new one so I stopped crying and helped make cookies and rode my new horse around a little but it never got to be a good horse like Neigh-Neigh because it was so new and the head was too big and fresh and yellow so I decided to stick by Neigh-Neigh but he smelled so bad he had to stay on the back porch for a long time and even after my Dad squirted the hose all over his head he still looked burned up so I just left him out on the back porch which my Dad said was putting him out to pasture and for my birthday I got a new scooter that went faster than Neigh-Neigh though I still thought Neigh-Neigh was a good old horse and no one ever dared throw him away though he completely disappeared when we moved to 3142 Lyndale Ave. So.

The Little King

Sometimes me and Janice just before we'd fall asleep wouldn't fight at all because we'd do THE LITTLE KING on the bedroom wall and the way we'd do THE LITTLE KING was to get a teeny Coca-Cola bottle about one finger long that any kid could get for free once a year at the Southside Picnic in Powderhorn Park and make the baby coke bottle stick to a finger by drinking the coke and then sucking the air out and smacking a finger right on the hole part of the top of it and waggling our coke bottle fingers around in front of lamps by our bed so the lamps would shoot shadows of the coke bottles on the wall and the shadows were fatter and bigger than the real coke bottles and were shaped like THE LITTLE KING who was a fat guy in a king suit in a comic strip and he never said anything or did much and was shaped like the shadow of a little coke bottle and me and Janice would make our LITTLE KING shadows walk all over the walls and ceiling and sometimes across our covers and faces and once even across my butt and we would try to say whatever we thought THE LITTLE KING might say and it wasn't hard because in the comic strip THE LITTLE KING never said anything so we could make our LITTLE KINGS say and do whatever we wanted and it was like running a whole comic strip by ourselves which had two LITTLE KINGS in it and when I got older and could read I didn't like THE LITTLE KING comic strip at all but I still liked to think of playing THE LITTLE KING with Janice and thought our shadow comic strip had been much better than the real one and even so good it was almost a movie.

The Christmas Panda

Although I was pretty crazy about stuffed animals I didn't love just any stuffed animal that came along and the Christmas I got an electric train that was supposed to be my number one present I got my Dumbo the Elephant which was the best animal I'd ever gotten and he was really my number one present and my electric train was my number two present though I pretended to my Mom and Dad that the train was number one because I knew it cost more but I also got another stuffed animal in the box that I thought the fire truck I didn't get would be in so that was already one thing against what popped out when I opened it which was a very skinny stuffed panda with one leg shorter than the other and as soon as I held it up I didn't like it at all but didn't know what to say so I said oh look at what I thought was going to be a fire truck it's really nice and put it back in the fire truck box and wasn't too proud of myself for not liking it because one reason I didn't was the legs and I thought about handicapped people and tried not to make anything of the funny looking legs in my mind but nothing helped and the whole panda was wrong it was so skinny it looked more like a black and white monkey than a panda and I thought about sticking a tail on it and making it into a monkey but I didn't know how to do it myself and if I asked my Mom to do it she'd know there was something wrong about the panda and she'd already told me how sweet he looked and that she hoped I liked him and that maybe there'd be a fire truck next year so I tried to play with him and get to like him but he'd always end up lying on the tracks when the train was coming and sometimes the train would smash into him and kill him and then I'd stick him in the fire truck box and bury it under some pillows or I'd have Dumbo save him and win medals but the panda never won any medals at all and the only name I could take time to think of for him was Pandy Panda which I knew was a stupid name even for a kid's stuffed animal and when one of his arms came loose I just took him to my Mom and said I guess that's it for poor old Pandy I guess we'd better throw him away but whenever Dumbo got a tear on any part of his cloth my Mom would have to make a new cover for the whole elephant except for the head which had a sort of fur on it.

Tooth Powder

Even though everyone in the family had always brushed their teeth with toothpaste one night during dinner my Dad announced that the only way to get your teeth really clean was to brush them with tooth POWDER and that using toothpaste was like eating pure sugar and it let your teeth get yellow and soft and no dentist would allow such stuff in their own mouths and dentists ALWAYS used tooth POWDER and from now on we'd all brush our teeth with tooth POWDER and he made a little can pop out of his pocket like a Jack-in-the-Box and it was red and white and said on itself COLGATE TOOTH POWDER and my Dad said why don't you kids march off to the bathroom and try it so me and Janice gobbled down the rest of our dinner and marched off to the bathroom to try it because we knew there was no escape and Dad followed us in with his red and white can and showed us how to put the tooth powder on our brush which was to pour a tiny white pile of it in your hand and then wet your tooth brush and tap it on the powder pile and then brush your teeth like usual but I breathed too hard on my powder-pile and it flew all over like a little blizzard so my Dad turned the can upside down to pour out some more but the more didn't come so he tapped the can but none of it poured out again so he slapped the can and a whole mountain of tooth powder fell in my hand so he made Janice take some of mine and then he took a whole lot of mine and yelled at Mom to come brush her teeth but she said she hadn't quite finished eating her dinner and she'd brush her teeth when she felt like it so I ended up with a pretty big pile of tooth powder all to myself and wet my brush but I didn't wet it enough because when I tapped the brush in the powder-pile so it'd be like toothpaste and stick on the brush nothing happened so I stuck my hands under the faucet for just a second to make it all mushy and sticky but it was a second too long and all the tooth powder turned into cream and ran out of my hand into the sink so my Dad yelled HERE LET ME DO IT FOR YOU and grabbed my brush and smashed it around in some tooth powder and said O.K. NOW BRUSH so I started to brush but the tooth powder tasted like flour powder and made me gag and choke and spit and Janice tried it and said ICK ICK IT TASTES JUST LIKE SAND DAD I'M NOT GOING TO USE IT YOU CAN'T MAKE ME USE IT and I joined Janice's side against my own Dad and shouted SHE'S RIGHT DAD SHE'S RIGHT but my Dad yelled YOU BET YOU'RE GOING TO USE IT BOTH OF YOU so I started to cry and asked him why he brought me all those baby tubes of toothpaste he got from the hotels at The Plumbers Convention if toothpaste was so poisonous and my Mom came in and said why don't you use it Dad and let the rest of us use toothpaste it probably won't kill us so he said O.K. O.K. BUT THEY DIDN'T EVEN GIVE IT A FAIR TRY FOR ALL I CARE THEIR TEETH CAN TURN YELLOW AND ROT IN THEIR MOUTHS JUST DON'T SEND ME THE DENTIST BILLS but we knew he did care and that our teeth wouldn't turn yellow and rot in our mouths and after a couple of weeks Dad crossed back over to toothpaste himself and we never saw tooth POWDER again and his teeth didn't turn yellow and rot in his mouth though none of us ever dared tell him they didn't.

Black Widow Spiders

Like funnel-shaped clouds and earthquakes and fires black widow spiders were one of the worst things in the world to me and I couldn't believe how some people were dumb enough to live in a place where lots of bananas grew because black widow spiders love to hang out in bananas and could hide there just waiting for you to try picking a banana so I made my Mom and Dad promise we'd never go live where bananas grew and whenever my Mom got back from the store with a big bag of groceries that had some bananas in it I'd watch those bananas until I knew it was safe and no black widow spider would come for me out of the bunch to bite me and kill me with deadly poison but even though they were such terrible bugs I always sort of wanted to get a peek at a live black widow spider and thought there might be one or two stray ones that didn't live in bananas but made webs in the corners of window wells or in between garages and would stay in their webs even if they spotted you and there were lots of webs in places like that around 3142 Lyndale so sometimes I'd capture ants and put them in webs so I could see what kind of spider would pop out of the web-hole and wrap up the ant but it was always a little brown spider with some dark lines on it and never a black spider with a fancy bright mark on its stomach which would make it a black widow but the little brown spiders were just about the right size for black widows and maybe some black widows got born kind of brown so sometimes I'd get a jar and catch a brown spider and feel like a hero to the ants and shake the jar around until I could see the spider's stomach but I never noticed any bright mark on any brown spider and the only black widow spiders I ever got to see I saw on a Field Trip to a Museum where they were dead and under some glass and one was upsidedown so you could see the mark on its stomach and the other was rightsideup so you could see how it'd look when it was coming at you and I stared at those black widows for a long time and thought AT LAST WE MEET and though they were dead I was glad they were under the glass because even an ordinary bee can sting you while it's being dead.

Buy Bonds and Stamps Today/Buy Bonds and Stamps Today

When I was in 2nd grade at Lyndale Grade School there was a big WAR BONDS AND STAMPS DRIVE to get us all excited enough to get money however we could scrape it up for buying WAR BONDS AND STAMPS so the U.S. would have enough money to make all the guns and bombs and bullets they needed to protect our Boys Overseas so they'd win the war for the Allied Forces and our DRIVE was made to be an Auditorium Program for all the grades and even Kindergarten and different classrooms had to do different things for the Auditorium Program and what Miss Holtz made our class choose to do was to have a WAR BONDS AND STAMPS DRIVE POETRY CONTEST and to have the writers of the five winning poems read them at the Auditorium Program and I wrote the first poem I ever made and it was one of the five winners because it went BUY BONDS AND STAMPS TODAY/BUY BONDS AND STAMPS TODAY/IF WE ALL BUY BONDS AND STAMPS/WE'LL HELP TO WIN THE WAR and I was pretty proud it was a winner and went home and made everybody listen to it and even made Janice listen to it and then I learned it by heart because I had to say it that way the next day in front of everyone at Lyndale except the janitor and my Mom helped me learn it and said she was very proud and the next day when our class walked in to the gym for the Auditorium Program and sat in our classes' spot me and the other four winners sat in a special spot in our classes' spot so when it was our turn to present we could walk right up to the stage without tripping over anyone and just to make sure I knew my poem by heart I said it over and over in my head until our class was called and when our class was called I tried to say it once more in my head before I walked up in front of everybody but nothing happened in my head at all so I tried it again and nothing happened again and all the other winners started walking up to the stage but I just sat there and started crying so Miss Holtz whispered over to me that it was O.K. Keith and you don't have to go up there so I stopped crying and liked listening to the other winners and clapped like mad for each one but I still wondered what my winner was like but I couldn't tell until all our winners came marching back to our classes' spot and I heard in my head again BUY BONDS AND STAMPS TODAY/BUY BONDS AND STAMPS TODAY/IF WE ALL BUY BONDS AND STAMPS/WE'LL HELP TO WIN THE WAR.

When the Lights Go On Again All Over the World

Sometimes while the War was going on there'd be Air Raid Drills at night which meant sirens and everyone in Minneapolis turning out all their lights and no lights anywhere except for the searchlights and it was real scary and we all hated hearing the sirens which were worse sounding than ambulances and our teacher Miss Bergstrom told us how lucky we were to be allowed to turn on our lights at all and how kids in London couldn't because they were going through true Air Raids with bombs falling and homes and buildings being destroyed and lives lost and we should pray to God and thank him for making our Air Raids just drills and somebody wrote a famous song about turning lights on and it became No. 1 on The Hit Parade and was called WHEN THE LIGHTS GO ON A-GAIN ALL OVER THE WORLD and it started out with WHEN THE LIGHTS GO ON A-GAAAAIN/ALLLLLL OVER THE WUUUURLD/AND THE BOYS COME HOME A-GAAAAIN/ ALLLLLL OVER THE WUUUURLD and Miss Bergstrom decided for our class to choose it to sing as our contribution to the Lyndale Grade School Patriotism Day Auditorium so everyone in the class had to learn it but most of us knew most of the words anyway because we all listened to The Hit Parade every Saturday night and the way Miss Bergstrom decided we should do the song was for everyone to hold up their hands and wiggle their fingers fast whenever we came to the words LIGHTS GO ON AGAIN and Stanley asked why she wanted us to do that and Miss Bergstrom gave Stanley a sort of fishy smile and asked if anyone in class could TELL Stanley why she wanted us to do that and Carolyn Kingfisher raised her hand and said she could tell Stanley why and told him that all the wiggling fingers looked like a lot of lights blinking and Stanley said oh and wiggled his fingers in front of his face and stared and wiggled them again and wrinkled his nose and didn't say anything more and me and Ronnie tried hard not to look at each other but it didn't work and Ronnie got thrown out in the hall for loud giggling though after a while he was let back in again to add a couple of lights to the song and even though we were both against the Axis Powers we had a hard time not giggling and biting our lips and doing fake coughing whenever the words LIGHTS GO ON AGAIN rolled around and those words came up a lot but we usually managed to get our fingers wiggling like crazy though sometimes we'd wiggle them real slow and pretend we were going to strangle the person in front of us and Miss Bergstrom usually spotted slow wiggling and would say FASTER RONNIE FASTER KEITH THAT'S IT THAT'S IT and when I got home from our first practice I wiggled my fingers at my Mom and asked her if she knew what it was and she said it looks like you're wiggling your fingers and I said nope it's the LIGHTS GOING ON A-GAAAAIN/ALLLLLL OVER THE WUUUURLD and flopped in the big chair laughing my brains out.

The Clean Plate Club

Part of the U.S.A.'s part of the Allied War Effort against the Krauts and the Japs which was what Jack said his Uncle Amil said you should call them was THE CLEAN PLATE CLUB and THE CLEAN PLATE CLUB was a club you could join if you cleaned your plate at meal times and didn't waste any food so you wouldn't be hungry so often and end up using too much food on the home front when our Boys in the trenches needed it to keep them going against the enemy but I never quite figured out THE CLEAN PLATE CLUB because I always thought of clubs as having just a few members and four or five members being the most any club could take and even the Cub Scouts of America wasn't a club because Pack 206 all by itself had almost a hundred kids in it but THE CLEAN PLATE CLUB was said on the radio to have millions and millions of Americans in it and when I got my card from the radio station saying I was a member of it I didn't know the names of anyone else of the millions and millions of Americans except for my Mom and Dad and Janice and Bob Hope and President Roosevelt so I asked Jack if he was a member of THE CLEAN PLATE CLUB and he said he was because his mom had sent his name in to the radio station which sent out the membership cards and though he didn't think it was much fun he was going to stick it out because his Uncle Amil was in the navy and had been at Pearl Harbor so I thought I'd better stick it out too because my Uncle Earl was in the army and had seen action and I wanted him to get enough to eat but I was never sure when I was being a member of the club and when I wasn't because sometimes I'd eat Spam sandwiches in a chair and not even use a plate so there wasn't anything to be clean about except my hands and sometimes my plate would be pretty clean except for a few carrots and I couldn't see how anyone except yourself could really check up on you all the time to know if you were following the rules of the club or not and I didn't even know who the officers of the club were so I asked my Dad and he said he was the president but I just dared to laugh in his face it was such a lie even my Mom wouldn't believe it and even though I didn't want to be unpatriotic I felt sort of unpatriotic because I didn't like being in THE CLEAN PLATE CLUB because what good was a club if you couldn't get to be an officer or know when to kick someone out of it?

Playing Worm

One night me and Jack and Margot and Renee were playing in the hall of 3142 Lyndale and I was sliding down the stairs from the 2nd floor to the 1st floor when Margot walked up the stairs which made me to see all the way up her dress to her very pants which were pink and I felt funny and nice all over and wanted to do it again not by accident but in a way so that if anyone looked at my looking it would look like an accident so I made up a new game I called WORM and I said I'M A WORM I'M A WORM HERE I COME HERE I COME and slid along the halls and up and down the stairs on my back and sometimes Margot or Renee would run by and I'd get a look but I couldn't go too fast on my back so if they ran too far I'd stand up and say NOW THE WORM CAN RUN NOW THE WORM CAN RUN and run until I caught up with them and flop myself down by their feet but once I went overboard and tried to wriggle between Margot's legs and she giggled and screamed and ran into her apartment so Renee giggled and screamed too and ran into Margot's apartment even though I didn't even try to make the worm go between her legs so that left just Jack and he asked me if I still wanted to be that dumb worm and that he didn't even know what the game WORM was and I said I didn't want to play WORM unless Margot and Renee came out because it was a game you only play with girls because they're afraid of them and run away when you're the worm and that once my Dad took Janice fishing and when he asked her to put a worm on her hook she screamed and I forgot to tell Jack that when my Dad asked me to put a worm on my hook I screamed too and even cried a little bit.

I Love You Very Mush

When I was only in 3rd grade and Jack was already in 4th Jack fell in love with Ann Bamby who was in 4th too and when he let me meet her

I fell in love with her even though she was a grade ahead because me and Jack were a lot alike and Ann Bamby had long brown hair and was cuter than Janice and almost as beautiful as my Mom and one night when Jack came over we felt like writing love letters to Ann Bamby and I decided that I would just write DEAR ANN, and then I LOVE YOU VERY MUCH one hundred times and then I GUESS I'D BETTER SIGN OFF NOW and SINCERELY YOURS, LOVE, KEITH GUNDERSON so I did and counted right and stuck all the I LOVE YOU VERY MUCHes in an envelope and addressed it to Ann Bamby and got a stamp from my Mom and Jack stuck whatever he wrote in an envelope and got a stamp from my Mom and said his Mom would pay her back and we didn't ask each other what we'd said in our letters but walked down to 32nd and Lyndale and plopped them in the MAIL BOX but as soon as my letter was gone a terrible idea came into my head about how you spell MUCH because the way I'd spelled MUCH was M-U-S-H and it was beginning to seem a little bit wrong so as soon as I got back to Apt. 24 I asked my Mom how you spelled MUCH and she said M-U-C-H so I asked how you spell MUSH like in corn meal mush and she said M-U-S-H so then I knew that the terrible idea was right and I'd told Ann Bamby I LOVE YOU VERY MUSH a hundred times and I could see her in my head opening my love letter and showing it to her whole family and everyone laughing and screaming and her big brother running next door and showing it around to the neighbors and Ann Bamby laughing too and telling everyone I was just a 3rd grade twerp and how Jack Hemken was her real boy friend and had sent her a letter no one else could ever see because it was so beautiful so I asked my Mom how you could get a letter back out of a MAIL BOX once you'd stuck it in and she said she didn't know how you could and my Dad who was reading the paper and eavesdropping too yelled out how it was illegal and a Federal Crime to break into a MAIL BOX so I knew it was all over because even Ann Bamby wasn't worth doing a Federal Crime for and that Jack and Ann would end up together and I'd end up the big joke of Ann Bamby's neighborhood and pretty soon the whole school would know about it but the next time I saw Ann Bamby she didn't say anything about the letter so I called her up and asked her to go to the movie with me at the Lyndale and she said she would and though she was already in 4th grade I dared put my head in her lap and say I LOVE YOU VERY MUCH and I said it how I hadn't spelled it and afterwards she let me buy her a coke at Walgreen's Drugs.

The Delicious Gravy

So when Mom was sick Dad did the cooking and me and my sisters wanted a good Sunday dinner as usual with meat and gravy and mashed potatoes so Dad make a chicken dinner with gravy and mashed potatoes but when we scooped the potatoes onto our plates we could see lots of little hard yellow lumps in them so we yelled LUMPS THERE ARE LUMPS IN THE POTATOES so Dad looked at the lumps but he couldn't see them and said you're all talking through your hats I don't see any lumps in these potatoes these potatoes are exactly like the ones your mother makes so we put some forkfulls of the non-lumpy potatoes in our mouths and screamed YOU CAN TASTE THEM YOU CAN TASTE THE LUMPS TASTE THEM DAD so Dad tasted his potatoes and rolled the bite around in his mouth and thought and felt and thought and said nope there aren't any lumps in these potatoes so we checked his potatoes again with our eyes to make sure he hadn't gotten a lucky scoop but he hadn't but we didn't say anything except please pass the gravy and planned at least to cover up the looks of the lumps so Dad passed the gravy but when we'd try to pour it it wouldn't pour and just sat in the gravy bowl shivering a bit so we shouted LOOK AT THE GRAVY LOOK AT HOW THICK IT IS IT DOESN'T EVEN POUR so Dad looked at the gravy but he didn't even try to pour it he just sliced a big firm spoonful out of the gravy bowl and smeared it around on his potatoes and said that gravy's just like the gravy your mother makes you kids are talking through your hats as we decided to ask each other to PLEASE PASS THE DELICIOUS GRAVY TO POUR ON OUR NON-LUMPY POTATOES AND UMM IT'S JUST LIKE WHAT MOM MAKES but we'd only take teeny little dabs of the gravy and wouldn't eat any and started to laugh and laugh until tears came and our sick Mom came out of the bedroom and said what's going on out here your Dad's a pretty good cook isn't he and I screamed and laughed and fell off my chair in laughing and tears and couldn't stop and Dad said for Mom to come and taste the gravy to see if it wasn't just like hers and she looked it over and said it certainly was the same color but that she still wasn't felling too well and wasn't hungry and me and my sisters kept on laughing and yelling PASS THE DELICIOUS GRAVY.

Grape Flavored Ice Cream Sodas

Once when my Dad and me were coming back from crappie fishing in Lake Calhoun without any crappies we stopped at SNYDER'S DRUGS for a treat and the treat I got was a grape flavored ice cream soda and it was really good and even so good I asked my Dad to taste it a little and he did and then snuck another taste and said it was really good and the next time we came back from crappie fishing in Lake Calhoun without any crappies and stopped at SNYDER'S for a treat we both got grape flavored ice cream sodas and told each other how really *really* good

they were and a few weeks later when it was hot and everyone was sitting around the apartment melting my Dad asked me if I felt like having
one of those grape flavored ice cream sodas and I said I did feel like
that and thought that him and me would be walking up to SNYDER'S
without Janice but instead my Dad had decided to make grape flavored
ice cream sodas all by himself for the whole family and said if you
think those up at SNYDER'S are good wait'll you taste mine I could
show that soda jerk a thing or two your old man almost went into the
restaurant business you know and I knew he sort of almost had because
he loved to say he almost had but I was surprised about the grape flavored ice cream sodas because I'd never seen him make one or even
heard him talk about them before I'd had one at SNYDER'S but he
said he made great ones and if I'd get my nose out of my comic and run
down to the basement store and charge twelve bottles of grape pop and
a quart and a half of vanilla ice cream we'd all have as much as we wanted and my Mom asked my Dad about just how much he thought we
wanted but he didn't even hear her and I yelled I wanted three or four
giant sodas and Janice said she wanted a root beer float instead because
she didn't like grape but my Dad said no root beer float could hold a
candle to his grape flavored ice cream sodas so I ran down to the store
and got six bottles of grape and the ice cream and then I ran down
again and got six more and when I got back upstairs I saw my Dad had
already poured the first bottles in the Thanksgiving Turkey Roasting
Pan and had begun to stab apart all the ice cream with a knife and
smash at it with a big wooden spoon and then he poured in the rest of
the pop and began to stir the ice cream around and around until everything began to look purply white and kept smashing away at any ice
cream lumps he'd spot bobbing around in the pop and none of them
escaped and pretty soon it all looked kind of soapy and you didn't see
what you'd see if you looked in your soda at SNYDER'S and my Mom
asked my Dad if he was sure he knew what he was doing but he said she
had to be kidding and kept stirring and stirring and then said ALL
RIGHT GET DOWN THE GLASSES and poured the funny looking
stuff into the glasses and gurgled his own down in a couple of gulps and
announced THAT'S BETTER THAN SNYDER'S YOU CAN BET
YOUR BOOTS ON THAT and my Mom took a little sip of hers and
said she'd never had one of them before and it certainly was different
and I tasted mine and yelled IT'S TOO WARM AND THERE AREN'T
ANY HUNKS OF ICE CREAM LEFT and my Dad said that's the secret
of my recipe it's much smoother than any soda you can buy in a drug
store so I almost began to cry but remembered I had my own nickel
and ran down to the store and bought a vanilla ice cream cone and
plopped the scoop into my soda and Janice said she thought it looked
icky and didn't want any but my Dad kept on drinking the stuff until
he said we could save the rest for later and it'd keep and if we wanted

it colder he'd make it colder and turned the refrigerator way up and yanked out a lot of jars and plates of stuff so he could get the rest of his secret recipe in but he had to pour it into three small bowls because the pan wouldn't fit and my Mom made popcorn and we all went into the living room to listen to THE SHADOW on the radio while my Dad's secret recipe sat in the bowls and the next morning me and Janice went to look at the bowls and there was just a lot of scummy stuff on the top of each one and purply white pop underneath so we laughed and laughed because Dad had already gone to work and I asked my Mom if she'd like some purple swamp for breakfast and in the afternoon I caught my Mom pouring the three swamps down the sink and when she saw me see her she said I don't think Dad will miss this very much and when Dad came home and looked in the refrigerator he said I see you've finished it off after all and my Mom said we sure did Dad we sure did.

SHIRLEY SCHOONOVER

Route 1, Box 111, Aurora

by Shirley Schoonover

I was born on a small farm that scrabbled and sprawled along the long lively road to Aurora, that brawling, Saturday night town. The ore-red road cut like a wound through the black wood of northern Minnesota, my black wood where mysterious gods hooted and squalled, the black wood that edged our farm. I'd follow the farm dogs down rabbit trails and around fallen trees where bears were sure to be lurking, those sullen bears, scruffy and baggy at the knees, foul-breathed, looking boozy, swearing bitterly when startled out of a nap. The black wood, where even in highest summer there'd be snow sulking in the knee-deep moss, and ice glittering within the moss so that a child could freeze her legs to the bone in July and throw snowballs at the dogs who'd blink reproachfully and nip off for home. The black wood, ominous with those big pawed bears, haunted by dawn gray owls who spat up mouse bones in furry cuds; the black wood with its old tall trees and many secret places and green halls where deer and unicorn grazed and gazed and the rare doves would make a pale lament. And I, brash and sassy, innocent as an egg, tough as rawhide, would yell, "Hello!" and the echo rang until I wished I hadn't said it at all because it roused ghosts and the loon whose voice stopped the spit in my throat and made my knobby knees leap high and wide for home.

149

The black wood was my secret place; the farm was my world. The barn, warm from the melancholy sighing cows, clattering with the chickens who meddled and gossiped, those hens who spurned the nests my father built, choosing to lay their eggs in the mangers and exploding red-eyed and vehement when the innocent cows would try to feed. The roosters, spurred and strutting, so near-sighted they'd hurl insults and challenges even at a milk pail. And the cats, going about their own business, mousing out the barn, stealing sips of fresh milk, and dropping kittens in the snuggery of the hayloft. Through this chicken-scratching, catcalling racket my father would come at the end of the day with the horses from the plowing, heavy-footed and certain, an eye on every living thing. The wise cats disappeared, the chickens squabbled out from underfoot. The horses, golden-eyed, ears delicately tuned, would move into their stalls to search for their oats while I ran to fetch buckets of water and the currycombs and brushes. My father would help me lift the heavy harnesses and hang them on the wooden pegs, and then I was left to brush and burnish to my heart's content. From head to hoof I'd brush those horses, gentling them with my hands, combing out the snarls from their manes, making love curls in their forelocks, wiping the sweat and froth from their sides, and pulling the tangles from their tails until the long black hair was shining and electric. The horses would listen to me talk, turning their heads to look at me and billowing their breath on my neck or nuzzling me with dusty kisses.

From the barn to the house along a path where the dogs, Shep and Pal and Rex, would fawn and bow to me, jumping up and falling back like waves around my knees. Beside the path the weeping willow tree where once I'd found a china doll, where later I'd retreat to hug my secret dreams or to spy on my parents when the minister came to call. He with potbellied piety and a diamond ring on his left pinky. Over-jolly, he'd wheedle coffee and cakes on Wednesday and rebuke us on Sunday. The willow tree where I'd scoot, dandered up from a scolding, to plan my escape to Africa or somewhere else where people would appreciate me. My green willow, where I'd pull the long branches together to hide me from my mother who wanted to wash and iron me on the summer days when I was dragged to Bible class, those long solemn classes in the church where I'd doze under the droning voice of the minister. But the church never dozed, it sat upright and ice-eyed, and I'd die of boredom waiting for the minister to oil his way through the day's lesson.

"You won't go to Heaven if you don't behave in church," my mother would say.

"Well, I ain't going to Heaven, anyway. I'm going to Africa." But I didn't go to Africa. Unrepentant and riddled with sin, I'd skulk under the willow tree.

The willow tree was my house, my castle, and I lived most of my summers there. But when the winter thundered into my world I decamped to the house, to the civilized but snug world of shoes and woolen underwear, underwear so long and rasping that I wondered if I'd have any skin left by spring. The house I lived in with my parents, I wonder now if I remember the house itself or more the way it smelled on Sunday afternoons when my socks and mittens were drying on the back of the stove, or the sunny starched smell of the kitchen curtains blending with the scent of the cardamom-spiced biscuits my mother baked.

The memories of childhood have no order at all but come lilting and spilling like the snows of all those winters. The snows of my childhood came shaking down the sky, mute thunderstorms that shawled the trees and capped the fence posts. Snowstorms that howled and nagged at the windows and drove the smoke back down the chimneys. Our snows made castles of haystacks and, one year, a turret on the outhouse. Our snows made royalty of us all, for we had crystal hanging from the eaves and frost-brocaded windows, not to mention the icy lace on our lashes and brows.

If there were snows to remember, there were the dazzling nights when your breath crisped inside your nostrils and the moon had blazing rings around it. Such clear nights that the stars sprang up at the edges of the pasture. And the Northern Lights spangled in silent fireworks all across the sky. Those cold clear nights so still that if you sang while carrying firewood, the man three farms away could hear you and yodel back.

Out of the clutter of memory comes the recollection of how we Finns fought the long winters: the sauna. If we didn't heat our own sauna, we'd wallow through the snow to someone else's sauna. Saturday nights and fifty below zero, we'd bundle our clean clothes together and be off to Aunt Martha's or Aunt Anna's, there to mingle and joke in the blustery, hot little kitchen as the children found each other and started to scrap under the table or under the feet of the red-faced fathers and the knitting mothers. We'd come in from the cold and have our coats, scarves, and mittens snatched away from us and be sent to behave ourselves, we uncorked, unruly children. The adults would sort themselves out for coffee and a chat before the ritual sauna began. And it seemed that just when we brawling brats would get a good fight going, that was when a mother would appear and haul the little girls off, usually by an ear, to the sauna where we'd be peeled like onions and stuck into the steam room to stew until we were scoured and scrubbed, our ears turned inside out, our necks, knees, and elbows scraped. Then we were rinsed with cold water and what was left of our skin was sanded off with the rough towels. A child had no privacy in the sauna. The slightest sniffle, the gentlest clearing of the throat, hinting at a cold (much wished for on Monday mornings!) exposed you. Your mouth was pried open for mother and aunts to examine; that sore throat you'd been encouraging by sucking icicles was revealed. Eyes glinting, my mother brought forth the jar of Musterole, which I thought I'd destroyed, and slathered me fore and aft. Then, deaf to my squalls, she forced me into the much despised long woolen underwear that chafed and itched even without the stinking Musterole. I raged and balked, but she had her way with me until it was time to put on my suspenders and long stockings.

"I ain't wearing that contraption!"

"You have to. You have a cold."

"Just socks," I begged. "Not the garter belt and stockings."

"Don't you want to get better?"

"It looks like hell."

"Don't swear. Here." And she snaked me into the suspenders, the garters snapping around my ears, the stockings lumping around my ankles.

I was done for and I knew it. Surly, greased, and gartered, I quit the sauna and went back to my aunt's kitchen, hoping no one would get downwind of me. But no wind was needed to carry my stench. My boy cousins were in the parlor telling dirty stories, and I tried to weasel in without being noticed.

"Boy, you stink!" Joel blatted, holding his nose at me. The other boys chortled, snorted, and backed away from me. "Stink! Ink, pink, stink!"

I lammed Joel one in the middle of his forehead, and he whacked me in the belly. Quicker than a cat could sneeze, we were rolling on the floor, gouging, kicking, and biting, our Finnish bloodlust rampaging. But then my father plucked me by the scruff of my neck and dumped me into the kitchen to sit behind the stove, where I glowered and sulked, one eye swelling shut and the smell of Musterole rising about me.

With winter, of course, there was Christmas. The Christmas I remember most was when we ate Petrice, our goose. She had come to our farm as a gosling. Thinking she was a gander, we named her Pete. When she laid an egg, we renamed her Petrice. She thought she was human and would have nothing to do with the other fowl. She always followed me around the farm, daffy, crooning to me, and I could never sit down without her getting into my lap and resting her head on my neck. She also wanted to mother puppies, and when our cocker bitch, Flicka, left her babes unattended once, Petrice nestled on them, wings outspread, crazy eyes soft and maternal. What a hooha there was when Flicka discovered Petrice gabbling there. The puppies didn't mind, but Flicka went mad. Foaming at the mouth, she attacked. Petrice did her best to fly, but, weighing twenty pounds, all she could do was lollop away, flapping her wings, while Flicka helped her along by grabbing mouthfuls of rump and feathers. Around and around the house they went, Petrice trundling, lurching, and honking and Flicka snapping and spitting out feathers. At last, poor Petrice ran headlong for the doghouse and stuck fast in the doorway, her fanny exposed, her cries dreadful, as Flicka lay down and promptly began denuding that plump backside. I scolded Flicka away and pityingly hauled Petrice feetfirst out of the doghouse. And when Christmas came and Petrice lay wreathed with parsley on the platter, I could not touch a drumstick or lay a fork on her white meat. I could not eat at all; cranberry sauce sparkled, sweet potatoes swam in golden sauce, apple pie bubbled and crisped, all to no avail, as I sat, pea green, at the table, poised on the edge of my chair, the brittle tears ready to break down my face.

But that was the only sad Christmas. All the other Christmases roll together into a white and woolly ball of remembering how it was to come to the rim of wakefulness on Christmas morning and lie there quilted and snug before flying out of bed to see what magic had happened during the night. There were always two kinds of presents. The practical kind included long woolen underpants and vests, always from an aunt who didn't know my size and so made them big enough to fit a cow, and knitted socks and caps that were too small, and a handmade pink satin brassiere trimmed with tatted roses from one of my daffier aunts, and the hated long cotton stockings with new suspenders from Santa Claus (my mother's handwriting), two suits of long underwear with trapdoors in back, and flannel pajamas to guarantee I'd never freeze at night, especially since I slept in my underwear. But the presents I liked were naturally not practical or useful to anyone but a child: candy canes and gumballs, red-and-green-striped ribbon candy, and a paper sack of orange bubble gum and licorice drops, once a gun that shot rubber-tipped darts with a real imitation leather holster, a whistle that made the dogs bark, a celluloid doll who wet profusely when fed (when she broke her head I used her to scoop snow cones), a bag of balloons, wax fangs that fit over my teeth. And a small blackboard with chalk, which was best of all, for in secret I practiced writing every dirty word I knew, only I was found out and got treated to another sitting spell behind the kitchen stove.

And then it was breakfast of oatmeal, which I dabbled at, mouth full of ribbon candy, hands sticky from sorting through the gumballs and candy canes. Then prinked and combed and stuffed into my blue rayon satin dress and tight black shoes, coated, hatted, and off to the Palo Congregational Church to discreetly suck on gumballs and pop tiny bubbles until my mother caught me and gave me such a pinch that I swallowed the gum.

Home from church, the long Christmas day spread out before us with aunts, uncles, and cousins coming by to kiss under the mistletoe. "Slobbering," I called it. All red-cheeked and smelling of Christmas colognes and after-shave lotion. There were the giddy, older girl cousins from Markham parading their fiancés and gaudy engagement rings while the spinsters whispered in the kitchen, "She *has* to, you know!" The uncles and my father would step out to the barn to look at the cows and to wet their whistles with a pre-dinner drink of Old Crow. The aunts and my mother tacked back and forth setting the long damasked table, carrying platters and bowls, scattering silver, folding napkins, unmolding the jello salad, basting the turkey, and hitting the head of whichever child got caught jam-handed or pickle-fingered.

Dinner was called and we all tucked in, barely waiting for manners; the plates were passed to my father, who laid on slices of turkey and handed the plates to my mother, who piled on mashed potatoes and ladled gravy, while aunts forked over the pickles, watermelon and dill, the walnut stuffing, and the vegetables, and we children lavished jellies and jam over our biscuits. We all ate beyond the bursting point and then begged for dessert: mince pies, marble cakes, raisin and cherry tarts, plum pudding, fruit-filled cookies, and chocolate candies — until one or another child turned pale and had to be led outdoors to be sick in the snow.

After dinner, the uncles and my father loosened their belts and shoelaces, belching behind polite hands, lighting their pipes and cigarettes, feet up, talking heavily and slowly, sometimes nodding into a doze. The aunts and my mother, elbows deep in soapsuds, coffee cups within reach, gossiped and creaked within their corsets and girdles. We children, adrift without a single parental eye tracking us, would sneak out to spy on the courting couples and snigger and simper in mockery at such moonstruck goonery, and if we caught them kissing we would smack our lips at them and howl like devils until some enraged swain came bangfooting after us, murderous and lusting for our blood.

But then the roistering day must end; the Christmas candles sputtered out, and the heavy twilight was now lanterned by the headlights of departing aunts and uncles and drowsing cousins. Then I sat in the starry tinseled Christmas glow and watched the snowflakes swaddling the earth anew with a white and silent light as the humming, holy night closed around me.

After Christmas came the New Year, wayward and relentless with school to be resumed, the wider range of my world, signaled by the lumbering yellow beetle of a school bus that shimmied over the ice-whining road to the chalk-smelling, paper-littered school-house that was filled by the big-bosomed, thousand-year-old Miss Dagney, dour as Dracula, with her energetic ruler that whacked my hands and her bleak ferret eyes that propelled me into the cloakroom for passing notes in geography class. And her hag's nagging that froze my wriggling restlessness and stifled the spitball urge, and her voice that cracked glass and shriveled my pirate's lust for red pencils and gum erasers in the next desk. What was school to me but a place of scandals, spilled inkwells, chewed pencils, learning how to howl the vowels and cough the consonants, trading sandwiches for comic books, squirreling gum under my desk, mumbling over the multiplication tables, and dreaming away the afternoons watching the dust motes dillydally in the sunlight, listening past Miss Dagney's voice to the drip of spring, knowing by the slant of the sun just when the school bus would grumble into the yard to carry us home again.

Winter. If I write more about winter than anything else, it's because I know more about winter. Laskiainen, the winter festival when the Finns came skiing in lyric patterns down the milky hills and from the snow-ruffed woods. Lakes with snow beaches where we left trails that ice dinosaurs might have envied and where the winter birds feathered the crusted snow with the whisper kisses of their landings. Winter in northern Minnesota where midday shone as bright and dark as midnight with all the sky shattered and falling into rings around the sun and moon. And, we children, stuffed and muffled with woolen mitts and scarves and the eternal long underwear, came trumpeting down the hills with wooden sleds and homemade skis and got in the way of the people with store-bought skis and fancy bindings, people who could ski the slalom. The slalom! Those whip turns marked by flags and fallen bodies. But anyone could do the ski jumps, even on homemade skis. And we Finns knew we could fly anyway, once launched on wax and supple wood and our own flaming arrogance. We'd take the downhill daredevil ice slide and, lifting from the lip of the slide, we would flatten along the skis, nose to tip, to soar in silence and then come down, baffling the wind with our bodies, hissing along above the snow to land with flexed knees and a flourishing snowplow.

Not just skiing, those Laskiainen days. Skating, not the figures,

but the blood battles of hockey and racing. The lean black skates
laced up the ankles and sharpened so that we flew on knife-edges,
and when the game got rough we'd kick and gouge. The figure
skaters were all indoors. But we took the Minnesota winds and
snow squalls straight, out on the lakes, and came home frozen
across the face, brows silvered with frost, even frost moustaches.
And me, at six and seven, I had learned to skate on clear patches
in the swamp, falling and bruising myself twenty-seven times in
one day. And I would slip into a game of hockey, snatching the
puck from the older kids, cutting it in and out between longer
legs, and bashing it into the net, only to be snuffed out by the
goalie who wouldn't let a punk kid play!

Snow and ice were our native territory. If we couldn't fly over
the lakes, we'd swim under the ice on Laskiainen. That was the
best, I thought. The brave boys and the whiskey-breathed men
would gather before noon in the sauna to brag and bully and drink
Old Crow or Teacher's, puffing up their courage to the swimming
point.

"I could do more'n a hundred yards easy," one of the boys
would say.

"Nah, a hundred's enough," the red-nosed gin drinker would answer.

"Oiva did more last year," the boys would claim.

And the rude sounds of belching and disbelief would belly
around the sauna. But it would be settled there where the temperature was one hundred and ninety plus as they sat around the bottles and the stove while the steam frisked over their heads and
they scratched and stretched before the plunge into the mother
heart of winter, the lake. Earlier someone would have gone out to
the lake to ax two holes in the ice a hundred yards apart. And now
the brave boys would drink straight whiskey or gin at a gulp and
run naked, high-kneeing it through the snow, to haul the harsh air
into their lungs and then dive headfirst into the first hole.

"Don't forget where you are," someone would advise them.
"Don't let the shock make you inhale."

Advice was dimly remembered at that first shock of icy water.
Then the garbled silence and the ice-gray world beneath. The first
to go were the toes; they turned lumpen dull. Ice formed over the

open eyes, it seemed; and one's genitals crept up to a safe warm place in the bowel. Sounds from the outside world were shrill, steps thumped overhead, the world drew skin-close, and the pulse of life was in your ears. Breaststroke was best, a long flat stroke and kick that took you a fifth of the way, the water purring around you like syrup, but cold! The breath came sliding through your nose, unwilled. Another gathering of muscles, contracting and stretching in the stroke, and the long glide while turning the eyes upward to measure how far, oh God! how far now? Not even half the distance and the god of death, Kalma, was breathing cold along your spine. A glance downward and there were all the pickerel and trout you'd never caught, asleep at the bottom of this ice-trapped world. You reached down and touched them: the spine of the sleepy pickerel, the fanning tail of the trout, all jeweled with cold, not moving, the gills and fins transparent. The sand beneath them dew-pearled with ice, prickling with air bubbles, the waterweeds drifting dark green and cold, slowly . . . slowly . . . and crawdaddies on the half shell with claws grasping at underwater dreams. The water world tucked up for the winter's night, and you, icy lunged, kicked off again to reach for the gray day world ahead. Heavy, the calves of your legs, the upper arms . . . heavy. Breath seethed from your nostrils, warming your belly in bubbles that rose and glimmered silver under the ice.

And then you broke for the surface, that shining circle of light, and you crawled and sprawled out of the water onto the ice and the brisk, rough clasp of the other Finns who had cursed and sworn and worried. You had come this long cold distance in silence and fear, and now they carried you, breathless, to the sauna and slopped more whiskey into you, doused you with hot water, scraped you with towels, and helped you into the bravado you now deserved.

Winter and water were our domain. We Finns were good at both. And after the sauna, at any time of the year, it was the lake or the river we sought. The sauna, for the child, was the baptismal, the place for laundering and scrubbing the soul. I, as a child, first saw my mother and father, soap-lathered and splendid, he with his fierce Finnish pride and my mother with her perky blue eyes and that biting scrub brush. Then, when I was seven or so, I was banished to bathe with only womenfolk: aunts, grandmother, girl cousins, and mothers. The men and boys kept apart, and I sulked under the blandishments of Aunt Anna, who pinched my fanny and chucked my chin. The sauna was just gab and gossip then, but I still had the coeducational juxtaposition of the sexes in the lake after the sauna. Then we were eels under the moon, diving from the sauna door to flash silver and black-wet under the stars. We all were hairless fauns then, I remember, with flat chests and just a cockleshell of sex. It was our time of innocence, and we were randy as lambs; the boys would pee from the tree branches and sprinkle our legs warm and laughing . . . we girls would trickle sly-ly into the lake, always knowing that we somehow had the magic of new life. Not for us, then, were the hooded eyes of lust. No, we kicked up our heels and danced back from the serious material of life. The glitterswim of the lake, the wreathing of waterweeds around our heads, the green gossip of fishes: those were our world. We wrote with scabby fingers on the sands and dreamed the dreams that lifted and billowed around us.

I can't make childhood lie still under the logic of a calendar of days or seasons, for it all comes tumbling out of the skein of mem-ory, bright-pricked with colors and tears and a laugh here and there.

Say childhood to me and I think of the high haymow where cobwebs drifted and gleamed and pigeons left feathered thoughts in the dusky light. Say childhood and my cousin Joel emerges, cussing and cussed, full-blown with mischief and malice. He came to stay on our farm one year, bringing with him such a bag of tricks and schemes that my grandmother locked up the good dishes and kept a night-light gleaming.

Joel and I met, collided, and fell upon each other in instant hate. We whaled away at each other, threw ourselves into a clawing embrace, fell to the ground, kicked, squalled, spat, swore, bloodied noses, tore hair, gouged genitals, and did our best to kill. Finally, we fell apart, eye to eye, spitting blood, satisfied. From then on, we were both sides of the bad penny. We sat, shank to scrawny shank in the outhouse, gassing away and reading Montgomery Ward or Sears Roebuck, wiping with the pages of ladies' under-wear. We hung upside down from the haymow rafters, letting our spit spiral down in long strands. We lassoed the hogs and rodeoed until my father caught us. Then we were hog-tied and threatened with isolation. Joel, with his white hair and evil blue eyes, smelling like a goat, with scarred knees, and spotted black and blue, was brave as a tiger by day. But at night he'd dig his scrubbledy head under the quilts, a frightened kidlet, and I would hum and buzz and weave stories for him, gabbling, happy as a goose, until he fell asleep.

And when they were about to take him back to live in the city, we stood, he and I, under the willow tree, without a word, scuffing our feet. Good-bye wasn't a word we knew, so there wasn't a thing to say.

After that, childhood was a solitary business. An only child, I had the freedom of loneliness. My best friends most winters were Orion and the moon. Orion paced the night sky, tracking the Great Bear, spilling a trail of stars and the northern lights. The moon and her pale sisters made a path over the crusted snow, and I and the buck rabbits would leap and frolic under the moon, madness and magic leading us farther and farther from the snuggery of house and forest, out to the virgin glitter of the frozen lakes where no one called, but I would answer, yodeling and dancing, wishing on the moon, not knowing that that moon had shone on other solitary dancers before me. Not caring either, because that was my moon, my dance, my dreams and wishes.

Childhood and dreams. One winter I had a dream come golden-eyed and living out of the lantern light in the driveway: Valko, white, with tangled mane, and lilting. My father bought a horse. My father bought him, but I owned him from the second I laid eyes on him. Valko was to be a light workhorse.

"Never been ridden," my father said. "He's part wild so stay away."

He might have told me to stop breathing. I followed them to the stall and watched that high-lifted head, the hooves that danced and sparked, the eye that flashed back at me.

"Let him settle for the night," my father said. And he, innocent with age, went back to the house.

I sat atop the feedbox. Valko nickered and nuzzled for feed, and I bribed him shamelessly with oats and half a loaf of bread I had stolen for my own snacking. He was a dream horse. White with a golden eye and silver stockings that curled over his hooves, and a silver tail that plumed behind him, and a curved crest of neck and shoulder that belied any plowhorse intentions. We talked, Valko and I, until my mother scolded from the house.

Mornings, before school, I ran out to feed Valko. And after school I changed from proper clothes to my worn cords and boots and was lost to humankind for hours, currying and brushing, wheedling and spoiling my horse. Before the week was out, I had sat astride his back in the stall, brushed his mane and braided his tail, cleaned his hooves, and let him discover the bread and snacks I had in my jacket pockets. And he kissed me with his bristled lips, let me lead him blindfolded around the barnyard, let me crawl between his hind hooves with only that golden eye turned to see where I had gone.

"He's half wild yet," my father said. "Don't you go riding him. He'll throw you."

But Valko followed me like a dog around the barnyard, kissing the back of my neck, nuzzling my pockets, calling me when I left him at last. So one day when my father was napping in the house, the newspaper over his face, and my mother was chinning with my grandmother about cousin Vivian who had married suspiciously fast, I, booted and illegal, took Valko out behind the haybarn, far out of sight, and, finding a pole fence, discussed the matter with Valko. He agreed, nodding his head, so I climbed the fence and eased myself across his back.

"It's not bad, is it?" I asked.

Valko turned his ears back, undecided.

I crept up to his withers and smoothed his mane. "You don't have to, if you don't want to. You just tell me if I hurt you and I'll stop." No answer. "You know I love you. I wouldn't do anything to hurt you," I crooned, carefully stroking his neck.

He turned his head and pretended to bite my foot. Then he took a step forward. Nodding, he decided we could go together around the barnyard. After that, we went round and round the yard and then through the gate and down the road. I held a strand of his mane in my hand and we walked sedately until he jounced into a trot, then smoothed into a run. A flick of his ears and we lifted into a soaring gallop, throwing up clods of snow behind us as we spurned the road and tried for the low-lying clouds. We were not earth-born, Valko and I, we were of another world, and we flew along the bare rim of this world, his mane stinging my face, my laugh chirruping him faster.

When we came back to the farm, my parents stood goggle-eyed on the porch, my mother's arms wrapped in her apron, my father's hands planted on his hips, a nasty look in his eyes. From the way his hair stood on end, I could sense his growing wrath. And the shaving strop in his right hand foretold my future. Quenched, I slid from Valko's back and led him to his stall. My father waited to make music on my backside.

But none of that mattered as long as Valko came nickering and nuzzling to my call. In the spring he would leap the farm fences when he heard me coming from the school bus, and I would ride him home. With my book bag on one side, my school dress hiked up, and my bare legs dangling down, we would canter into the farmyard and scatter the chickens and horrify my mother because my pants were showing.

Sunday mornings Valko and I would disappear for the day, taking a lunch of bread and cheese, exploring the ferny, magic black wood. And we would swim in the gleaming secret lake. I would braid water lilies, ferns, and violets in his mane and tail until he was a walking flower garden, and he, unsentimental, would eat the flowers, gleaming at me with those golden eyes. And he loved me.

But childhood ends. And late that spring my father had to sell Valko. Because I had loved and spoiled Valko. So when Valko went, I ran away from home.

I didn't run far. I went to live in the willow tree, scowling out from the green shadows and spurning all entreaties from my parents. I didn't starve: I raided the chicken coop and cooked the eggs in my doll's pot over a birchbark fire. I did accept bread from my grandmother, and I crept into the barn for warm milk from the obliging cows. I slept in my old quilt, lulled by the willow's green song. I sulked through the summer, teasing the cows with willow wands, swimming alone in the lake, garlanding myself with waterweeds, scaring myself silly on midnight prowls through the black wood when owls would swoop to rabbit kill; and loons would weep their madness across the dark and echoing nights. I knew that lost souls were whispering just above me in the tree branches and snatching my hair as I crept past them, and I could see those lost souls lifting and drifting above the lake just before the moon rose, and I could hear their laments as they moaned alone, lonely, waiting to catch such sprats as I. The long wan faces they had, the spindle fingers that plucked and touched the grasses and left wet prints on stones came creeping even to my willow tree to steal me out of my green snug place. I heard the owls moan and the foxes bark and then those silent sliding hissing sounds of the lost souls, and my hair would rise along the back of my neck. And I didn't pray because I was too proud, too angry, too lonely. And because I knew my willow tree would protect me, would keep the lost souls from touching me with their cold, wet fingers.

And fall came tricking me with its colors, and the leaves flamed and fell, and a box of crayons, waxy and blasphemously bright, tumbled out of the willow tree, and I knew that it was time to go back to the house. And what was a Minnesota fall but the cry of geese as they came bugling out of the north, moving across the moon to promise a return once they had been south. October, I remember, always lied, it was so flaming and lyric, strumpeting its way just before November quenched it and left the gay leaves draggling in the freezing rain, and the wounded sun sank lower and lower, and only the birch trees still stood vivid white against the raging wind. And we were left, all of us, with winter and ice that creaked and castled and snow that made a new world.

And what is left now, spinning from the wild and woolly skein of childhood memory? Spring! When the snow foamed in the gullies, scorched by the resurrected sun. The crooked-fingered trees threw off their widows' weeds to flirt green and tender on the hilltops. Spring, when my weeping willow trailed green ribbons and chuckled seductively, holding hands with the wind.

Minnesota spring mornings that shone clear and calm so that I always wakened clean and newborn, sassy as an Easter egg. And bounding out of bed to yodel and sing through breakfast, wearing my knees bare, the long underwear abandoned, the suspenders dangling from a doorknob. Somewhere along the knotted string of growing up I had eased out of my patchwork, prickly kidhood into adolescence, that time of moods and daymares when I was this-tle-witted and hiccuping inside while my legs and arms went spi-dering off beyond control. My parents, who must have wondered at the fate that dumped me down their chimney, quit giving me chores to do: I would forget myself while whipping cream and churn it into butter, or sitting at the table with my long legs I would spill the table leaf and send the mashed potatoes into my father's lap along with the gravy and the green beans, or I would slam the barn door on my own head, or sent to fetch the cows I would idle and dream in the pasture until the cows, painful and heavy with milk, would come home by themselves. Minnesota spring days when I thought I could reach out of myself and touch everything around me, could somehow hold the morning song of the lark, could always taste those wild rose days, would never lose my cockleshell dreams.

One of those spring mornings I can remember waking before the rest of the world and climbing to the top of the barn, its corru-gated roof dew-iced and silver, to look at the farm and our farm-house, smoke wisping from the sleeping chimney, the windows heavy-lidded, the house itself still asleep with my parents inside, their dreams quilted close around them.

And down the road, my grandmother sleeping too, in her little salt-white house. I wondered if she dreamed fresh dreams or slept with her heart rocking with ancient loves now gone. Did she dream even now of the cuckoos and their round-songs, so long ago heard in the forests of Savonlinna, that castle, a real castle, where she had been a girl? Those ancient loves, were they safe and chaste within her memory, as my yet unknown loves were untouched, our griefs known and unknown, still pulsing, past and future and not in our arms? She always wore her hair in a bun during the day, but at night it fell across her pillow like silver seaweed drifting from the warm, worn, time-carved ivory of her brow. She was my moon, my grandmother, the light that gleamed always across the darkest moments of my childhood. All the times I had run away from the grown-up world, I had never run away from her, but rather I spun her coronets of ferns and violets and clover buds, wrapping myself close to her in the silken loops of love and trust. And she, ancient yet ageless, had time and place for me, rocking me in her chair or letting me comb her long ash-silver hair with her ivory comb and braid it, or letting me parade her back and forth between the lilacs and bleeding hearts that magicked under the shining birch trees. And she was always there with the glowing night-light when nightmares shrieked me out of bed; and she saved for me the broken beads from lost necklaces, even a teal's wing I had found, and the old glass doorknobs, so old they were lavender and shadowed with memories she might have known.

Minnesota childhood. The mornings of my life, moving out of darkness and sleep into the newly born, innocent, exuberant-as-roses days of love, leaving behind me the pillows where kisses feathered my cheeks. The memories of childhood, lilting as candles, come chuckling like the rain, with no order and no end.

TOYSE KYLE

Minnesota Black, Minnesota Blue

by Toyse Kyle

When the governor of Minnesota stood on the cover of *Time* sometime ago — blue lake and green trees in the background, his happy
hand holding up a big northern pike on a stringer and his happy
mouth smiling like a pickerel — I started to think about Life. "The
Good Life in Minnesota," the caption said. *Not for the fish!* I
thought to myself.

Why did I identify with the fish in that photobit of the time of
our lives? How did the Minnesota utopia help to shape me as black
woman, mother, student, teacher? What's fishy in this picture?
Am I crazy? Is this society crazy? Or are we all happy as motorboats in the land of the sky-blue laughing waters?

I was not born here. My family — all eight of us with two more
soon to come — swam upriver to get here. Was it worth it? To try
to tell you my answer to that question, I'll have to begin in the
spawning grounds.

We lived, before coming North, in Kansas City, Missouri, in a
black ghetto that stretched for days. The grocery store we shopped
at was operated by blacks. The congregation of the Baptist church
we attended was all black. My school was also black — students,
teachers, and administrators. I remember too well that neither the
teachers nor the administrators would hesitate, at a moment's

notice, to indulge in "ass-kicking" with a leather strap for the least infraction of the innumerable rules.

Whippings, in or out of class, were often administered for being "dumb." I had my share of those. Miss Jackson, my second-grade teacher (may a white devil have her on his stringer) recognized a mental block I had concerning one particular word. I can't remember the word now — I'm certain it was something simple, like "good" or "life." Anyway, she would wait until some student was reading orally, stop him at that word, and then call me up to the front of the class to continue the reading. Invariably, my mind would come to a complete blank on the pronunciation of that word, and then she would get her kicks by whipping me long and hard. I would go back to my seat, repeating the word over and over again to myself, but the whippings and the mental repetitions never seemed to help. The teacher would call upon me the next time the word showed up, and the whole cycle would begin again.

I was unnerved by the experience — the pain, the embarrassment, and the mental anguish. And yet Mama would manage to make it worse when I got home: "If you got whipped in school, you deserved it! And you'll get a double whipping when you get home!" Mama always followed through on her warnings. The welts I had gotten at school betrayed my sins no matter how hard I tried to conceal them. Even now, when I go back to Missouri and happen to pass by Booker T. Washington Elementary School, the blue welts rise again on my black skin. What did I do to be so black and blue?

On my way to school each day I would pass by Miss Day's Orphan Home. Like the school, the orphanage was a large, rather ominous structure. The three-story building was surrounded by a fairly sizable but totally barren dirt yard — no grass, no trees, and no playground equipment for its several hundred black children. All of this was surrounded by a wire fence about six feet high. The children inside the wire amused themselves as best they could by lining up along the fence and watching the world go by. I felt superior to those children. I lived with my mother, father, and five younger sisters and brothers — Jackie, Morris, Marie, Puddin', and Ronnie. We had a home of our own with grass, trees, and even a grapevine. Mama, who may have detected my haughty attitude toward the orphans, said that I should feel sorry for them and always acknowledge their greetings. So I did, but very condescendingly.

Not long after, when I was six, I found myself on the other side of that fence. Mama and Daddy were always in financial straits, and they finally ran our family ship on the rocks. They had to sell the house. They moved into a rooming house with Ronnie, the youngest child. The rest of use were moved — like falling into a nightmare — to Miss Day's Orphan Home. Miss Day seemed to be a pleasant woman when Mama took us there, but she turned out to be a dragon — quick with the strap, like those school administrators, and the employer of bad cooks. Though we had been poor and sometimes hungry at home, Mama was a good cook and managed to give us tasty meals. But at the orphanage our diets were bits of stale bread dunked in milk, or half-cooked oatmeal, or grits without gravy or even a dab of butter. Whatever meat we had depended on our ability to find and separate those slivers of it occasionally present in the chunks of salt pork which ever so slightly seasoned our navy bean soup.

The garbage we ate was a delight, however, compared to the treatment we received from Miss Day and her staff. Even the other children, who seemed harmless enough while I was on the outside of that fence, were tough and mean. They enjoyed harassing my younger brother Jackie, who was highly nervous and a stutterer, baiting him until his stuttering got worse. Like Morris, Marie, and Puddin', Jackie soon developed hideous sores which covered his entire body. These sores were never attended to. They festered in the hot and unshaded yard, attracting flies. I noticed that after a while the kids would not even bother to swat the flies away. They seemed totally resigned to their plight, and I would — on and off — despise them for their apparent weaknesses. They seemed to whine and cry all the time, like Job on his dungheap multiplied by five. And they never fought back. My own fights were attempts, often feeble, to defend them from some bullying Bigger Thomas. If I wasn't whipped or locked in a dark closet for this infraction of the rules, Miss Day would force me to swallow a ladle-sized dose of cod liver oil. She would probably be sad to know how much this punishment contributed to my usual good health.

Mama visited us rarely. When she did, it seemed like a holiday, even though she never took us away from the home: she was with us and our family seemed close again. We would gather about her, all talking at once and some of us weeping, trying to tell her how horrible the place was and begging to go home with her. She never seemed to understand our anxieties, or, if she did, she never revealed her compassion to us. The only emotions Mama ever showed were anger, frustration, and resentment — and bitterness toward the world around her. And during her visits to Miss Day's she never displayed even these feelings, much less the love and compassion we needed to salve our bodies and minds.

I decided to run away. But where? We had other relatives in Kansas City, but I knew too well that they would probably resent my going to them for help. They disdained us as the darker-skinned and poorer relatives. My only recourse was to go to Mama and try to convince her that I would be very little trouble if she would only let me live with her.

One hot and sultry day I walked out through the wire gate, heading for Mama. The rooming house where she and Daddy stayed was only about a mile from the orphanage. When I arrived there, Mama was sitting on the front porch in a rocker, apparently trying to find some relief from the oppressive heat. As she rocked, she flicked flies away with a paper fan. She saw me before I had opened the gate. I never did get the chance to give my prepared spiel. Mama jumped up and ran out into the yard toward me, screaming and cursing and warning me not to come near the place again. She told me to go back to the orphanage where I belonged. When I, quite stunned, didn't move fast enough, she began tossing rocks at me, threatening to call the police. I cried all the way back to the orphanage. I did not know then that Mama's behavior was an early sign of her mysterious sickness.

Despite my bitterness at Mama's rejection of me, I was still glad to see her on her rare visits. After we had all been ushered into the visiting parlor reserved for such occasions, and I had convinced myself that we had complete privacy, I'd again pour out our grievances. I dramatized our mistreatment in the hope that Mama would be infuriated enough to withdraw us from the place immediately. But even the added pleas of the younger kids didn't help; Mama seemed to listen only halfheartedly, passing off our complaints by saying that we would all be together soon. She said that she and Daddy were saving all their money to buy a house for us in Minneapolis — a place that was far away and much better than anything we had ever known. I couldn't grasp what a Minneapolis was all about. To my six-year-old ears Minneapolis sounded as phony as Santa Claus, but "that great getting-up morning" arrived. After we had spent about a year at Miss Day's, Mama gathered us all up one day and took us to the rooming house to prepare for our move northward.

The rooming house was full of relatives and friends who had come to see us off. Some were helping Mama to pack, others were preparing fantastic baskets of food with fried chicken, fruit, biscuits, and other delectables we hadn't tasted since we had gone to the orphanage. I was beginning to wonder if there was food in Minneapolis because of the abundance of things being prepared. I remember hearing such resounding phrases as "great opportunity," though I didn't know what that phrase meant. And for the first time in my life I noticed the phrase "white people." While my grandmother was helping me get into a dress that I had never seen before, she warned with that shrewd all-knowing eye of hers that I had better be very good and be particularly respectful to all white people. She told me then that whenever white folks talked to me I should always answer "yes, ma'am" and "no, ma'am" and "yes, sir" and "no, sir." I didn't know what "white folks" meant, but on the night train north — Daddy worked for the railroad as a cook and had secured a compartment for us — I practiced yessing them. And sure enough, when we arrived in Minneapolis, at dawn, there they were. We were surrounded everywhere by white people — human beings without color whose speech was strange. I remember asking Mama if it hurt to be without color. She pinched me for gawking and not moving fast enough with my share of our paraphernalia. We were whisked from the Milwaukee Depot in a taxi (my first cab ride) to our new address. It was a three-bedroom bungalow on Sixteenth Avenue and Eighth Street. The house didn't look very grand, but it was better than Miss Day's pokey. I was happy that we had any house at all and that we were all together again.

The neighborhood was what nowadays would be called "multi-ethnic," although we all had our poverty in common. Our arrival changed the neighborhood to "mixed," for we were the first black family on the block. I quickly learned a new meaning for an old word. That word was "nigger." I'm sure that I must have heard that word many times before moving to Minneapolis because blacks — we called ourselves Negroes then — often jocularly addressed one another as "nigger." But somehow the word had never stood out enough in our old environment for me to take notice of it. Now it was poured like poison into my ear.

The white neighbors came out of their houses and apartments to watch the black family move in. While the adults were muttering their disappoval to one another, the less inhibited children were chanting and shouting "Nigger!" "Dirty niggers!" "Blacky!" and "Pickaninnies!" When we got into the house and had fairly settled ourselves, I asked Mama what the word "nigger" meant. She tossed my query off by saying that it was not nice and that I shouldn't have any business being bothered by it. But I was bothered. I felt insulted. It hurt. I went out to investigate our yard. The white kids were still there. They began their verbal assaults again. I, in turn, called *them* "niggers," which turned some of their white faces red with confusion. Some of them ran to their homes to check out my vocabulary, and my mother began receiving complaints from enraged parents. Mama scolded me for causing trouble and warned me not to use the word again. However, she did say that I could call them "rednecks" or "peckerwoods" if they bothered me again, and so I did just that.

I was enrolled the next day in Adams Elementary School. It was an old school then, though it has only recently been torn down. Still, it seemed like a palace compared to Booker T. Washington Elementary School. Mama went with me that first day to a second-grade classroom for registration. I was a little afraid of my all-white classmates and even more of the white teacher, who did not conceal her annoyance at having a black student in her class. While she was talking to my mother, several of the bolder kids were shouting out "Nigger!" "Aunt Jemima!" and "Black Sambo!" And the teacher said, quite loudly, "I don't see why all you Negroes think you have to come up here anyway when you'd be much better off down South with your own kind!" But I was even more surprised at my mother's behavior. At home, Mama was a mighty force, and I thought that she was always that way. But in the presence of that bigoted white woman, Mama was docile, submissive to her arrogance, soft-spoken. At one point she even thanked the woman for her time and kindness for allowing me to be enrolled in her classroom. I was astonished and confused by what I was witnessing. This was the first time I had seen either of my parents involved with whites in any interchange. I understood that Mama was losing.

It was only some years later that I was able to analyze the dynamics of that situation. The year was 1948; little had been done in the way of civil rights for blacks, and even less had been done to rectify the common abuses that blacks had been undergoing since the time of slavery. I know now that Mama not only acted a role of inferiority to that white woman but also *felt* inferior. And the white woman automatically acted out the assumed superiority of her whiteness.

The teacher shoved some papers toward Mama and directed her to fill them out. Mama tried to use a small corner of the woman's desk; while she was writing, the woman yanked the pen from her hand and asked rhetorically, "Don't they even teach you people how to hold a pen down there?" The classroom was in an uproar of hilarity as the woman grabbed my mother's hand, folded her tiny fingers around the pen, and disdainfully instructed her in the white folks' way of pen-holding. I only then noticed how physically small my mother was compared to that strapping northern woman. I kept hoping that Mama would hit the woman or at least say something really cutting. But Mama was all compliance. She just smiled and nodded, nodded and smiled. Maybe she winced occasionally. She seemed bowed from her usual proud stance. I despised the woman, I despised the children, I despised the circumstances, and momentarily I despised even Mama.

For nearly a year after my ritual initiation into white people's territory, I was often teased and taunted: "Your mother doesn't even know how to write!" But the assaults were directed toward me, also, because I spoke with a southern accent and used many words and phrases that were strange to the Minneapolis whites. I resolved very quickly to learn white people's speech, so that they could never again laugh at me for the way I talked. But this new way of talking — my Minnesota dialect — became such an integral part of me that when I went "home" on occasional summer visits to Kansas City, my relatives were amused and sometimes annoyed by my new way of speaking. Sometimes my grandmother would rebuke me by saying, "Just because you've been up North don't come around here trying to act like no white girl . . . you ain't no Miss Anne . . . you home-folks just like the rest of us, so talk like you got some sense!" Finally, I found much merit and safety in deliberately becoming bi-dialectal, especially since I had to move with uncomfortable frequency between two disparate culture groups.

There were two other blacks in Adams Elementary School then, both boys. The older of them was as mean as a white kid. He would often beat me up. If he couldn't catch me, we would stand at some distance from one another and play "the dozens":

> I fucked your Mama
> Till she went blind.
> Her breath smells bad
> But she sure can grind.

I wasn't very good at this game of verbal warfare when I entered the school, but it didn't take me long to master the nuances of it:

> Baboon and your Mama
> Learning to screw.
> Baby came out
> Looking like you.

In retrospect, I know now that I was being exposed to a special kind of overt racism — black against black. This Minnesota black boy was contemptuous of my obvious southernness, but in addition, since he was also considerably lighter in skin color than I was, he wasted no time in letting me know that being "lighter and brighter" was better than being "blacker and badder." It was from him that I learned another biting jingle:

> If you're white, you're right!
> If you're brown, stick around;
> But if you're black, stay back!

The sting of those words was too sharp to shake off easily. I felt very black in contrast to my glaringly white environment, and the feeling was hard to live with in those days before black was beautiful. The "negativeness" of my color was constantly reinforced at home and elsewhere. All swear words and insults were prefaced by the words "You black . . ." If you gave a negative response to a request, the retort would be, "All you really have to do is to stay black and die!" And one particularly devastating barb went, "You can kiss my black ass . . ."

My experiences with both blacks and whites in Minnesota — a land of milk and honey and a distant promised land for those of us who identified with the children of Canaan — turned out to be a bit of a "trip."

Not long after we moved to Minnesota and two more children were born — making a total of eight of us within a nine-year span — it seemed as though Mama was always sick. She didn't look sick, but she acted strange. We were too young to really understand the myriad problems that would bring on Mama's deep and prolonged depressions. When the electric company turned off the lights, or when our phone was disconnected, or when the heat didn't come on in the wintertime, or when we didn't have clothes to wear to school when it got really cold, or when we had too little to eat, my sisters, brothers, and I adjusted to the situation, but Mama would fret and worry, complain and nag. More often than not, she would vent her anger and frustrations on us.

We were most happy and most contented when Mama was out of the house at work or at a friend's home. But when she would leave us for hours or for a whole day, she would lock us in our bedroom until she got home. We couldn't afford babysitters, and Mama wasn't quite certain of my ability to take care of the younger kids till I was eight. I intensely despised her act of locking us in; I could adjust to the fact that we couldn't go to the bathroom when we had to or "steal" food when we were hungry, but I couldn't adjust to our total immobility and restricted freedom. The younger kids would cry and whine, and they never seemed able to contain the urine in their distended bladders. And they would ask me for food. I used to feel guilty because of my impotence: an eight-year-old mother without any milk.

My parents constantly reminded me of my responsibilities toward my younger brothers and sisters. I became a surrogate mother for the unattended babies that my mother ignored and sometimes abused if their incessant crying got too much for her nerves. In one frightening instance when Mama was whipping the baby with a leather strap because she wouldn't stop crying, I overcame my terror of Mama and fought with her for the belt. Though she got the best of me, she had stopped whipping Sandy. Sandy was the fattest of us all because when I was left alone to watch the kids I could stop Sandy's crying only by giving her pieces of bread and crackers. Sandy was also bowlegged, Mama said, because I carried her around all the time on my hip with her fat legs clasped around my waist.

Mama was an impossible woman to please. It seemed that nothing I ever did could escape some biting criticism from her. She castigated me because I hadn't gotten home soon enough, or because I had overcooked the beans, or because she thought I had punished one of the other kids unjustly in her absence, or because I had dropped the heavy groceries on the way home, or because I had scorched one of Daddy's shirts, or because I hadn't polished her nursing shoes white enough, or because I had taken too long to wash our endless succession of dishes, or because the baby hadn't been changed in so long that he was found to have maggots in his diaper. (In later years she explained that the diaper incident was why she had given me a subscription to a commercial diaper service for one of my own babies.)

I was a creative, "artsy" kid, despite the elements of drudgery in my Cinderella existence. In my fantasy world I always knew whose foot the glass slipper would fit. I envisioned Mama as the wicked stepmother. But Mama was ambitious for her firstborn. As soon as I could walk, Mama had enrolled me in dancing school. And she made me rehearse for what seemed like endless hours every day (until I was old enough to become her housekeeper and babysitter). I took ballet and tap-dancing lessons, acrobatics, baton twirling, and piano lessons. I appeared in Kansas City stage shows, doing little song and dance numbers practically from infancy. In Minneapolis, too, I appeared in one benefit performance after another, in talent contests and fashion shows, and eventually on television programs — anything Mama could think of. Our family photo albums are laden with newspaper clippings and snapshots of me in assorted costumes that I hardly remember — for instance, a ballet tutu with matching leotards and satin toe shoes on one occasion and an abbreviated satin tuxedo with a matching top hat and enormous satin bows adorning my tap shoes on another. In those show-biz photos I appear very black and shiny, grinning like Al Jolson, as if deliriously happy.

For several years in a row after we arrived in Minneapolis Mama managed a neighborhood marching and baton twirling group. I was expected to choreograph the routines and to teach the other kids the intricate maneuvers. Our annual objective was to win awards in the Minneapolis Aquatennial Parade. I was the group leader and I usually marched alone several paces ahead of our motley crew, strutting like hell and blowing on my whistle to signal the routines. In the old days the parade ended at Parade Stadium, and because we knew the judges were there we used to save our last bit of strength to put on a particularly entertaining act for them. That strategy worked, at least sometimes, because we did win awards.

Ours was a mixed-race group, and on that basis alone we were quite a novelty to the large numbers of people who lined the street and hung out of upper-floor windows to watch the spectacle. Sometimes when we would pass by a particularly enthusiastic group of spectators, some of the whites would throw nickels and dimes at our feet to watch us scramble for them. But a high-stepping baton princess with a whistle could not break stride to scoop up the man's filthy lucre — I would prance right over the money, and Mama, who always accompanied us along the sidelines, would scold me afterward for being so stupid.

Even during my stage performances Mama was always in the wings coaching, doing the same number on the sidelines out of the audience's view and calling out improvised routines as they occurred to her. She would shout out, "Smile, goddammit!" and "Get down on your knees now, get down on your knees . . . now throw them a big kiss!" and all that old-time bullshit. Though the applause was sometimes deafening, all this would be drowned out by Mama's usual complaints in the wings that I had made so many mistakes, or that my taps weren't loud enough and people couldn't hear them, or that I should have taken off my white satin top hat and tossed it in the air as she had directed.

I truly believe that Mama's aspiration was for me to become the black Shirley Temple from the ghetto or a female reincarnation of Bill "Bojangles" Robinson. She seemed desperate in her zeal for my career, never realizing that she was preparing me for a show business specialty that was soon to become obsolete.

In time I began to understand that Mama wasn't just "mean" — she had problems that disturbed her deeply and bound her on a wheel of fire. The mad society into which she was born had cut her to the brain.

I was nine or ten when I discovered while snooping through my parents' drawers (my usual occupation in their absence) that Mama's sister had committed suicide. We were told that our aunt died because of a heart attack, but I knew otherwise. The news clippings I read from the *Kansas City Call* said that she had jumped off a bridge onto a railroad track. Mama was extremely distraught. She left us for a few days to attend her sister's funeral in Kansas City. When she came back, she seemed even more depressed than usual, and she and Daddy argued more intensely and more frequently than ever. After a while Daddy left us. Mama still kept going to work — the 3:00 to 11:00 evening shift at the hospital — but when she was at home she cried a lot and told her woes to sympathetic friends on the telephone. Daddy was terrible, she said, for having left us.

One night after Mama came in from work, she woke me up and told me to put on my school clothes. Then the two of us walked from our house to downtown Minneapolis. I was terribly afraid of what she might do. When she noticed my tremors, she asked me if I was cold. I said yes because I was afraid to let her know how really scared I was. Finally we reached our destination, the Third Avenue bridge near the old post office. My worst imaginings had become reality: Mama was going to kill herself. I started crying as we waited for the whole city to go to sleep. When the traffic had stopped, Mama grabbed my collar and tried her best to pull us both over the bridge railing. I was screaming and begging her to stop. We were so absorbed in our struggle that we did not notice a cab which had stopped in the middle of the bridge. Its white driver left the vehicle running, its doors open, and raced toward us. The man pulled us off the railing. Mama, who had been cold and apparently calm during the whole episode, began raging hysterically. The man forced Mama into the back of the cab. He drove us home, carried Mama into the house, and put her into her bed. Then he told me to watch her and to call him if I ever needed any help with my mother, who in the meantime appeared to have passed out. The man left his name and number by the phone. (How could he know it had been disconnected!) I was thoroughly shaken by Mama's attempt to take us away, but I was even more stunned that that white man — a total stranger — had gone out of his way to help us. He didn't even charge us for the fare. Mama slept most of the next day, then got up and went to work as if nothing unusual had happened.

The situation at home went back to normal, but Daddy did not come back. Once, while Mama was at work, Daddy came by the house to see how we were getting along. He didn't stay long, and he seemed wary, tense, worried, ill at ease. But he did give me some money to buy food. I loved him very much and missed him terribly, but even then I understood his absence.

Some time after that surprise visit my mother again came home one evening extremely distraught. She claimed that while she was riding on the streetcar she had seen Daddy walking down the street with a woman. In a rage she called her mother in Kansas City and said, "Mama, I just called to say good-bye. I'm blowing this house, myself, and these goddamned kids up!" Everybody started crying then. I quickly considered grabbing the kids and running out of the back door, but as usual we didn't have any place to run to. My problem was solved, though, when in a few minutes policemen were banging at our front door. Mama ran around and turned out all the lights. She told us not to open the door and not to make a sound. The policemen kept banging at the door, shouting "Open up!" and shining their flashlights in through the window of the door. I decided I was more afraid of Mama than I was of the policemen. I bolted for the door and let them in despite Mama's threats. Those enormous men brushed past me and raced for my mother who by now was completely hysterical. As the policemen roughly forced Mama into a straitjacket, she cursed me and let me know that as soon as she was free she would kill me. I immediately assumed that I would have to figure out a way to take care of my brothers and sisters, and before Mama was even out of the house I was already thinking about quitting school and finding a job. But the social worker the policemen sent for told me to pack our clothes and to gather our valuables so that she could take us someplace else for the night. I informed her that we had only the clothes we were wearing. Our valuables wouldn't take much room either, since they amounted to only the handful of small change we kept in a vase on a dining-room shelf. We were driven in government style to the examining room at the Minneapolis General Hospital.

I recall being terribly humiliated by the attitudes of the doctors and nurses who examined us. After removing our clothing a nurse picked up one of the garments I had been wearing and held it between her thumb and index finger with her pinky extended. She asked, "What shall I do with this god-awful thing?" The doctor shouted over his shoulder, "Burn it!" There was much laughter and apparent amusement on the part of all the adults present at that mass examination of our unwashed and obviously undernourished bodies. But the doctor who examined me appeared to be very angry, too. He muttered to himself and shook his head. Occasionally he addressed gruff remarks to the interns who were watching: "Look at the distended belly . . . gross malnutrition . . . bleeding and puffy gums . . . pyorrhea . . . look at the jaundiced eyes . . . some scar tissue here . . ." I didn't understand some of the words he used, but I made mental notes to check out their meanings later.

I was very much relieved when those miserable examinations were over. Before they were through, one of the smart-assed nurses asked rhetorically, "Don't you people eat?" I sensed that she really didn't expect to be answered, but I spoke up in my most adult voice, saying that we did eat and that I fixed the meals. When she asked what we ate, I quickly outlined the menu of the better-sounding items in our diet: "Peanut-butter-and-jelly sandwiches . . . grits and gravy . . . navy beans and ham hocks . . . cereal . . ." The adults laughed some more.

We were all hospitalized after that ordeal for about a month. We thoroughly enjoyed our hospitalization. It sure beat Miss Day's! We were fed three meals a day, and we had meat at every meal. We were told that we could have food between meals which they referred to as "snacks" (another white folks' word). We hadn't realized that we were sick, but they told us we were. So we enjoyed ourselves. When we were bored with staying in bed, we were allowed to go into the nursery playroom where there were games, toys, and many books to read. Even in our confinement we had more privileges and freedom than we had ever experienced before. We were ready to snack on endlessly.

I was annoyed one day, therefore, to see the social worker who had brought us there. I thought she was going to take us home. I asked her where Mama was. She said that our mother was in Cambridge State Hospital; I remember feeling very relieved. We were resigned to going home when I realized that the woman wasn't going in the right direction. The scenery we passed on our mysterious journey was like that in a movie. There were trees along the boulevards, and the houses looked as though they had been taken right out of a storybook that talked about the way white people lived. There were well-manicured lawns, flowers, shrubs, and white picket fences. I asked the woman where we were going. She said that we were going to a wonderful place where there would be a lot of children to play with and good things to do.

I suspected a trick. I began dredging up memories of Miss Day's orphanage in Kansas City. I told the social worker that I would rather go home and take care of the others and myself. But she just kept on driving through the movie set until we arrived at what might have been the estate of Douglas Fairbanks, Jr. The granite-pillared entryway had a sign on it that read "Vince Day Center" or maybe "Vincent Day Center." (It was across from Lake Calhoun where an insurance company now stands.) We followed a curving drive to the top of a low hill — and the most magnificent mansion I had ever seen in or out of the storybooks. As we got out of the station wagon and walked toward the mansion, I wondered if Stepin Fetchit would open the door, but as it turned out we were greeted by a white maid. The foyer was illuminated by a chandelier that was bigger than I was. I could see high-ceilinged rooms, marble floors, and wide, curving staircases. I couldn't believe that it was all real!

Soon we were ushered into a spacious dining hall where thirty or forty other children were having lunch at long tables, and we were seated at different tables with children in our own age groups. This initial meal was as grand as its surroundings. For the first time in our lives we tasted lamb chops. I knew all about Little Bo Peep from the General Hospital Library, but I didn't know people ate the lost sheep. Besides the chops, this wonderful meal included potatoes with gravy, fresh peas, rolls, an abundant supply of milk, and ice cream. We were told that we could eat as much as we wanted. Since we never really trusted anyone, and we never knew how long anything good would last, we gorged ourselves. Long after all the other children had gone out to play, we remained at the tables stuffing ourselves — and then our pockets — before we grudgingly left the dining room.

The rest of the afternoon continued the fantasy. We were introduced to some of the other children, and we played with them. Nobody seemed to notice our color, though we were obviously the only black beings in the place. Then, to our amazement, we were served an evening meal of the same lavishness and quality as the noon lunch. We weren't quite up to it! After dinner we played some more, and then the younger children were sent off to bed. Since I was older, I was allowed to amuse myself by banging away at one of the pianos in a downstairs parlor until I was told to get ready for bed.

I was escorted by a social worker to one of the second-floor dormitory chambers for the older girls. The other girls were already in bed and, ostensibly, asleep. The social worker pointed out my bed. It had a top sheet and a bottom sheet (we couldn't afford such luxuries at home), a blanket, and an extra blanket folded neatly at the end of the bed. It all seemed so lovely. The young woman handed me a pair of pajamas (which were pressed, yet), a fresh towel, and a washcloth. She pointed out the bathroom and told me to bathe before going to bed. But, when I went into the elegant bathroom, I couldn't find the tub! At the end of the room there were some small cubicles with walls that didn't go all the way to the ceiling; each cubicle had a plastic curtain, a floor drain, a soap dish, and a nozzlelike fixture with faucets. I considered the possibility of bathing in one of those rooms, but there was no stopper for the drain. Even if I succeeded in filling up the cubicle, there would be no way to prevent the water from spilling out through those plastic curtains onto the floor. And how would you get into the thing even if you had managed to fill it up?

After about fifteen minutes the social worker stuck her head into the room. She asked if there was something wrong. I told her everything was just fine. But she stood there staring at me, and I began to feel the heat rising from my collarbone to my face. Had I been white, I would have looked beet red. Finally she asked why I had not bathed. I managed to inquire in a small voice, "Did you want me to bathe in the sink?" I was so grateful that she didn't laugh at me as white people usually did when I was confusedly trying to respond to their strange world. Gently, the woman asked me if I had ever seen a shower (another new word) before. When I told her I hadn't, she very patiently began to instruct me in how to use a shower.

What a marvelous invention! I remember thinking that white people had all the good things, and we nothing. But the delightful sensation of warm water pelting my body kept me from starting a revolution that evening. It was comparable to standing in warm summer rain completely naked. It was luxuriant, soothing, and oh such a beautiful experience! Several times the young woman stuck her head into the room to ask if I had finished. Gleefully, I shouted back, "No!" She then said I could take as long as I liked, and so I did. Eventually, my young aide — Charmian to my Cleopatra — told me through the shower curtain that she would have to go home but that I could stay in the shower as long as I wished. She had turned down my bed, she said, and she would probably be back the next day before I woke up. She said that she would introduce me to my new roommates in the morning. Above the roar of the plummeting spray I yelled, "Okay! And good-night!" I figured that I would probably shower till the next day. The shower was so exhilarating that I even let my hair "go home."

But my ecstasy was rudely interrupted. While standing there my face lifted toward the water's source, I began to notice scufflings and murmurings in the room outside the shower stall. Little heads appeared above the walls of the cubicle, and the curtain was roughly jerked back. And all of those pale bodies began dispassionately discussing my black-skinned nakedness. My ears seemed to burn with all those familiar old sounds that I had heard in the past. For what seemed like an eternity, the name-calling rituals were punctuated by questions and comments among the children outside the stall: "See, you lied. They don't have tails!" "Look! The black doesn't even come off!" "She looks like a monkey!" "Why is her hair so crinkly? How come it doesn't get straight like ours when it gets wet?" The lone boy among the pallid bitches asked me directly, "Do you fuck?" A white girl responded, "Of course she fucks!"

I was mortified. I screamed and cursed at them to get away. I tried to cover my body with my hands. No one, absolutely no one, had ever seen me completely naked; even doctors, when they examined you, covered you with a sheet or a towel. I was more embarrassed by the fact of my nakedness than by the discussion of me as though I were some peculiar animal in a zoo.

Grabbing my clothes, I ran past the huddled group. I heard one of the girls scream hysterically, "She touched me!" Without drying myself I hurriedly dressed under the sheets in my daytime clothes while heatedly damning them all with the worst swear words I could think of and assuring them that I would kill them as soon as I was dressed. In the midst of the screaming, cursing, and crying, with the shower roaring in the background, a night supervisor entered and tried to bring calm to the bedlam. By this time some of the little monsters were even hiding under their beds. I had been waiting all day for the catch in that beautifully decorated, gossamer world. Despite my customary caution, I found myself entwined by that web — the white spider was there all the time.

I didn't sleep a wink that night or the next night either. I was keeping watch, awaiting the next trick. For the first week or so I kept to myself at all times. I refused all overtures to join the recreation groups which were going picnicking, swimming, and biking, and enjoying other really interesting activities. Though I tried to warn my sisters and brothers to stay away from the others, they totally ignored my admonitions and seemed to be having a great time, much to my own irritation. Finally, my defenses were broken down, and quite by accident I found myself having fun. More and more, I began to relax and I had to admit — even to myself — that I thoroughly enjoyed my stay at the white people's orphanage. We spent part of the school year at Calhoun Elementary School, where most of the students were upper-middle-class white kids. I even thought I met a prince or two.

But eventually we were wrenched from that elegant splendor back into the cinders. Mama was released from the state hospital. She and Daddy got back together (although they were divorced a few years later), and reluctantly we returned to the realities of the old neighborhood — physical pain, grief, deprivation, and the ever-present odor of garbage mixed with an equally nauseous odor from the decaying bodies of rats caught in the spaces within the walls of the houses. And always there was the unceasing noise of street traffic, passing trains, and the ambulance and police sirens which usually followed neighborhood and family brawls. But these human-made sounds never quite drowned out the little noises and scratching sounds below the surface at night which signaled that mice or rats were making new holes for entrances into our larger territory. More subtle, but almost as repulsive, were the sounds that the roaches made when they began their nightly treks in search of crumbs and debris left by our carelessness.

Another species of vermin showed up during the day — social workers, truant officers, private investigators, bill collectors, process servers. The social workers were snooping on those who were on welfare, trying to catch them in some kind of trap so that they could justify taking away what little money the people received from the state. They watched to see if the boyfriend stayed in the house or if the ex-husband came back on the sly. They watched to see whether anybody was making a few extra bucks on the side. Somebody was always being served a summons or having his meager wages garnisheed or his home attached or his furniture reclaimed. White neighborhoods got the street cleaners, the street-repair crews, the tree surgeons, and the exterminators. Black and racially mixed neighborhoods got the rats, the roaches, and the human vermin.

Growing up was not always traumatic. I particularly cherish those occasions at home when on Saturday mornings at around eleven o'clock Daddy would get up and begin making breakfast. Daddy worked as a cook on the train and was exceptionally skilled at his tasks. He would cook fish, grits and gravy, biscuits, and sometimes greens. Occasionally — with the help of certain porters, cooks, and waiters on the train — there would be pork chops and potatoes. The back of our lot went right up to the tracks, and sometimes our friends would toss out to us large parcels of "the man's" food. Then for a while we could eat high on the hog.

Other moments that I relish were those few times when our relatives from Kansas City visited us. On these occasions everyone, even Mama, seemed to be in a very happy mood. All of the adults took turns at displaying their particular culinary talents. And music, always present in the background, supplemented our gaiety. On the tabletop record player that Daddy had won in a poker game we listened over and over again to the blues, jazz, and big-band sounds of Count Basie, Duke Ellington, Ella Fitzgerald, Billy Eckstein, Sophie Tucker, Dinah Washington, and Billie Holliday. Totally immersed in these rhythms, the adults showed off the latest boogie or bebop step. And the other kids and I stood on the fringes of the frolics, clapping our hands, snapping our fingers, and shaking our hips, trying to imitate those frenzied, yet smoothly syncopated movements. It was common knowledge in our group that you really couldn't teach somebody to dance — all he had to do was to "get with it"!

I noticed that our Kansas City relatives and friends were disappointed on their first visits to our house because they had come expecting to see a lake right outside our door. When they discovered that the nearest lake was three or four miles away and that you had to get there by car or on the streetcar, they would remark, "This sure as hell don't seem like the land of ten thousand lakes. Where the hell are they? That's just a bunch of bullshit!" Even though the kids and I had visited lakes while we were at the orphanage, our family had not visited a lake together because we didn't have carfare enough or because our clothes were not "good" enough to wear on a streetcar or at a beach where white people might see us.

Other particularly happy memories in the back roads of my mind were those Saturday or Sunday afternoons when, after we had finished our assorted chores, we would be given a dime so that we could visit the local movie theater. The films presented my fantasies much more beautifully and vividly than anything I could dream up as a way of escaping the usual ugliness in our lives. I never tired of watching Betty Grable or Rita Hayworth being made love to in glamorous settings and silly episodes. Later, when I began reviewing my childhood fantasies, I was startled to realize that I had always imagined myself as a white heroine, with long blond hair. I also remember laughing when Mantan Moreland would holler, "Feets, do yo' stuff!" after being "terr'fied of de ghosts." The black-skinned dupes in those films — Moreland, Willie Best, even Louis Armstrong — appeared always so stupid, so bug-eyed, and so ignorant. I could dig Dorothy Dandridge or Pearl Bailey — but not often enough. I was annoyed later when I realized that I had sat cheering Roy Rogers and Dale Evans and the white cowboy heroes who slaughtered or drove off the Indian "savages." I had also jumped up from my front-row seat and cheered as Tarzan and the great white hunters beat off vengeful black "savages."

At school I was easily moved to daydreams about the idealized family lives of Dick and Jane and their dog Spot, whose episodes were told and retold in our elementary school primers. The fiction-alized family appeared to live so happily and perfectly together. They had gardens, flowers, and vine-covered trellises. They all ate their meals together around the dining room table, and how they really seemed to love and care for one another. I often wished that we could live that way. In my daydream world we did.

Of course, there were also truly good friendships with white children that I still treasure in memory. Blanche and Clara West-over, who lived next door to our house on Eighth Street, became — after our initial battles — my bosom buddies. We played together, fought against our enemies together, mulled over the mysteries of sex together, dreamed and fantasized together, and — always — we went to school together. One day, as Clara and I were walking home arm-in-arm after a skirmish with our adversaries, Clara became reflective. She announced that she had hit upon a solution to my problem. She said that her mother had a big washtub and some really strong laundry soap and that if we both scrubbed my body very hard my black might come off. It was a minor thing, but I was dismayed to discover that, regardless of how well we knew each other, she still couldn't understand why her idea wouldn't work.

My color didn't become an issue in my relationship with Clara and Blanche until others brought the differences to our attention. Usually I was recognized as the brains and the mouthpiece of our little clique. When we were caught stealing from the local grocer, I invented a complex circumstantial story for the old man who owned the store. The basic plot was that some older boys in the neighborhood had forced us into a life of crime in spite of our protests. I knew he would believe me — or would at least pretend to. Most adult whites I had encountered couldn't adjust to Brer Rabbit — to any kind of intelligence in a black child. It was on that ironical twist that we won. But we really didn't care *how* we won. As we grew older, my deviousness became more sophisticated.

Opportunity knocked again when I thought of a bigger hustle than ripping off candy from the corner grocer. I fashioned our new caper on the pattern of the experts who milked the school children on behalf of the American Red Cross, the March of Dimes, and the local Community Chest. The teachers would insensitively harangue us if we didn't bring our dimes and nickels to school so that our class might win some contrived contest over another class. It never seemed to occur to our educators that we were as poverty-stricken as the people they were, ostensibly, trying to help. During one fund drive I decided that I would get some money by going from house to house with my friends and asking for contributions. We were so successful in our venture that I concluded that it was an easy way to get money whenever we needed it. I selected our victims, being careful never to approach the same residence twice, and I did the talking, backed up by my friends. It was a great hustle. We divided the money equally and spent it all on candy and bakery goods and anything else we could devour before we had to go home.

The game ended, however, when I "jumped noble" about an old

white man who was our mark for a contribution. When we rang the bell at the dilapidated duplex, the shriveled, feeble old man came to the door. As I looked past him, I could see a level of poverty about seven nicks below mine. What little furniture the man had was falling apart. My conscience snapped at me, but I felt compelled not to blow our cover. After I had given my spiel, I hoped that the man would tell us that he didn't have any money. Instead, he hobbled over to one of those old-fashioned built-in buffets, lifted a sugar bowl (of all things) off the shelf, and pulled out a sock containing some coins. He began to count out pennies and nickels. Then he hobbled back to us and gave us that small pittance.

The lump in my throat took a couple of days to dissolve after that stint. To my friends, who were often annoyed because I would jump noble at the weirdest times, I announced that our contribution hustle was over. Though I had been going to church, it wasn't religion or the thought of sin that had dissuaded me: it was my realization that I was doing almost the same thing that the teachers who supervised the fund drives were doing.

After we entered Wendell Phillips Junior High School, I deliberately broke off my associations with Blanche and Clara. I felt guilty about it afterward, because I recognized their hurt and pain at being rejected. And, after all, rejection was the name of the briar patch where Brer Rabbit was born. But I had found new friends — black friends — who were more exciting, more adventurous, and "badder" than any of my old friends. And, probably because my parents, teachers, and old friends had condemned this group as a wild, undisciplined, immoral, and loud bunch destined for trouble, I found myself drawn closer and closer to them.

Through my new friends I fell in love with rhythm and blues music, which was never played at home. My parents' few records consisted only of jazz and bebop music. And, though I often listened to pop tunes on the radio, I couldn't relate much to "Peg o' My Heart," "Sentimental Journey," "Oh, You Beautiful Doll," "Take Me Out to the Ball Game," and similar tunes. But I quickly learned to love rhythm and blues as played and sung by B. B. King, Johnny Ace, Little Richard, James Brown, the Temptations (an old but still popular group), Chuck Berry, Fats Domino, Odis Redding, Little Anthony and the Imperials, and many other black artists. Accompanied by "git-box," bass, and drum, they wailed, purred, and sometimes screamed lyrics, variations on spirituals, and up-tempo jazz sounds — all communicating a contemporary version of how black people felt when times were good and how they felt when times were bad. The dance vogues that developed around this music accentuated its sensitivity and sensuality. Since we didn't have a radio station in Minneapolis then which featured black "sounds," I learned to tune our radio to Little Rock, Atlanta, and Memphis stations after the sun went down.

My new friends and I would blatantly and loudly sing, dance, and bang out these new rhythms in the school halls, in the lunchroom, and even in the classrooms, much to the disgust and dismay of our white teachers. We were always in trouble for our loud "signifying" displays of disrespect for adult whites. I was invariably singled out as a target. Those omnipresent teachers said they had expected better things from me since I was supposed to be so bright. I was embarrassed by this because it exposed me as an enemy in the eyes of my black friends who hated school, who were looking forward to dropping out, and who often did poorly in what little we were expected to learn in school.

In a way I was never completely within the group because they all seemed to have unlimited freedom. It was common knowledge that because of my large family and my sick mother I was never allowed out of the house at night. I was expected to come straight home from school so that I could cook, clean, do laundry, and take care of the younger kids. Often I was late getting to school because I had to fix the morning meal, see that everyone had something to wear, prepare lunches, comb and braid my younger sisters' hair, and get everybody else off before I could leave.

Although I greatly resented the innumerable "strings" that restricted my freedom, I know now that those strings probably kept me out of the escapades that some of my friends became involved in. Some of them were parents at twelve and thirteen. Others ended up on the street pursuing one hopeless hustle after another. A few died from overdoses of drugs or from botched abortions in somebody's kitchen. Two of the old gang died from stabbing and shooting. And occasionally I would read in the papers or hear via the grapevine that one of them had ended up in prison.

Still, there were others of us who somehow managed to move through the sick world we hadn't made without suffering much permanent damage from all that we were exposed to. My own escape was made possible in part by my father's persistent striving against those uncommon odds. By the time I was fourteen, Daddy, spurred on by Mama, had fought his way out of the black lower class.

After many years of work on the railroad, Daddy went tardily to college — to the University of Minnesota, where he earned a degree in business administration. He was brilliant, sensitive, earnest, educated, beautiful, and black. It was the last of those qualities that kept white businessmen from hiring him. So out of a desperate need to provide his family with a better way of life, my father went into business for himself. Many times he worked his several jobs from early morning to late at night — free-lance accounting, construction contracting, and finally selling real estate. In this last business he prospered for several years, but eventually he lost everything and went into bankruptcy.

Mama, too, when she wasn't ill, worked at assorted jobs as a doctor's assistant and later as a nurse. She also did some free-lance writing, and she gave dancing lessons at the Phyllis Wheatley Settlement House, at the Hallie Q. Brown Community Center in St. Paul, and at the Emmanuel Cohen center in North Minneapolis.

Everybody worked in our house, including my little brothers, who did odd jobs, sold newspapers, and made deliveries for grocers and pharmacists. And we stepped up two rungs on the economic ladder — one too many, maybe. We moved out of the old neighborhood into an expensive home in South Minneapolis. To all outward appearances we were a successful, prospering family.

In recognition of our new status Mama joined one of those black "booshie" (bourgeois) garden clubs. We started to spend money as though we had always had it. For example, Mama began sending my younger sisters and me to the local "grease, press, and curl" shops. And she began buying our "company clothes" at stores like Sears, Penney's, and even some of the uptown shops on

Nicollet Avenue. Our parents began the inevitable charade of giving elaborate lunches, dinners, and garden parties that were always written up in the local black "booshie" papers. The articles usually went something like this:

Mrs. Clyde W. Williams, a popular Minneapolis socialite, entertained out-of-town guests and local friends at a prettily appointed, catered brunch in her spacious and beautifully appointed Portland Avenue residence. The champagne and hors d'oeuvres were served on the spacious lawn. The only hitch in the splendid affair occurred when some of the local matrons discovered that they had mixed up their assorted minks and other furs in Mrs. Williams's prettily appointed powder room. But the good-humored mistake never daunted the high spirits of the affair. Those in attendance were: Messrs. and Mesdames _____, Dr. and Mrs. _____, and Mr. and Mrs. _____, who drove up to the twin towns especially to attend the lovely festivities. A good time was had by all.

Never did the prettily appointed guests or the gossip columnists notice that Mrs. Williams's children were not so prettily appointed and were still scavenging — like black fish in blue water — behind the show-and-tell façade. Our real existence had changed little from what it was in the old neighborhood.

For me, our move to Portland Avenue became an emblem of the desperation in both black and white American life — the need to be Dick and Jane. We live in the delusion that at the end of *Home of the Brave* white Mingo will ask black Peter Moss to become his business partner and that we will all live happily ever after. But even in Minnesota — this northern utopia — life goes on below the surface of what most people are willing to see. Moreover, those who wrench themselves to the surface, or who at least manage to delude themselves into believing that they have surfaced, are likely to end up on the governor's stringer or to live on with the scar tissue after they spit out the lure.

Since our move to Minnesota, the kids in our family had all "turned Catholic." My parents weren't involved in this little Chartist movement, though Mama bragged about it to her black friends. I remember when the local nuns in our old neighborhood on Eighth Street discovered our presence. The black-garbed sisters came to our house and asked Daddy if they could give instruction to his children. His response was, "I don't give a damn!" His mild blasphemy was sufficient approval for the nuns to begin their programmed proselytizing. The nuns lured us to Saturday catechism classes by offering us treats — which turned out to be stale doughnuts — that interested us more than the church and its dogma.

Despite the nuns' zealous instruction, my visit to my first Mass turned out to be another culture shock. Our previous experiences at church had been somewhat like Flip Wilson's parody of the "Church of What's Happenin' Now." The black Baptist church in Kansas City, a small storefront establishment, was my only point of comparison. Everybody sang, stomped, and clapped. Some played tambourines, and there was always a rollicking piano player who pounded out the rhythmic spirituals that heightened the pitch of our emotions. The minister got a lot of feedback when he was doing well — "Praise Jesus!" "Hallelujah, I'm coming to God!" "I hear yuh, Lord!" and "Amen, brothah!" In the church and on the street we always called one another "sistah" and "brothah," the way blacks do now. At services, after a particularly spirited address, people would start shaking their heads, clapping their hands, "truckin'" down the aisles, and "gettin' the spirit."

Everything was different at St. Elizabeth's Church in Minneapolis. St. Elizabeth's was a large, ornate, Gothic structure with many statues, pictures, candles, and an elaborate altar which glittered with gold and intricate design. The whole environment reeked of incense. Most of the ceremony was in Latin, but when the priest garbed in many layers of strange-looking vestments, delivered his sermon in English or the vernacular, I still couldn't understand a word he said. I recall feeling very sorry for him because he wasn't getting the feedback I was accustomed to hearing. I thought he had flopped, and I was on his side. But he was obviously holy, and so were the heart-thumping, crossing-themselves parishioners. After that first display of white piety, the nuns had an easy time in their conversion of us blacks from the South.

The nuns were good women, according to their lights. At my First Communion I showed up without the conventional white dress, white veil, white stockings, and white shoes. For weeks I just *knew* that Mama would buy or make them for me. She said she wouldn't, but I was convinced even until the morning of the ceremony that she would surprise me. When I came to the church in my everyday clothes, the nuns sent kids running in all directions to get the white things their sisters had worn the year before. And after we had all eaten God's Body for the first time, the nuns had little "family" presents for us — crayons and holy pictures all wrapped in tissue and ribbons.

I suspected later that the nuns and the parishioners were responsible for the mysterious — but always welcome — baskets of food which appeared out of nowhere at Thanksgiving and Christmas time outside our front door. (The baskets stopped when we moved to the big house on Portland.) The new faith was a hustle, but one that made me feel good, and I practiced it with devotion and commitment.

At home it was difficult to follow through on our indoctrination because Daddy thought it was all a big joke. He would tease us when we were fasting to take Communion the next day. He was even more amused when we piously informed him that we couldn't eat meat on Fridays. I soon noticed that the rare occurrence of meat in our house tended to be on Fridays. Though we desperately wanted that meat, we nobly rejected the temptation and ate only the potatoes or rice and vegetables, much to Daddy's annoyance. Still, he never stopped us from regularly attending Mass or the Saturday confession sessions at the church. Before we left the house, however, he would say, "Goddammit, if you've done something wrong, you need to be telling me about it instead of going up to that goddammed church and telling some damned white man what you've done!" Basically, I agreed with him, but that didn't deter me from pursuing my newfound beliefs.

I became intensely involved in Catholicism. I enrolled in Holy Angels Academy in Richfield. I seriously considered becoming a nun. But one of the sisters informed me, during a religion class, that I couldn't join her order because the Sisters of St. Joseph didn't allow black women to enter their novitiate. Oddly enough, I had not expected nuns to be racists. After all, they were the guardians and purveyors of the so-called Christian ethic. They preached love. I thought that they were better than most white lay people I had known. Ultimately, it turned out, they were as racist as everyone else, especially when it seemed as though my black body might cross the threshold of their private world. That incident precipitated in me the beginning of the end of the religious bit.

While attending Holy Angels I began to shake off the final remnants of my youthful naïveté! Sometimes, in my close friendships with whites and in my truly rewarding experiences with a few white teachers and counselors, bolstered by Mama's covert innuendos that "white was right," I forgot the fact of my blackness. At least, I would force myself to accept minor slights — having white store clerks ignore me, or running into the occasional brat who would yell out in a crowd, "Look, Mommy, at the nigger lady with the dirty face," or having bus drivers pass me by at clearly designated bus stops if no whites were standing there, or watching white people on the bus stand with an armload of parcels rather than take a seat next to me.

It was about this same time that Rosa Parks began her crusade to integrate Selma buses, and Martin Luther King had begun his bus boycott crusade in Birmingham. White folks in the North watched the sit-ins and racial unrest on their wide-screened television sets. They condemned the white South and placated their own guilt by talking about how liberal they were.

In Minneapolis, on a Nicollet Avenue bus heading toward the school, I encountered "the problem" in person. The bus was extremely crowded, and the white driver kept yelling, "Move to the back of the bus!" Because my arms were full of books, and because I was too short to reach the handstraps comfortably, I had to hold onto the backs of the seats as I was moved along with the crowd. Before the bus had traveled more than two blocks, a white woman began to kick at my feet and legs while muttering incoherently to herself. After a while she stood up and screamed, "Niggers should never be close to white people! Niggers have no business being here!" She started to slap and pound me wherever her fast-flying fists could land on my body.

I was too stunned to react appropriately. I really should have tried to kill her, but instead I just did my best to ward off the blows. The driver and most of the passengers left their seats to get a better view, but no one came to my assistance. When the woman had fully vented her hatred, she pushed her way to the back door and rang the bell to get off. One white man did attempt to help me gather my books and papers from the muddy floor. I was hurt emotionally more than I was physically injured by the whole episode. I was wearing the Holy Angels uniform, and my first dumbfounded thought was, "Can't she see that I'm a Catholic?" I believe that I had subconsciously assumed that my school uniform — my public symbol — had somehow obscured the fact of my blackness.

This new revelation of my naïveté shamed and angered me. Pressing the kinks out of my "nappy" hair, acting like whites, dressing like whites, doing those things customarily ordained to be "for whites only," I deluded only myself. All the pressing creams and bleaching creams — Mama used them for years and only grew darker — the "special" uniforms, and the prettily appointed home were clearly but outward signs of my inner delusions. To the bigoted whites a nigger was always a nigger.

Fannie Lou Hamer, Dr. King, Stokely Carmichael, Willie Hicks, Anne Moody, Malcolm X, and many others were fighting racism — tooth and nail — in the South and in the East. But blacks in Minnesota pretended there was no race problem in their own state and held that the activists were only troublemakers. As I grew up, I had absorbed the idea that blackness was something "bad," something that made you different. The "good" white people were those who pretended that they didn't see those differences. In our encounters we mutually pretended that those differences weren't visible or important. What a sham!

I can't erase the past, including God's creation. Those early pains can never be forgotten. They must be remembered. I now arm myself quite proudly with my differentness. In doing this I find myself less vulnerable and more able to cope with objective reality.

So now my childhood is over. Daddy and my sisters and brothers seem scattered to the winds, although we try to keep in touch with one another from time to time. Mama is dead. She died in 1973 at the age of fifty-one. Even she has left Minnesota and returned to Kansas City. At the wake everything seemed irreverent to me because people were laughing and talking and reminiscing about old times. Though at first I was angered by the apparent irreverence, I began to remember that in our not too distant past our people bemoaned births and celebrated funerals because life was so grim and our people believed so firmly in a happy hereafter.

I was not alone in my grief over Mama's death. My sisters, Marie and Sandy, were hysterical, and my brothers, Ronnie and Julian, did their best to console them. My brother Jackie grieved separately in a distant city. We couldn't find Morris, who lived someplace in Hawaii — the last we heard — near a beach and under a bridge with a knapsack (which somebody later stole) as his only possession. We hadn't seen or heard from my sister Marion (Puddin') for about five years. We were informed by the funeral directress, later, that Marion had come from California. She had heard about Mama's death through a medium, but she didn't want her presence made known to the rest of the family. The directress told me that Puddin' had arrived at the funeral home after the wake and that she had sat alone all night patting Mama's dead body and crying. My brothers raced around Kansas City after hearing that Puddin' was there, somewhere. They never found her, but Puddin's fancy signature appeared as the last name on the funeral home's guest ledger.

I am still woefully sorry that Mama's life was so muddled and confused. Because of her mental and physical fragility, she was too easily buffeted about in life. Her few happinesses were ever so brief, and her miseries (which burdened her children's lives also) seemed unceasing. I know, too, that I contributed greatly to Mama's grief when I married young to get away from her. I deliberately cut myself off from her because I knew I couldn't cope with her endless succession of problems that neither she nor I could resolve. Mama always seemed to drain from my mind and body what little strength I had. All eight of us knew, too well, that Mama could destroy us, and so we had left her. Several of the kids ran away from home before they were twelve. A few stayed with her well into their teens. Her last husband, the fourth after Daddy, was also never a part of Mama's complex life or of ours. Mama died alone.

After I received word from Fairview Hospital that Mama was having a heart attack, I went immediately to the hospital. I sat with her body for nearly an hour before I realized that she was dead. I remember arguing with the nurses, telling them that she couldn't be dead — at least not until I could tell her I was sorry for so many things. But it was too late.

I was haunted by the fact that on my thirty-third birthday Mama had called on the phone, and, as had become my custom, I was very brusque with her. Before I could tell her I had to hurry off, she said, "I only wanted to tell you that I love you." I was shocked. Mama had never said those words before in my whole life. I hardly knew how to respond. Those words were too incongruent with all she had said and all she. had done while we lived together. I remember her voice ringing through my childhood: "I hate you . . . I hate your black filthy guts . . . you ugly black thing, I wish you were dead . . . I despise you all!" I let a long and awkward pause drop between us before I could finally muster a ridiculous "Thank you." Only at her deathbed could I bring myself to say, "Mama, I love you! I'm sorry!" She did not hear.

Every now and then, in one of those clumsy mixed social gatherings when race relations and blackness inevitably become the topic after we have run out of small talk, one of the "colorless" individuals will ask me (because I am the token black guest and the presumed authority on all that's black), "But, don't you find that things are really much better for you people here in the North?" Depending upon my mood (tolerance, anger, patience, bitterness, caution, or trust), I usually attempt to muster a response. It might be a caustic "No!" or it might be a less emphatic retort followed by polite and yet pointed exposition. Regardless of the circumstances, my response is never without the twinge of those old pains, which are often freshened and reinforced by the actions of die-hard bigots and pseudoliberals.

Racism was here in Minnesota before the area was a state or even a white man's territory. It came down the St. Lawrence and through the Great Lakes. It came up the Mississippi, like me. It reached America before it reached Minnesota. It arrived in Greece before it hit Rome. It won't leave this year. And then, of course, there are always the "concerned" few who worry that I might be one of those black racists who never seem to be satisfied with the great changes society has made. What can I say? Power makes culture.

I often wonder whether this will be a better world for my children — my oh-so-black and beautiful Kim, and Earle, and Lance — who are also growing up in Minnesota. For me, it has been a trip, and it still is. Even for the fish! I can say with that jive-ass Socrates, referring to the bureaucrats who made him drink the poison, "They have done me no harm. But they didn't mean to do me any good. For this I may gently blame them." He might have added, "Sure the society is crazy. But so far it's the only one we've got." So far!

ROBERT BLY

Being a Lutheran Boy-God in Minnesota

by Robert Bly

An old milk delivery wagon my uncle had used once to deliver milk all around town stood near the smokehouse. Some disaster had happened to him — I didn't know what it was at the time, and the milk wagon stood there floating, pale, deserted by human beings. And the smokehouse had walls of stone, all smoky and blacked on the inside, the roof a frail contraption of boards, soaked in wood smoke as if in ocean water, but frail and liable to die compared to the walls.

There were six people in the household. The only children were my brother, James, and I. He was a year and a half older, but we began school together and were in the same grade. My mother worked at the courthouse during the day, and so a wonderful woman named Marie Schmidt took care of us for years. My father always had a hired man, and one, Art Nelson, was with us for eight or nine years.

My father wearing a large black coat stands near the windmill, holding a baby up over the snow; it is my brother or myself. The windmill is stark, my father has had to become a man too soon. At sixteen he quit school, being the oldest son, to work. Always around him there was a high exhilaration, pursued by grief and depression, and a tough mother, who believed in rules. He had a gift for deep feeling. Other men bobbed like corks around his silence, and around his swift decisions; that did not bring him more company, but did help carry the burdens higher up the mountain. His heart beat very fast, and he felt himself tied to this earth. At church he kept his arms crossed over his chest. He had the sturdiest respect, grained and unplaned, for some men and women; when others were mentioned, you were astounded to find out how little he thought of them. A brooding secretly lifted the short sentences he said. And he stubbornly refused to be carried away on easy judgments that serve to bind a company together and resemble stones bouncing over the surface of the water. He preferred weight, even if the stone sank all the way to the bottom.

And those hot days, the top of the threshing machine hot and shaking, my father standing there with legs wide, how good to feel all that shaking beneath you, coming up through the soles of the feet and the legs, the horses stamping to scare flies, as they wait for their load to go, the earthy and good machine, friendly to man except when it took a finger or an arm, its great front choppers coming out and down, to warn the bundles their time had come.

Our time has come! It is all right. How good it is to give the end of it all away, to let life go . . . so that the female shapes floating in the sky can be told what they already know, that waterfalls are wet, that water pours down, that we too are unassimilatable by objects, and we are born to sail sideways through the spaces between objects, between stars, between our deaths — and how often we have died . . . so many times eaten by wild animals, as we waited, dozing, beneath a tree, the water gourd and dried meat nearby, the tribe gone on to the hive, and all our anguish in this life is a sideways step in the darkness, slipping between two heavy posts we cannot see . . . so on the threshing machine the legs always gave thanks to the Father, the Son, and the Holy Ghost . . .

My brother and I went to a country school. It had one room, the teachers were just and kind, and I liked everything that happened to me there. By the time we started, most of the country schools had closed, and District 94, where I went from the third grade on, was to have been closed. But if one parent in the township insisted, it had to stay open. My father refused to agree to the closing, and my brother and I were sometimes the only students in the school; there were never more than five or six. That was a wise refusal.

We usually walked the mile to school, or rode two on a thin mule. We had two teachers there in eight years. Esther Kemen, calm and affectionate, had a boyfriend with a moustache and kept a pan of water on top of the coal stove in case we wanted to heat our cocoa for lunch, and a wire popcorn popper we could hold inside the stove and toast our cheese sandwiches. She had gone to this school, and her father also. For seventh and eighth grades, we had Marie Skulborstad, excitable and full of good energy. I kept a diary when I was eleven, and in the sixth grade, and I'll set down a few entries from it.

Jan 10.

> Went to school. Took down some decoration. A new boy La Verne Shelstad. He is 14 years old and is in the 8th grade. My foot hurt so after school took boot off. Thinks my little toe has infection in between toes. Daddy and Mom went to a church meeting. Daddy was appointed delegate for church convention in June.

Jan 25.

> Neither James nor I went to school on account of blizzard. I practised my music lesson in grandma's room on Clara's piano. Got my magnifying glass from Post Toasties.

Jan 26.

> Went to school. Walter and La Verne were there too. Got my 40 stamps from Grape Nuts Flakes. Got our report card from school. Couldn't go outside all day. La Verne couldn't either. Marie washed clothes.

Jan 27.

> Went to school. Had spelling test sent out from Wroolie. I got 102. James 81, Walter 82, La Verne 82. My toe started to hurt again.

Feb 2.

> Ground Hog day. Went to school. Got wet in school, walked home. Brought home book "Widow O'Callahan's Boys." James brought home "Black Beauty." Walter got "Dark Frigate," and La Verne "Robinson Crusoe." Marie washed clothes.

Feb 3.

Went to school. Walked home. Played ping pong in school. Studied singing lessons. Finished reading book "Widow O'Callaghan's Boys." Art just came home today. His face was scratched.

Feb 13.

Went to Sunday School. Was going to Litchfield but was too icy. We got twin lambs from Western ewe. Daddy bought it from Julius Lund. We brought lambs into house. One was a buck and the other a ewe.

Feb 15.

Went to school. Got letter from Grandma. Got whistling ring from Jack Armstrong. Marie washed and waxed floor. Snowed in night.

Feb 19.

Went to singing lessons. Found out I had to sing in musical. Have Key of D this time. Went over to Nelson's and shot a pigeon. Got package from Helma. It contained necktie and three handkerchiefs. Put sled together. Marie washed my head. Took bath.

Feb 20.

Went to Granma and Mervin's and Rueben's. I threw up just before we came to Willmar. Played Monopoly at Grandma's. Were going to Cities on Monday but Daddy decided not to.

Feb 21.

Went to school. Got six lambs. We have now 17 lambs. Mom, James and I went to show "Merrygoround of 1938."

Feb 23.

Went to school. Didn't get any lambs and none died. Mom had awful cold. Margaret Ehlenz died of double pneumonia just before 6:00 in the afternoon.

March 2.

Didn't go to school on account Teacher's dad was worse. Cut off 22 lamb's tails which were upstairs. We couldn't cut off one lamb's tail upstairs. Worked on model planes. Fixed pen in chicken house for James' lambs and ewes and ones we raised on bottle. James has one old ewe and his old ewe. Mom and Daddy went to Roy's up at our old place. They moved a couple of days ago. Started reading "Hans Brinker and His Silver Skates."

March 3.

Went to school. Had Arithmetic, Geography and Spelling test. In Spelling I got 100, James got 94. In Arithmetic Test I got 94, James got 77. In Geography I got 92.

March 4.

Went to school. Had science test. I got 97. James got 95.

March 7.

> Went to school. James got his Charlie McCarthy from Chase and San-
> born Coffee. It is just a cardboard. You can make his eyes and
> mouth move. Worked on plane. Got funny papers from Alvin. Had
> musical at Mrs. Smith's. I had to sing, "What Can I Give Him?"
> "Going Skating" and "While We Sleep."

March 23.

> Went to school. La Verne wasn't there. James batted ball into ditch
> full of water, and it went into culvert. It lodged in middle of culvert.
> It got lost at last recess. Worked all last recess and til almost 4:15
> after school. We still didn't get it out. Rode bikes.

March 24.

> Went to school. La Verne did come. I brought fish pole and James a
> flash. Rode bikes. The fish pole was not long enough to reach ball.
> We sent in Walter's dog but it didn't do any good. Then we blocked
> up one end and washed it out. James took fish pole and flash home.
> I took lunchbuckets and my kite. La Verne had kite in school.

March 25.

> Went to school. Had declamatory contest. I won in Humorous Read-
> ings. A Fudge girl was after me. In Dramatics a Fudge girl won. Also
> had spellings. Walter, La Verne, then James went down first. I was
> the 5th to last. I went down on Recipe. Name of my piece was
> Jimmie Jones Likes Geography. Worked on things in school. I
> stained 3 boards. Couldn't take bikes. I got haircut.

I grew up as a typical "boy-god." As I understand the idea, boys
toward whom the mother directs a good deal of energy, either
warm or cold, tend to become boy-gods. They are boys, and yet
they feel somehow eternal, out of the stream of life, they float
above it. My mother was and is a good mother, without envy or
malice, affectionate, excitable, living with simplicity and energy —
one of the servants of life. I had a brother a year and a half older,
but I was the favorite son.

This embodied itself in a sense that I was "special," and so in a
general lack of compassion for others. If someone were suffering,
or in a rage, I would feel myself pull away, into some safe area,
where I did not "descend" to those emotions, and get entangled in
them, but neither did I help the person at all. What helping I did
tended to be from above. We all know of people who bring Christ-

mas gifts to the poor, or "help" old ladies by taking tea with them, who do not move others and are themselves unmoved. I was that sort.

The mood of Lutheran Sunday School only speeded up that tendency. It taught us that the body — that is, woman — was evil, and that purity lay in the eternal, in what was "up" . . . I already knew that. Rilke mentions the white dresses that girls wear at confirmation, but a woman will soon have to come down into her own body, certainly when she has a child she will. A man can remain floating for years, as I did.

In 1953, when I was twenty-six, I gathered into a little folder the poems I had written to that time, almost every one the poem of a boy-god. Here is a poem I wrote when I was twenty-two.

> You wonder why we take so many trips
> And why our hours all are violent —
> I speak of vegetation and the tide —
> But when December storms the continent
> And breaks the seas past any strength of ships
> Now I remember Christ the crucified,
> Who hurt his Mary, could not help but say
> At feast, "What have I to do with thee?"
> Leaving for Jerusalem. This push
> A baptist said was set in every knee
> By that club-footed shape behind the bush
> When life bent down to fire Adam's ribs.
>
> There are peeling ferns inside Skid Row
> Gospel missions in New Orleans
> Where summer watched a woman put her hands
> Around her husband, twenty years ago.
> They spoke of love. He said, "Yes, forget it."
> He left and walked to where he sleeps,
> Where he eats his pork and beans from cans
> And keeps a whore who has no teeth. These things
> I heard. Learn them. They make some belief.
> And I will leave you. That is another grief
> That cannot be atoned in Copley Square
> Body to body in the Christmas air.

In the Skid Row passage, when I referred to the experience there, it was not mine, but someone else's. That is typical of the boy-god. The cry "I will leave you" is the everlasting cry of the boy-god. He wants to be tied down to no one, especially not to a woman, and so he is always with "his hand on his lips, bidding farewell." The boy-god also typically explains the reason for his departure (which to him is the most exciting part of the love) as caused by vast, whirling forces, so cosmic that to obey is to be "pure," and so complicated in their working, that they could, of course, only be understood by "special people." The boy-god has a great sensitivity to the different resonances — which he interprets as dissonances — of the notes given off by spirit and body. The last line catches that perception of dissonance, in a tone which amounts almost to satisfaction.

The boy-god is often curiously cheerful — and I was cheerful almost all through childhood. This habit too becomes intensified in the Norwegian-American culture of the farms, where the social tone is a maddening cheerfulness, with no one ever admitting to being depressed or suicidal. No serious conflicts are ever found between separate areas of church doctrine, nor between capitalist practice and Christian practice. Only the oldest settlers, born in Norway, and socialists when they came, went around muttering in indignation at the latest news of corporate takeover. All deep conflicts of opinion are potentially depressing to one of the people arguing, if not to both.

In the middle of the Vietnam War most people would limit themselves to "Well, we should have never gotten in there in the first place," a sentiment hard to build on. I was troubled all through my twenties by this insistent cheerfulness, and a little surprised at being troubled by it, since it had fit so well into the moods of high school. I finally realized it did not fit the moods of ancient civilization at all. I wrote this poem when I was twenty-four.

> When once astrologers read frozen stars,
> The stars said cold and death, and it was there.
> The blizzard of stars then shed remorseless snow
> Of terrible Novembers unborn yet,
> And earth was moving toward its death forever.
> We pore on men, and find the hoped-for June,
> And therefore to divine the mortal spring
> Deny the earth and contradict the stars;
> We, like musicians, read from written bars
> And ask musicians to be more true than stars.

It is still a boy-god's poem, with its obsession with stars and height. The poem notices that despite the love of stars, the boy-god, when pressed, will deny both the earth and the stars. He is just not sensitive enough to any heavy object outside himself. The movement toward secularization in recent history, the increasing emphasis on human beings instead of stars and "inhuman" forces, and the movement away from a close life with nature, have both increased the power of the boy-god plague.

The poem also makes it clear that a symptom of the boy-god syndrome is his insistence — despite his conviction that he is special and thereby spontaneous and free — on reading music from written bars, that is to say, clinging to the safety of mind-concepts. Everything in the poem is mental. The mind-grids, developed over centuries in the seed, and over twelve years in the schools, interpose themselves between the boy and all sense experience. They "lift" him out of it. How high I was all through high school! What a terrible longing to come down!

And many hours shocking grain. That meant we went out in the morning with gloves, took two bundles of oats, and set them up on their butts, their foolish heads straying into each other. Then we found two more, and set those next to the first couple. Then we found two more for the far side. When these three pairs were in place, a mass of prickly oat spikes and itchy dust and smug straw, we put an outrider, or leaner, on each of the two sides, for good measure, making a total of eight bundles.

How many marriages we left in the field! And it was so beautiful to look back, and see all the houses standing in rows, not even rows either, but sometimes a shock poking out a little this way or that, and the ground all around cleaned of its burdens, naked, open to moonlight.

And I loved the nights after threshing, when the moon would hover over the strawpiles, all alone on some hill, far from the cluttered farmyards, with their itchy hens, stacks abandoned by the earthbound threshers whose horses obeyed them and took them home in the dusk. Sometimes I went back out into the fields, now so oddly silent — it was as if we went back to the Renaissance, where the fourteenth century lay in moonlight, only the people gone, the blood in all the marble — and sat on a new strawstack, looking at the moon, which was like a body just come from the bath, or the wheel of a bundle wagon everyone liked, or that round twist of hair at the back of a woman's neck.

We always had some suspicion of men from the town, who did not work with their hands. In town, they thought themselves better, but my father did not share that view, and he shielded us from its destructive radiation. He ran a threshing rig, and stood on it, respecting a number of grown men and even horses who worked with their hands, shoulders, and hooves all day. At times if we were threshing a field that the bank owned, having foreclosed during the late disastrous thirties — perhaps six or seven years before we were threshing — then the bank, to make sure the grain was divided properly, would send a cashier or teller out to watch the wagonboxes being pulled up to the thresher, and pulled away full, and where they went — from their cars — the bank often accepting their loads at a different elevator than the renter was using. How we pitied these creatures! Getting out of the car with a white shirt and a necktie, stepping over the stubble like a cat so as not to get too much chaff in his black oxfords, how weak and feeble! What a poor model of a human being! It was clear the teller was incapable of any boisterous joy, and was nothing but a small zoo animal of some sort that locked the doors on itself, pale from the reflected light off the zoo walls, light as salt in a shaker, clearly obsessed with money — you could see greed all over him. How ignoble! How sordid and ignoble! What ignobility!

A joy in growing up on a Minnesota farm at the time I did is that there was a place for men and women who could do only physical work. I knew mainly men of this sort, often bachelors. They never really knew that they were "dumb," because the farm culture was a hive that needed them. Their mother might mention to a neighbor in his hearing that the boy was "not cut out for school," but the tone of the sentence implied that a teacher was a curious kind of bird-trainer, whom one humored. They all knew that the real core of a boy lay in whether when sent out to the black fields he would go on working through the darkening light, whether he would get up in the middle of the night to check his ewes — for lambs born in midwinter can live only a few hours if they are not dried with a towel and taught to suck — or whether he could put on harnesses in the halfdark, still keeping the horse calm by not being irritable. These boys, when they grew to be men, were usually patient with children, patient with cow dung and poorly lit barns, patient with slow horses and lodged barley. They could see they were needed. They hired out and lived forty or sometimes fifty years with the same family, at the start upstairs in a bare, unheated room, later perhaps in a small house or converted railway car, where they stayed snug through Sunday and never went to church. If you are needed, what does the rest matter?

Soon big machines began to appear, and we know what happened then. Only those with a fairly high IQ in the technical parts of the brain are allowed to farm. The reason for the spread of these large machines is not clear to me: historians usually mention shortage of labor. But there was no sign of that at all in the early forties, when they started to appear.

D. H. Lawrence, in his frightening essay "Men Must Work and Women As Well," says that one of the most important changes in the life of humanity had occurred during his own lifetime. That change amounted to the acceptance among all classes — he was speaking of England — of this idea: one should not do physical work. Other variations are, "We must go upward. Work with the head is higher than work with the hands." "Whoever is not fit to work in an office does not deserve respect." This idea appeared in China in Imperial times but was only accepted by the governing and scholar class. Here it is a secret sentence whispered in the four-minute gaps between high school classes, and through the walls of churches and government offices. It is especially whispered by stylish clothes and by the glazed fenders of the cars coming out of Detroit, where the models change every year: "We are angels, physical work is a mistake for us."

And what happens to the farm machines if physical work is bad? The early tractor, up to about 1950, was only a cast-iron engine with four wheels and a seat, made to pull heavy things, as clean in its way as a hammer or a spoon. First a simple cab was put on over the seat. Now the cab is luxurious, with a bucket seat, a dashboard that curiously resembles the communications panel of the executive's desk, side panels of imitation grained leather in black, tape decks for cartridge rock, and air conditioning. It seems to say, "All mental people deserve comfort."

The men who are not "cut out for school" now, when they reach eighteen, drift away into large cities, where they float like heavy steel washers enchanted by a medium, floating a foot or two below the ceiling of their small apartments. Others collect Social Security and sit with a television set, where they see the physical body killed again and again.

The unconscious does not hear well. It is a little deaf. It gets things wrong, because for two million years it has always done things its way and has only been talked to for the last three or four thousand years. If you say to it, "Physical work is bad," it may lose a word or two of that sentence. For some time it has been acting as if it heard, "Physical is bad."

Many college-educated people in their twenties and thirties are returning enthusiastically to work with their bodies, avoiding machines when possible. But on the farms no one has heard of the Whole Earth Catalog. Men in their twenties in western Minnesota getting into cars gesture with every motion their apology for having a body at all. In the living rooms of farmhouses one more and more often meets women without opinions. It is astounding, as my brother and I found out by throwing bundles of grain around twelve or fourteen hours a day, how much energy the body is capable of pouring out and then replenishing. That is a magical act, because you never really understand where all that energy comes from. Men and women who have experienced that are more likely to understand the idea that spiritual energy can also be poured out and replenished from mysterious sources. It is interesting to discover that those ecstasies involving high spiritual energy which we associate with the early Middle Ages in Europe continued well into the twentieth century in Tibet, a country so stark and cold the body has to pour out energy in amazing amounts simply to travel, or to stay warm, or to get food.

I'll tell you a story about my father. Each year men from south of us — Kansas, Missouri, Arkansas, even Alabama and Tennessee — would move through the country, following the small grain harvest north. They would end up in North Dakota or Canada about late September and would then go home again. My father, since he ran a threshing rig, would hire one or two of these men each threshing season. Sometimes I went with him, and at 6:00 A.M. before the rig had started, we would drive uptown to a small park in which some of the men had slept that night. If he saw a man with a face he liked, he would ask him if he could pitch bundles and drive a team of horses.

On one of those mornings, he hired a man whom I will call Garth Morrison, who had come up from a small town in Missouri. Garth turned out to be a good worker, and he and my father got on together very well. He stayed with us during the week. On Saturday night, the teams put away, he would go to town, and be gone Saturday night and Sunday night. But early Monday morning he would always be back and ready for work.

One Monday morning he didn't show up. My father was puzzled, and at about 9:00 A.M. he put someone else in charge of the rig and drove to town to see if he could find Garth. Asking around here and there, he heard that Garth had been picked up by the sheriff Saturday night. Apparently he had made a date with a waitress at a cafe, who had agreed to let him walk her home. At 11:00 he had gone to pick her up and, probably to his surprise, she did let him walk her home, where she lived with her parents. A few words were exchanged — probably a series of misunderstood signals between a southern man and a northern woman. He slapped her face. She went inside furious and complaining. Her parents called the sheriff. The man was from out of state. The sheriff and the judge had a secret court session the next morning — Sunday morning — having refused all along to let Garth call my father on the telephone, and sentenced him to twenty years at Stillwater prison. By Sunday noon he was on his way to Stillwater. By Sunday night the sheriff was back in town. It was said he always tried to show proof of his vigilance shortly before an election.

My father, once he got the story from the reluctant sheriff, was enraged. He shut down the threshing rig, and with his best friend, Alvin Hofstad, got in the car and drove to St. Paul to see the attorney general of Minnesota. The attorney general agreed that the facts gave off a bad odor. He went with my father and Alvin Hofstad to Stillwater, where they talked to Garth and verified the story. He then had Garth taken out of the prison and returned to the county jail in Madison to await trial. He stayed in the county jail a month or more, and we as boys would go up to talk with him through the window. My father hired a lawyer and paid for Garth's wife and infant son to come up from Missouri for the trial. They stayed with us and she testified at the trial; I remember her holding the baby on the stand. The jury convicted Garth of simple assault, and the judge ruled that the time already spent in jail more than served out the appropriate sentence. He was released and the family returned to Missouri.

My father never spoke to the sheriff again for the rest of the sheriff's life. Garth did not come north again either. The spring following the trial, Garth and his wife invited my father and mother down to Missouri for a visit. They drove down, and it turned out that everyone in that small Missouri town knew the story. When my father went for a haircut, the barber would not let him pay, and whenever he and mother went into a restaurant, the owner would not accept their money.

To be able to respect your father is such a beautiful thing! I learned then that the indignation of the solitary man is the stone pin that connects this world to the next. The more easy-going businessmen in Madison, who had so many friends, would have left Garth sitting in his cell for twenty years. They would have been afraid to put their hand into the web of social friendships, afraid the web would not be repaired over night, or that the spider of loneliness would bite them. I learned too that when you have been unselfish, people respond not in words but by feeding you. I learned so much from that one story! We don't need to read books on ethics or to see documentaries on television; one moral example will do for a lifetime.

It is good to be alone near wood. I sometimes went to the top of the loft, where the hay was deep and a small high window looked out over the eastern fields. Up there someone had built a small shelf, just right to sit on. Its pale boards were miraculously strong so high in the air. I loved the knotholes, and the dusting of hay chaff in them, and in the corners and groins of the two-by-fours. Each one was a tiny intense house! Places looked at with such intensity on the day the barn was built and then never looked at again.

We had brought the hay in ourselves. Horses pulled the wagons right up and onto the second floor. Before throwing the first hay on the rack, we would lay down two ropes lengthwise on the rack floor; their ends, with snaps, hung down over the edges. When the hay was about to overflow the sideboards, we put down two more ropes on top of it for the second layer. Once the load of hay was in the barn, one of us would stand, his legs like a swimmer in deep water, rocking on top of the load, waiting for the lifters to be lowered from the track running way up in the skull of the barn. When they had come down, we snapped the rope ends of the top layer on and jumped off.

Then my father and perhaps Art below on the floor would pull on their long delicate rope, thick as a thumb, and slowly, with groans, the upper half, from the heart up, would begin to rise. What joy to see it lift, go up, farther and farther, into the dark top, darkness ascending into darkness, there was no end to its richness, the stomach sweaty and alive with dust, the body ready to run. Then the spreading of coarse salt, thrown in handfuls from a bucket — it salted the cows and the hay.

I wrote a poem with that barn in it later.

> We are approaching sleep: the chestnut blossoms in the mind
> Mingle with thoughts of pain
> And the long roots of barley, bitterness

As of the oak roots staining the waters dark
In Louisiana, the wet streets soaked with rain
And sodden blossoms, out of this
We have come, a tunnel softly hurtling into darkness.

The storm is coming. The small farmhouse in Minnesota
Is hardly strong enough for the storm.
Darkness, darkness in grass, darkness in trees.
Even the water in wells trembles.
Bodies give off darkness, and chrysanthemums
Are dark, and horses, who are bearing great loads of hay
To the deep barns where the dark air is moving from corners.

Lincoln's statue, and the traffic. From the long past
Into the long present
A bird, forgotten in these pressures, warbling,
As the great wheel turns around, grinding
The living in water.
Washing, continual washing, in water now stained
With blossoms and rotting logs,
Cries, half-muffled, from beneath the earth, the living
    awakened at last like the dead.

EDNA and HOWARD HONG
and MARY HONG LOE

Remembering Is a Forward Movement

*by Edna and Howard Hong
and Mary Hong Loe*

If the five of our eight children who no longer live in Minnesota abstain from Minnesota Old Home Picnics in southern California or Texas, it is not because they have lost interest in the Land of Sky-Blue Waters or that they cannot stomach potato salad and cole slaw — it is only that they cannot abide remembering backward.

True nostalgia is not merely or essentially a backward movement, a heart-rending longing for a bygone, a once before, a something lost. It is a remembering forward, a carrying into any experience in space and time — not dead remembrance, but a green and growing recollecting that is strong enough to dye that new space indelibly green and make that new time as memorable as the vibrant past. Those who go away from a time and space when and where they were happy take the aura of that happiness with them. Separating from that time and that place is not a cutting or tearing up of roots. It is a moving out into a wider world, a vaster existence, but the center remains the same. The earth turns methodically in space, the wheel of life moves erratically over the earth, but the quiet recollection of the root-life where one grew up is the hub. Thus five of our eight children have indeed left Minnesota, but Minnesota has never left them, for growing up in Minnesota has helped to give all ten of us the organic capacity to be everywhere and anywhere and always at home.

Not that each of us is moving ahead in time and space on the same current of memories or with the same angle of vision! After all, we have different whences and whens. Father Howard was an infant immigrant from North Dakota, and Mother Edna a belated immigrant from Wisconsin. Erik and Irena, our adopted children, came from Latvia and have dark memories of terror, flight, and hunger when they were only five and seven years old. But the fact that the six other children were all born on the same floor in the same hospital in Northfield, Minnesota, does not necessarily add up to shared common memories. Shared in telling and retelling, yes, but each one's personal history is unique. Only Edna had in her childhood a nicked and gashed woodbox and the never-ending chore of keeping it filled — and a brother whose big toe was split neatly down the middle when he was chopping wood for that woodbox. Only Howard sorted vegetables and fruit at the Gamble-Robinson Wholesale Fruit and Vegetable Company in Willmar in his early teens and has a disproportionate amount of rotten cabbage leaves and soft potatoes in his web of memories. Only Judy nearly died in the polio epidemic. Only Mary (who will tell our North Woods story some pages hence) nearly drowned at the age of two when she fell off the dock at Hovland, Minnesota, into the crystal clear waters of Lake Superior. Peder alone started school in Heidelberg, Germany, in October of 1947, scared and protesting — until he discovered that his American teacher was from his own hometown, Northfield, Minnesota.

All these memories, the personal as well as the tribal, may be conjured up by memory and imagination at will and may be lovingly looked at by the eye of the mind, but they could never have been invented by even the flightiest of fancies. They had to be most intimately experienced firsthand. Our daughter Judy could sit with her brown Hawaiian babies on a stretch of white beach fringed with coconut palms and conceive of a white-water river swirling darkly around huge boulders, plunging through black basalt gorges stained with orange lichen, dropping into two enormous kettles before rushing on to lose itself in the cold depths of Lake Superior, *only* because she had subjectively experienced that river. Without her experience of the Brule River her imagined river would be an artificial river, a plastic river, not an incarnate river. Having had a long love affair with this Minnesota river, her Brule River recollected in Hawaii was as real to her as the real waves breaking on the real coral reef out in the real lagoon.

To be eligible for core-of-being stuff, the experience has to be total. A jet-set visitor to Minneapolis on a twenty-degrees-below-zero weekend in January certainly does have an authentic frigid experience *in* Minnesota and may truthfully report with appropriate dramatic effects to New York friends on the cru-el-l-l climate, but one most assuredly does not have an authentic experience *of* Minnesota and of Minnesota's weather. For it is Minnesota weather that is missed most by anyone who has totally experienced it, particularly if one has become weary of a flat climate elsewhere, however benign it may once have seemed to the Minnesota expatriate. All the weathers of the world suffer by comparison with the weather back home in Minnesota, for the weather back home is not a matter of statistics, mean temperatures, average precipitation, etc. — it is a matter of a total assault on the total man — and his antiphonal response to the assault. Fragmented men scuttling from overheated hotel lobbies across ten feet of sidewalk to heated cabs do not know Minnesota weather. Apartment-reared children who are bussed to school and toted by fond parents to the YMCA for swimming lessons do not and cannot know Minnesota weather. The sum total of their abridged and minimized experiences never equals rhapsody. The capacity to be rhapsodic about Minnesota weather comes from being massively assaulted (gently or brutally) in every tissue of one's being.

Genteel the weather in Minnesota is not! Even when it is most charming and full of grace, it has the potentiality of swiftly veering and delivering a rude clout, a stinging slap, a knockout blow. We do not forget November 11, 1940, which began with good duck-hunting weather — temperatures in the high twenties, mild rain — but swiftly (so swiftly that dozens died) changed into a blizzard with hurricane winds, sharp biting snow, and paralyzing cold. An evening class in the history of philosophy scheduled to meet in our unfinished-as-yet basement house on the north edge of Manitou Heights met as planned, even though every member literally fought his way to the door from tree to tree, bending almost double against the fury of the wind. If a philosopher is a person of judgment and practical wisdom, the members of the class were not philosophers that night. If a philosopher is a person who keeps his serenity under trying conditions, they were all philosophers that night. But their teacher was supremely a philosopher, for after his students left he and his man Friday, a guileless freshman who had volunteered to exchange faithful labor for rough bed and rustic board, cheerfully planed, fitted, and installed storm windows throughout the wild night. As the indoor temperature relentlessly descended and the snow sifted through the temporary roofing, the philosopher's normal good humor became high glee, and, without premeditatedly meaning to, he drove out the ice devils of apprehension that were invading his young wife. She had her gloating glee, however, a week later when her fear that the roof would blow off proved to have been justified. The roof *had* lifted that night — enough to admit a mound of snow which, in the Indian summer temperature that trailed the storm, promptly melted, dripped through the ceiling, and for several days and nights volubly filled the pans set out all over the floor.

There is no doubt that Howard's ecstatic response to what some would call Minnesota's "meanest" weather was patterned in that Willmar childhood: sleeping on the porch of the cottage on Eagle Lake in the worst of weather, calmly peering out from his blankets and tarpaulin at the commotion of driving rain, thrashing branches, and whitecap waves — tramping, with a pocket of cheese and old bread, during snowstorms through the dry cattails around Foot Lake to Robbins Island and back — skating in the bitter cold with his pals at the Sand Pit and roasting potatoes in the hot ashes of a fire they built in a dug-out fireplace in the bank. Each such experience deposited its gossamer threads of palpable, sensuous delight. No, he is neither an anachronism nor an accident, that white-haired man who climbs in his battle-scarred World War II jeep at midnight (if that is when the snowfall abates), pulls down the earflaps of his fur cap, clamps a lighted cigar between his teeth, and chugs forth to plow driveways all up and down the road. He is a prodigal squandering his inheritance.

Coveting the same inheritance for our children, we resisted becoming "totin' parents" and sent our children forth on foot to their destinations in fair weather and what some call foul. Their walk to elementary school skirted a fringe of woods, dropped down a hill through a thicket of lilacs, crossed the St. Olaf athletic field, and continued down tree-lined streets to Longfellow School a mile away. The two-mile walk to high school crossed the Cannon River. In his senior and most decadent year our firstborn discovered that we lived a fraction more than two miles from school and were eligible for the country bus. "I knew it all the time," grumbled his father, "but I didn't tell them." The firstborn rode the bus, quite legitimately and legally, only one week, for reasons he did not choose to elaborate.

We did not and do not exhortingly encourage our children to walk; we did not and do not walk ourselves in order to develop lungs, hearts, thews, and thighs, although being in fine fettle is not to be scorned. We merely wanted the children to be stroked as we had been stroked by that incredibly soft, moist southeast thaw-wind that reminds us here in Minnesota in the dead of winter, after a long siege of Canadian air, that there is a southland, a mild and genial warmland. Conversely, or perhaps reversely, we want them to know the flippant feeling, the tactile ebullience when our wonderful Minnesota ventilating system drives away a midsummer invasion of hot humid air. We want them to savor snow on the palate, to tipple the April rain, to get stewed on the hard cider of pungent October air, to become well educated in the acoustics of weather (walk-taught, not laboratory-learned), to be able to discern from the sound of the train whistle at midnight whether the temperature is above or below zero, to be alert to the articulation of sounds obscured by snowfall so heavy and silent that the walker himself becomes as anonymous as a snowflake, to be able to stand at a window inside a warm house on any winter morning and decide from the complexion of the nude trees whether one should wear a Russian fur cap or a French beret on the three-quarter-mile walk to the college. In other words, we want our children's "five and country senses" to be trained as our five and country senses were trained — by total exposure (both pleasurable and painful) to Minnesota weather.

How much of our own and our children's attachment to hearth

and home do we all owe to Minnesota winters? Has anyone ever made a study of home-feeling and climate? Is there a relationship between the feeling of home as a sanctuary and the austere, shut-in months when the sun rises late and sets early, when darkness and cold bear down and press in, when the besieged house creaks and groans in the night? Does the simple act of coming in out of the cold into the brightness and warmth of home, repeated again and again, make home a harbor of harbors?

But what scientific device or psychological test could ever compute such a relationship, if it does indeed exist, when it is so difficult to isolate the ingredients of the warm air that meets the blast of cold air at the door of home? The air that met our respective frost-nipped noses was not only warm — it was usually redolent with the fragrance of bread baking, beef bones simmering in a soup kettle, or some other unpretending odor that also exuded something of home as a place where no harm came.

And if home does indeed become a hundred times home in Minnesota winters, it is a companion truth that bed becomes a hundred times bed. And what a patron of the conjugal relationship is the cold bedroom! Having slept in frigid bedrooms as children (we seem even to recall a dusting of snow on our beds some mornings, or are we perhaps confusing ourselves with Abe Lincoln?), neither of us can abide heated sleeping rooms. And if we happen to have had more or less of a disagreement and more or less cannot abide each other when we go to bed in winter, an exploring toe soon slides across the frigid sheet and asks forgiveness of its mate. Marriage counselors could well recommend icy bedrooms for icy marital misrelationships.

No doubt there is some connection between the bitter, bitter winter of 1936, when for the whole month of January the temperature did not rise above zero, and the fact that a certain auction-goer sometimes buys an old-fashioned wood range or a Round Oak heater. Howard was a graduate student at the University of Minnesota that year, a student of David F. Swenson, who whetted his embryonic interest in Søren Kierkegaard. Huddling and all but hugging the hard-coal heater with its glowing isinglass windows during that interminably arctic month, he developed an affection for palpable instruments of heat that went far beyond stoves and heaters and included saunas and volcanoes. Yes, returning from Denmark in 1966 he even hired a Piper Cub plane and a pilot and flew over Surtsey, the newest Icelandic island aborning. As he peered down into the glowing eye of the volcano, was he remembering Minnesota in 1936 and those glowing isinglass windows?

There also seems to be a link between the shut-in months and reading habits — at least there was before the advent of television. Each of us in our separate childhood households, miles apart, became wedded to books in childhood on long winter evenings. As parents we adamantly resisted piteous pleas for a television set until our youngest was sixteen, and we watched our children, one by one, discover our not-so-secret joy in reading. For the hours of television which we denied our children, we substituted reading aloud to them story after story, book after book. Even when the late, light evenings returned and the children played outside, there was many a reading before bedtime. It seems that we are indebted to the classic Minnesota winter weather also for the wondrous enjoyment of reading aloud as a family!

It started early, this reading aloud. Unexpectedly returning early the first night out after the arrival of the firstborn we almost lost, the young mother found her partner reading Coleridge's "Frost at Midnight" to his month-old son in his basket before the crackling fire. The son slept, and the quiet intruder listened:

> The frost performs its secret ministry,
> Unhelped by any wind. The owlet's cry
> Came loud — and hark, again! loud as before.
> The inmates of my cottage, all at rest,
> Have left me to that solitude, which suits
> Abstruser musings: save that at my side
> My cradled infant slumbers peacefully.

Solitude, that substance starved to a shadow by our proliferating mass society, is another legacy of growing up in Minnesota. Only in the gift of time and space and in the experience of aloneness can the human spirit become attentive to its potentiality and relations, for attention is the power of the human spirit to be present to spirit — to oneself, to the spirit in whom we live, move, and have our being, to the spirit in another person, to the spirit in all that which we in our arrogated superiority call subhuman in creatures and creation. Solitude is needed for the green-growing of spirit and for the power of spirit to meet spirit with attention. Growing up in Minnesota provided us with solitude in good measure, "pressed down, shaken together, and running over."

We two parents found ample solitude in our own parental homes, for each of us grew up in one of those old-fashioned castles of beneficent solitude that people rarely build anymore. It is popular now to sneer at the architecture of those nineteenth-century houses as examples of conspicuous consumption; yet may it not rather be a necessary but not conspicuous assumption that the spirit of man needs attics, basements, closets, lawns, hedges, grape arbors, barns, haylofts? Even the outhouse in the back was "a place apart" such as the modern bathroom can never be. One of our grandpas had a habit of overstaying nature's invitation there. As children we thought he was having a hard time. Now we know that he was answering the invitation also of another nature more easily but more devastatingly thwarted.

We provided our own children with a stone castle of solitude in a remnant of Minnesota's ancient Big Woods on the edge of the St. Olaf campus. When the campus sidled over and crowded in and a Frankensteinian monster of a boys' dormitory was closer than the raucous bedlam of radio station WDGY, a Lakeville mover, Charles Wren, picked up our stone castle, body and soul, and moved it without a creak or crack in either its body or soul to the bluffs of Heath Creek. Here we enjoy once more the ingredients that make for solitude.

In the sixth grade children begin to be assaulted with a battery of psychological tests that are supposed to track and run down in the secret recesses of the subconscious of the unsuspecting innocents all the unnormal and abnormal attitudes and sick-sick complexes to which they may have fallen prey in their family life. ("All the better to counsel you, my dear!") One day one of our eight complex psyches, a virgin to these tests, came home from school troubled.

"We had a test today, and I think I gave a dumb answer to one of the questions."

"What was the question?"

"Where do you like best to be?"

We two parents looked at each other significantly, perhaps fearing the fierce face of some hidden truth.

"What did you write for an answer?"

"I wrote that I liked to be at home best." (Secret relief. Hurray for us!) "But it isn't that," she went on. "It's what came next. Then they asked 'Why?' and I wrote, 'Because that's the only place in the whole world I can be alone by myself when I want to be.'"

Solitude has indeed been efficacious in our family, but when solitude was combined with primitivity, the roots of our several selves absorbed what cannot be measured by any tests or any computer (after all, one cannot feed into computers the hearing of river sounds and the call of loons and the seeing of the orange-stained lichen on ancient rocks). It was up north in the vast wilderness at the tip of the arrowhead which Minnesota arches over the end of Lake Superior that our several selves found our nerves changed to sensitively seeking rootlets that absorbed peace, unity, and continuity from the awesome quiet, the regularized change, and the vastness and delicate fragility of nature there.

It was Howard's chronic hay fever that sent us there in the first place some thirty years ago, but it is the place itself and its gifts that draw us back summer after summer. We may go there with spirits torn and fragmented, but we never leave without being put together again in a quiet kind of healing that goes on without our knowing it at the moment.

That the primitive experience of wilderness was meaningful to our children we suspected when our youngest became so alert to the word "north" at the toddling age that if in our southern Minnesota home a visitor casually mentioned the word in quite another context, he would ask us later, "Do they have an Up North, too?" But we did not really know that taking ourselves and our family into the Minnesota wilderness was one of the very best tangible things we ever did for ourselves and for them until one of them wrote about it with such quiet exuberance that it must be incorporated in our reflections on growing up in Minnesota. Come in, Mary Hong Loe, you who literally fell into Lake Superior at the age of two and figuratively have never been rescued and apparently do not want to be!

Each summer our family migrated up the Brule River which chases itself down the northeastern wedge of Minnesota and catches up finally in the blue bowl of Lake Superior. We tucked ourselves away in a cabin shanty shelved on a high river bluff, back over logging roads, past stingy farmsteads forgotten by hands that could not force the red clay soil, across Mons Hanson's Creek and beyond the big meadow, cinched smaller each year by its belt of poplar trees. The red peaked roof and a window-wide view of the rushing river were the brightest trimmings of the sixteen-by-twenty-four-foot cabin. The climate at times might have dismayed Mother Eve and Father Adam, but to us children our wilderness watering grounds took on the aura of a Garden of Eden. Our parents found something far greater than a pollen-free, cheap vacation for ten; they set us down in a world swept clean, and we unwrapped space and time and silence and ourselves. In an age of disposables we received experiences we could use again and again.

The size of our cabin encouraged us to leap the outdoor spaces. Dad wanted a roof over our heads, nothing more. This was a child's dream come true, and those of us who were past seven contributed some work, more complaining, and lots of sentiment to its construction. The area was cleared of trees and brush. Cedar posts were positioned in the ground to support our meager cabin, which was weighted on the east by a rescued wood cookstove and on the west by the promise of a fireplace. Above the kitchen and the bedroom was a loft full of beds, which, as any child would agree, was the best of sleeping rooms. It had a narrow window to catch the falling stars and climbing sun, nails to hang jeans on, candles to read by, and siblings to confer with in the profound nightness. Beds lined the living area, too, but that room focused on the river and was dominated by a twelve-foot tabletop balanced on a redwood coffinbox purchased from a mortician and esteemed for its mouseproof storage.

The table was the only work space in the cabin. Consequently our paraphernalia of books, letters, armies of chessmen and checkers, collected rocks, dried bear tracks, pickle-jar vases of daisies, buttercups, and unidentified weeds, local maps, driftwood curiosities, birchbark scrolls, cigar ashes, sprinklings of last night's lantern-crazed insects, half-grown candles, and bread rising like pale moons always threatened to overwhelm its forty-eight square feet. Mother saved the most valuable treasures by hanging them from the rafters as mobiles or tacking them on the walls, and managed to keep the table clear enough to serve anything from stuffed cabbage to baked northern pike for two or twenty. Evenings we sat in the circle of lantern light reading heroic stories or the current events of 1910 to 1924 in old issues of *Youth's Companion*, listening to Mother's rocking and her reading aloud, or we hunched around the table unscrabbling wooden words.

Contrary to all the work our Spartan quarters might imply, household duties were wonderfully minimal. Lack of electricity spared us the usual plethora of specialized conveniences, and we found two basic tools, the wood-burning stove and the broom, adaptable and sufficient. The iron stove ("the best lefse maker," its former owner, Mrs. Flaten, had said) generously and simultaneously fried bacon, heated dishwater, baked muffins, steeped coffee, simmered soup, boiled clothes white in Felsnaphtha, took the chill off the morning air, toasted bread light or dark, disposed of the sweepings from the floor, and gave us the pleasant spice of burning wood as we breakfasted. And it did all these services graciously and gratuitously, asking only that we feed it dry wood, empty its ash box, and give its top a waxed-paper wipe now and then.

Meals were served twice a day — simple fare of cheese, fresh breads, canned meats, occasional trout or pike, eggs, and vegetables that kept well, which meant a glut of cabbages and carrots. We liked to picnic on flat table-rocks in the middle of the river, making quick fires from sun-dried driftwood. We speared strips of steak or sausage and lumps of cheese and wrapped them sizzling in leaves of river-washed lettuce. We gleaned our share of berries when the harvest sufficed both bears and us. One summer would be creeping with sweet nestling strawberries, tiny to try the patience of a good-sized pail. Another would spare us many bowls of raspberries, mixed with limp, piquant thimbleberries by small, undiscriminating hands. The aging apple trees at an abandoned farm responded once or twice to hearty shakes, but they seldom gift us now, and the blueberries that used to stain the big, white bowl have given way to huckleberries. The forest foods were as capricious as the weather, yet there were abundant wild supermarkets that we should have patronized but did not: the swamps greened with thick, multipurpose cattails, the birches sailed up their sap, untapped, and hazelnut bushes draped the paths with fruit almost unplucked except by chipmunks. Most regrettable was the cosmos of mushrooms nursing on old logs or shielded under the skirts of spruce and fir — a wealth we never learned to identify positively.

A spring supplied delicious water and refrigeration of sorts. Rising from the cold depths, the water seeped, clear as glass, into a sunken oak cider vinegar barrel. We carefully took off the lid and dipped our pails, slowly so as not to unsettle the silt, drew them up, and quickly climbed the path. Our shoulder bones were yokes, our arms hangers stiff with weight, but going to the spring was an essential chore with an obvious reward, and we all shared it. Some enjoyed the spring trek more than others; although the low, wet spot often stewed with mosquitoes, it was also indulged by brilliant water-loving flowers and visited by deer.

In a second open barrel small amounts of butter and milk in glass jars were kept, encased in an old ten-gallon cream can with a bear-defying deep cover. That was the extent of refrigeration, except for the cans of juice left on the porch overnight to catch cold for breakfast. We did make one abortive experiment with a cold storage box in the ground, only to lure a nosy bear who easily toppled the huge rock on the lid and shredded a month's supply of cheese and cabbage into slaw. We avoided highly perishable foods, drank our powdered milk with some effort, and came to realize that refrigeration never had a monopoly on preservation.

Not all in our neighborhood of several families were enthusiastic hikers, fishermen, stone-hoppers, or swimmers, but no one escaped addiction to the North Woods air. Washed by lakes and combed by trees, it was the first and last we tasted of the woods. It was not sipping air, but stuff for filling one's bellows. It was redolent and bracing, with an edge that made one feel keen and defined against the elements, and yet the summer sun stroked the open meadows and sifted through the trees to soften the windless pockets into warmth and make the berries blush. It was an uneven layering of lake breeze and soaking heat, usually distinctly warmer than the climate on the shores of Lake Superior. The most dramatic difference surprised us on a sleeveless July morning when we drove the thirty-odd miles into Grand Marais to cash in on its "Crazy Days" sale. There the wind was frigid enough to sprinkle snow on nearby hills, and sidewalk vendors rubbed their hands for warmth and pleasure as they sold their racks of thermal underwear and sweatshirts.

Our summer mode of life dispensed with middlemen and took us to the source. It informed us with a degree of self-sufficiency, probably its most positive and radical ingredient. No distant pipes delivered energy. No meters measured what we used. No bakers baked while we slept. Telephones did not abridge our thoughts; the only voices from afar were echoes of our own. A white-throated sparrow piped the five o'clock news. Father took his watch off upon arrival, hung it from a nail, and from then on slept a depth he seldom slept elsewhere. Even as we never got sick for lack of germs, we quietly, almost innocently, avoided the complications inherent in an overspecialized society. Frustrations lost their sting because we were our own ombudsmen. If the stove smoked or did not heat, it was because the damper was not up or we had not dried the wood. When rain stained pictures on the ceiling, we had to tar the roof. If perchance we were bored, no jester appeared upon a screen or organized a game for us — we had to venture and find something to do.

Every morning there were chores for us to do. The drinking pails and the stove's reservoir had to be filled; firewood had to be chopped and stacked; the breakfast dishes had to be doused in boiling water; a batch of something had to be baked in the oven's lingering heat; and table crumbs had to be set out on a rock for the scurrying chipmunks to hoard. Then the young trees competing for our view might have to be clipped or a disagreeably close wasp's colony might have to be smoked out. These were daily or annual tasks and were expected, but every summer seemed to evolve its special project, too.

My father had an eye for such undertakings. He said the river begged for a sauna, and he was right. So we children clasped a clattering of boards under each arm and made two dragging trips per day down the lumpy path until a sauna was balanced between four boulders and anchored with cables against the spring tide. Since then we have been Finnish clean. Another summer Dad conjured, or otherwise propelled, two small log buildings, previously serving a homesteader's family as washhouse and guesthouse, across the creek's precarious bridge and up our gullied road. The one that became a study was sidled partway down the bluff and perched between two towering spruces; it looked as if it grew there on its own. The second building sat half-neglected by the path to the swimming hole. "The witch's house!" my own three children tell me now as we tiptoe past. A pending project, I tell myself, but it will have to wait until the fireplace is built.

And so the summers spun themselves out, and work was fun and fun was work, with lots of lolling time between. We grew up before families "stopped at two"; and so in the families of the neighborhood there were enough Johns, Marys, and Pauls to gambol in the twilight playing "kick the can," to push an expedition to the beaver dam, or trapperlike to explore the Brule to the very end. We discovered animal paths, a spectacular gorge gouging through the rock, an abandoned cabin deep in the woods, and a loon's dream of a small lake, lost to the world behind its shield of handclasping pine. The forest was veined sporadically with logging roads in various states of overgrowth. Gradually our sense of the region's geography increased, especially when a '39 Chevrolet truck joined the trappings left to winter in the woods. One afternoon we meant to drive three miles to a fishing lake. One turn led to another as we bullied the truck around fallen trees, through frog-cold puddles, and ended up making the first star's wish that we would have enough gas to make it out of the woods and down the Gunflint Trail to Grand Marais, where we could retank for the cabin on the Brule. The three-mile trip turned out to be a seventy-five-mile trek through the wilderness!

If our outlooks do indeed change as we grow older, and thus for the ten of us those woods became eighteen kingdoms and more, the Brule ribboned through each kingdom and tied them all together. Our acres of spruce and birch cross the Brule at its best, where it descends into leaping, handspringing white water, channeled by huge boulders that are increasingly exposed as summer wanes. Nowhere down the river's seven miles to its mouth, or upstream as far as we have ventured, does it exhibit so well its several moods and manners. Within a few hundred yards the water pummels powerfully enough to slap one's strongest rock-grip loose and broadens into mirror pools for water bugs and babies. Below the scuffling rocks and water and encircled by an audience of unblinking boulders, the river rests a moment in deeper channels before it tumbles on. There where the river sings a slower song we became amphibians.

We paddled circles in the shallows until seaworthy for our first river crossing. One by one over the years we thrust our scared-daring bodies against the current to the landing rock on the other side. Our watchful families cheered, celebrating the initial success and giving encouragement for the much harder struggle back again. The strange fact that I do not remember my own maiden voyage may indicate how much sympathetic energy was spent on successive river crossings. We all learned to swim with gust and joy, if not economy of movement. The dynamics of the river set up a jungle gym of swimming things to do. We would slide down the smaller falls headfirst, shoulder ourselves, sleek as otters, against the somersaulting water, push our heads back to force a watery oxygen tent over us, vibrate in the plunging falls, ride a flotilla of capsizing inner tubes down the current, spend our limbs and lungs in whirlwinds of water tag, and wash our hair squeaky clean, taking all the time we wanted "in the shower." Hour upon timeless hour we swam the golden water, drinking when thirsty and climbing onto sun-hot rocks to rest, like seals, each with his own territory. We swam in twos, respecting chance, but swimming in the Brule was so infectious that the pool usually glistened and thrashed with legs, thick as smelt in spring.

The swimming hole was a peopled place, a playful place. Up the river, however, among the scattering of room-sized boulders we dramatically called the Castle, and downstream where the water swirled around nut-smooth reading rocks, the river generated a quiet, restorative mood. The sounding, speeding water appealed to some relic memory in us and became the pervasive core of our North Woods life. Dad had set a row of windows in clear view of the river's southward glisten and had raised the cabin up around them; we drifted asleep to the water's windy lullaby and woke to watch the lakeward-stealing fog, fitted to the river like a coverlet of softest down; and every day we descended the steep billy goat path and lived in easy intimacy with it, walled in by river roar and a backdrop slice of cliff.

In that amphitheater we stepped beneath unfailing trees and hopped the same tried stones out into currents running yesterday's very course. We learned to expect the solitary seagull mapping the morning and evening river. Someone would spot a dirt-brown beaver hiding against the dirt-brown bank, the bear cub bumbling across his bridge of stones by the island, and prolific signs of ghostly deer and moose. The air startled with metal-blue-and-red dragonflies, and teams of waterskaters cast their curious shadows on the river bottom. Out of the warm, wet rot of logs, seedlings and fairy worlds of mosses came alive. We saw endurance, chance, and law. We knew transience but glimpsed eternity. We learned that nature's flux is constancy and we were at ease. That familiar bend of the Brule, with its company of rocks and veils of slender birches cascading into waterfalls, cycled through our lives as faithfully as we returned to it.

I married a man who readily rooted into the northern woods of Minnesota, and much of our hopefulness about life blossoms from our experiences there. Struggling in the labyrinths of close urban society, we have come to believe that the catch-your-breath months are no longer merely a luxury but a necessity. Every summer we transplant our three young children to the banks of the Brule and watch them unfurl and thrive like the fiddlehead ferns. Gently pulled by the rolling sun and nourished by a river of liquid amber and the rich rot of log and leaf, our children will soon discover that the boulders, the birch, and they are blood brothers.

Blooddaughter Mary's rhapsody about summers in northern Minnesota fails to mention that the man to whom she is married has an Indian name, registered with the Red Lake band of Ojibway Indians: Ned-wa-ghe-no-nins (also spelled May-dway-gah-no-nind), meaning "He Who Is Spoken To." The Indian name given to him by his part-Indian mother is the name of the one-time hereditary chief of the Red Lake band, one of Bishop Whipple's first converts to Christianity. The "other grandma" of Mary's children has the Ojibway name of Ki-we-din-ok, "Woman of the North Wind." All of which leads to the third unique aspect of growing up in Minnesota — the Indians.

Visiting three ancestral farms in Norway with our children has made no greater impact on us and them than the slow, cumulative impact of growing up in a state that was the home and the history of the Iowa, Dakota, and Ojibway tribes. Although none of us became Indian artifact hunters (although a stone hammer in the Brule River and an arrowhead on the shore of Union Lake, Rice County, did happen to find us), some of us have become infiltrated by the history of the Indians in Minnesota. Specialists we are not and do not wish to be. All we have done, after all, is to raise the antennae and become attentive to the messages coming in. The messages came and keep coming.

The most recent message came quite by accident when last spring we came upon the grave of Good Thunder, a Dakota chief, on the west bank of the Minnesota River near Morton. We are quite positively sure that we are neither romanticists nor sentimentalists. It was not these emotional juices that quickened in us as we stood near the tombstone Bishop Whipple erected to his good Indian friend, Chief Wabasha, Wakinyanwaste (Good Thunder). It was a kith-and-kin feeling. Whether Good Thunder would claim us, we do not know, but we claimed him and loved him. Loved him for having the quiet courage to say to the bishop, when the latter reproved him and his tribe for a scalp dance, "White man go to war with his own brother; kills more men than Wabasha can count all his life. Great Spirit look down and says, '*Good* white man; he has My Book; I have good home for him by and by.' Dakota has no Great Spirit's Book; he goes to war, kills one man, has a foolish scalp-dance; Great Spirit very angry. *Wabasha doesn't believe it!*" We loved Bishop Whipple for having the grace to report that story and many like them in his *Lights and Shadows of a Long Episcopate.* Is Good Thunder's little daughter there beside him, the one who died of tuberculosis and was buried "somewhere on the prairie," as the old account relates, and whose grave the Indian women heaped with wild roses? Since then, whenever we see wild June roses, we instantly think of Chief Good Thunder and his daughter, resting in the good earth of which they were shamefully robbed.

How could we be sentimentalists, we two parents who in the span of our our lives have experienced the transition from the white men's history of the Sioux Massacre of the pioneer settlers in Minnesota in 1862, which Howard avidly read and heard described in his childhood in Kandiyohi County, to the Indians' history of the rape of the Indians, which we and our children have read in *Bury My Heart at Wounded Knee*.

Yet long before his children discovered the tragic story of the Indians in *Bury My Heart at Wounded Knee*, Howard, growing up in Willmar in the twenties, found it in a volume in his book-laden home — *The Aborigines of Minnesota*, published by the Minnesota Historical Society in 1911. Poring over the fascinating, profusely illustrated, and very detailed historical treasure, he came upon this account of the Mendota Treaty by an early writer who certainly was no sentimentalist at all about Indians or their unhappy fate. We quote it at some length only to resurrect it from a book that is largely or totally unknown to the present generation of Minnesotans. Or is that the only reason? Are we perhaps also trying to establish that previous generations did not live in a Dark Age of Total Unenlightenment with regard to the fate of the Minnesota Indians! On pages 553-54 Howard in his parental home in Willmar read:

There was therefore a loud and persistent demand for the privilege of settlement on the west side of the Mississippi, and hence for the acquisition of the lands of the Dakota. At once Gov. Ramsey applied himself to the task. It is needless to state that the people were unanimous in aiding in this westward movement. The traders, the chief factors of the industry of the state, perceived in it the shortest way of collecting their claims against the Indians for goods advanced; the land speculators knew that it would open a wide door for almost limitless dealing in agricultural land; lumbermen looked longingly upon the pine forests of the upper Mississippi; farmers and all homesteaders had their plows ready for the soil, only awaiting permission to cross the Mississippi, and a numerous horde of vagrants, such as hover about the frontiers of civilization, rent the air with hazzahs [sic] for the encouragement of the politicians who were active in the initial plans. There was a hurried and sweeping plan formulated. The legislature of 1849, at the instance of Gov. Ramsey, petitioned Congress for the purchase, and the cession, of the lands west of the Mississippi, and it was less than five months after the arrival of

Gov. Ramsey (i.e., in October, 1849) that the Sioux were summoned to treat for the surrender of their lands.

Long before white Minnesotans were forced to be honest about their history, Howard read in this book, just published when he was born, that the first council was abortive for want of a sufficient number of Indians and that a second one was called in July of 1851 at Traverse des Sioux, resulting in what is known as the Mendota Treaty. The boy read on:

> That, however, was only a temporary check in the execution of what may be called, from the Indian's standpoint, a monstrous conspiracy, the final consummation of what was disastrous to both the Dakota and the whites. To the former it spelled extinction and to the latter expansion through the bloody path of massacre. It was sanctioned by the formalities of "treaty" in 1851. There was pitted the diplomacy and power of civilization against the simplicity, ignorance, and hunger of a barbarous people. A shipload of provisions, including cattle, for feasting the Indians, had been sent to Traverse des Sioux. When promise and palaver failed and the Indians refused to cede their lands for the payments that had been offered, and the council was about to break up without the desired results, the chiefs were informed by Governor Ramsey, who "understood" the aborigine and his peculiarities and also understood the persuasive effect of an empty stomach, that immediately the issue of further food would be stopped. That struck the chiefs with consternation, as they had brought with them their women and children, and they knew that there was no game in the region on which, in such an emergency, they could rely to prevent starvation. That was the final coup, and the chiefs, one after the other, made their "marks," giving assent to the first step to the final doom of their people.

The Willmar lad went on reading about things he never heard discussed by adults and never read in his school histories. He read of payments delayed, of starvation. He learned that there was yet another treaty in 1858 which sold half again of the Dakota's shrunken domain, the part of their reservation north of the Minnesota River, and that although the tribe as a whole had approved the treaty of 1852 the treaty in 1858 was never approved by the whole tribe. He read Taliaferro's statement, which was made two years after the tragic events of 1862.

> But for the treaty of 1858 the Sioux bands of the Dakota nation would have been a peaceable and thriving people, but the wrongs perpetrated by the white men under that treaty mainly caused the murder of many innocent people in 1862. The Crow [Chief Little Crow] and his Indians realized their

fate in 1858, at Washington, at the last treaty with the government; they were as children led to the slaughter, no man seemed to care for them, and they became desperate. The young men could no longer be controlled, their lands were sold, and the traders got the proceeds through the connivance of men called respectable citizens by evil doers.

Thus it was that long before the American conscience was prodded to know the white man's perfidy, long before the Indian's side of the history of the American West came to painful light, a man sat in front of his fireplace and told his children of how eight thousand Indians were cheated out of thirty million acres of some of the best land on the face of the earth.

Does this early encounter with the true facts account for that man's Christian pacifism, for the two sons who are conscientious objectors? Perhaps even for his youngest son's emotional outburst in the Thorshavn harbor in the Faroe Islands, where Howard, Edna, Theodore, and Nathaniel stood in 1966 watching in horror the slaughter of 120 whales in a long and complicated theatrical ritual that once, but no more, had its justification in keeping an impoverished people alive? A harpooned and dying whale thrashing in the red-red water of the harbor smashed a shiny new boat, throwing its owner and his harpoon into the water.

"Do it again!" the boy screamed in revulsion, tears streaming down his face. "Oh, do it again!"

It may be so. And if it *is* so, then it proves that remembering is not a pathological backward looking at a past time or place, but a healthy forward movement into the present and future. Remembering the history of the Minnesota Indians explains the present frictions and sends the ten of us into the future chastised and hopefully wiser and more loving sisters and brothers in the family of man. Just as the solitude still to be found in Minnesota helped make us whole, it continues to integrate our fractioned selves and helps us face a hard present and a darkening future. As for Minnesota weather, it has been a splendid teacher, has disciplined us well. We can shiver out or sweat out any weather — and love every minute of it!

Biographical Notes

Biographical Notes

MERIDEL LE SUEUR was born in Murray, Iowa, in 1900 and has spent most of her life in the Middle West, from Texas to Minnesota. In the North Star State she has lived in Minneapolis and St. Paul as well as in the countryside. She was educated at the American Academy of Dramatic Art in New York, and in the 1920s she worked briefly in Hollywood as an actress. But, as she said thirty years ago, "I go east and west, but I always come back here because I feel this is the rich humus of anything I will ever be able to write."

Le Sueur's first story appeared in the *Dial* in 1927 and was reprinted in *O'Brien's Best Short Stories* that year. Since then her work has appeared in *Scribner's*, the *Saturday Evening Post, Mademoiselle, Seventeen*, the *Yale Review*, the *Anvil*, the *Kenyon Review*, the *New Republic*, the *Nation, Mainstream, New Masses, Harper's*, and other magazines. One of her best-known books is *North Star Country* (1945), which appeared in a series edited by Erskine Caldwell. Her most recent books include *Corn Village* (1971) and *Rites of Ancient Ripening* (1976). A collection of her stories about the Great Depression will be published by the Feminist Press in 1976.

◇◈◇◈◇◈◇◈◇◈◇

HARRISON E. SALISBURY was born in Minneapolis in 1908 and graduated from the University of Minnesota with a B.A. degree in 1930. He started his newspaper career in Minneapolis and later worked for the United Press in Chicago, Washington, New York, London, and Moscow. He joined the staff of the *New York Times* in 1949 and served as the *Times* Moscow correspondent through 1954, when he returned to the United States. He received the Pulitzer Prize for international correspondence in 1955 for his reporting from Moscow. He was the originator of the *New York Times* "Op-Ed" page and associate editor of the newspaper until his retirement in 1972. He was given the Distinguished Achievement Award of the University of Minnesota in 1955. He is presently president of the National Institute of Arts and Letters and conducts the PBS television program "Behind the Lines."

Salisbury is the author of many books including *American in Russia* (1955), *The Shook-Up Generation* (1958), *Moscow Journal* (1961), *The Northern Palmyra Affair* (1962), *The 900 Days: The Siege of Leningrad* (1969), and *The Gates of Hell* (1975).

GERALD VIZENOR was born in Minneapolis in 1934. He is of Anishinabe-French heritage and is enrolled on the White Earth Reservation (where his father was born); he is a member of the first generation in his paternal families to be born off the reservation. After his father died, he lived with several foster families in Minneapolis. As he once said, "I grew up in cold places before the energy crisis, but I did not appreciate how poor I was until I studied about my disadvantages in college social science courses." He attended public schools in Minneapolis through the eleventh grade, completing his high school courses while serving in the army in Japan. Following military service he studied for one year at New York University, taking courses in writing from Louise Bogan and Eda Lou Walton, and completed his degree at the University of Minnesota. He continued at the University of Minnesota with postgraduate work in Asian studies and library science. He also studied at the William Mitchell College of Law and the graduate school of education at Harvard University.

Vizenor has published three books of haiku poems: *Raising the Moon Vines* (1964), *Seventeen Chirps* (1964), and *Empty Swings* (1967). Several of his haiku poems are included in *The Haiku Anthology* and *From the Belly of the Shark*. His longer poems have appeared in three anthologies: *25 Minnesota Poets*, *Voices of the Rainbow*, and *An American Indian Anthology*. His work has also appeared in *Dakotah Territory*.

In addition, Vizenor has published traditional tales and songs of the woodland tribal people in two volumes entitled *Anishinabe Adisokan* (1970) and *Anishinabe Nagamon* (1970, first published in 1965 under the title *Summer in the Spring: Lyric Poems of the Ojibway*). His recent book *The Everlasting Sky: New Voices from the People Named the Chippewa* (1972) is the only contemporary history of Anishinabe tribal people. His work is also included in *The Way: An Anthology of American Indian Literature*. A number of his editorials (written for the *Minneapolis Tribune*), magazine stories, and investigative reports about tribal consciousness, the trial of Thomas James White Hawk, and radical and religious tribal movements have been published in a volume entitled *Tribal Scenes and Ceremonies* (1976). He is currently writing a novel about tribal visions and terminal beliefs.

Vizenor has been employed as a social worker at the state reformatory, a journalist, a community advocate (for tribal people in urban centers), and a civil rights organizer. He has lived and worked on several reservations and small towns in northern Minnesota. He directed the first Indian studies program at Bemidji State University, and he has taught tribal literature and history at Lake Forest College, Macalester College, and the University of California at Berkeley.

KEITH GUNDERSON was born in New Ulm, Minnesota, in 1935. His family moved shortly thereafter to Minneapolis, where he attended Irving and Lyndale grade schools, Jefferson Junior High School, and West High School. He holds B.A. degrees from Macalester College in St. Paul and from Oxford University and a Ph.D. degree from Princeton University. He has divided some of his adult energies between philosophy and poetry, teaching philosophy at Princeton, the University of California in Los Angeles, and the University of Minnesota, where he is professor of philosophy and research associate at the Minnesota Center for Philosophy of Science.

Gunderson's poems have appeared in *Chelsea*, the *Massachusetts Review*, *Epoch*, and other magazines, his philosophical essays in *Mind*, *Inquiry*, *The Journal of Philosophy*, and other periodicals. His books of poetry are *A Continual Interest in the Sun and Sea* (reissued in one volume with *Inland Missing the Sea* in 1976), *To See a Thing* (1975), and *3142 Lyndale Ave. So., Apt. 24 — Prose Poems (20 Selections)* (1975). In philosophy he is the author of *Mentality and Machines* (1971) and the editor of *Language, Mind, and Knowledge* (Minnesota Studies in the Philosophy of Science, volume 7, 1975).

SHIRLEY SCHOONOVER was born in Biwabik, Minnesota, on the Iron Range and was educated in the public schools there and at the University of Minnesota and the University of Nebraska. She is the author of two novels, *Mountain of Winter* (1965) and *Sam's Song* (1969), and many short stories. Two of her stories, "The Star Blanket" (*Transatlantic Review*, 1961) and "Old and Country Tale" (*Atlantic Monthly*, 1963), won O. Henry awards. She has taught fiction writing at the University of Rochester (New York). She is currently working on two new novels, *Flowers for Leah* and *The Finns*.

TOYSE KYLE was born in Kansas City, Missouri, in 1938 and came to Minneapolis in 1948. She has degrees in arts and in education from the Metropolitan State Junior College, Minneapolis, and the University of Minnesota, where she is completing her M.A. degree in speech communication. She is an instructor in the Department of Arts, Communication, and Philosophy of the General College at the University of Minnesota. Although she has written television scripts and has produced educational tapes for KTCA-TV, the essay in this book is the first of her work to appear in print.

ROBERT BLY was born on December 23, 1926, in Madison, Minnesota. He attended the local country school and high school before studying at St. Olaf College and Harvard University, where he received the A.B. degree in 1950. He is founder, publisher, and editor of The Fifties Press (more recently known as The Sixties Press and currently as The Seventies Press), and he helped to organize the Minnesota Writers Publishing House, a cooperative which has published eight volumes of poetry by Minnesota writers in the last few years.

Bly's books of poetry include *Silence in the Snowy Fields* (1962); *The Light around the Body* (1967), which received the National Book Award; *The Teeth Mother Naked at Last* (1970); *Jumping out of Bed* (1973); *Sleepers Joining Hands* (1973); *Old Man Rubbing His Eyes* (1975); and *The Morning Glory (1975)*. Bly is the editor of *Forty Poems Touching on Recent American History* (1970), *A Poetry Reading against the Vietnam War* (1970), and *The Sea and the Honeycomb* (1971).

Bly has also published a number of translations from Swedish, Norwegian, German, Spanish, French, Russian, and Japanese. His poetry translations include *Twenty Poems of Georg Trakl* (with James Wright, 1961); *Neruda and Vallejo: Selected Poems* (with James Wright and John Knoepfle, 1971); *Lorca and Jiménez: Selected Poems* (1973); *Friends, You Drank Some Darkness. Martinson, Ekelöf and Tranströmer: Selected Poems* (1975); *The Fish in the Sea Is Not Thirsty: Versions of Kabir* (1975); *Rilke: Ten Sonnets to Orpheus* (1975); and *The Kabir Book: Forty-Four of the Ecstatic Poems of Kabir* (1976); He has also translated Knut Hamsun's *Hunger* (1967) and Selma Lagerlöf's *The Story of Gösta Berling* (1962).

HOWARD V. HONG was born in Wolford, North Dakota, in 1912, EDNA H. HONG in Thorpe, Wisconsin, in 1913. They both graduated from St. Olaf College, where Howard received his B.A. degree in 1934, Edna hers in 1938. After Howard received his Ph.D. degree from the University of Minnesota in 1938, they studied together at the University of Copenhagen in 1938-39.

Together the Hongs have translated many of the works of Søren Kierkegaard, beginning with *For Self-Examination* (1940) and continuing through *Works of Love* (1962), *Journals and Papers* (seven volumes, 1968-1977), for which they received the National Book Award in 1968, and *Armed Neutrality and an Open Letter* (1968). They also wrote *Muskego Boy* (1944) and *The Boy Who Fought with Kings* (1946) and translated and edited Gregor Malantschuk's *Kierkegaard's Thought* (1971).

Edna Hong is the author of *Clues to the Kingdom* (1968), *The Book of a Century* (1969), *Turn Over Any Stone* (1970), *The Gayety of Grace* (1972), *Grateful Ground* (1974), and *Bright Valley of Love* (1976). She has also published poetry and stories in various magazines.

Howard Hong is the author of *This World and the Church* (1955) and the editor of *Integration and the Christian Liberal Arts College* (1956) and *Christian Faith and the Liberal Arts* (1961). Since 1972 he has been the general editor of *Kierkegaard's Collected Works* (Princeton University Press) and the director of the Kierkegaard Library at St. Olaf College, where he has taught philosophy (except for periods of leave) since 1938. A conscientious objector to war, he served in field positions in Scandinavia, Austria, and Germany from 1943 to 1949, aiding war prisoners and refugees.

MARY HONG LOE was born in Northfield, Minnesota, in 1944. She received her B.A. degree at St. Olaf College in 1966 and her M.A. degree in library science in 1970 from the University of Iowa. She is a homemaker and a librarian in Oswego, New York.